For Sempai.

Best wishes always.

Sensei [illegible].

[illegible]

Advances in Political Science: An International Series

As an expression of its commitment to global political science, the International Political Science Association initiated this series to promote the publication of rigorous scholarly research by its members and affiliated groups. Conceptual and theoretical developments in the discipline, and their explication in various settings, represent the special focus of the series.

Titles include:

Christa Altenstetter and James Warner Björkman (*editors*)
HEALTH POLICY REFORM, NATIONAL VARIATIONS AND GLOBALIZATION

Asher Arian, David Nachmias and Ruth Amir
EXECUTIVE GOVERNANCE IN ISRAEL

Dirk Berg-Schlosser and Jeremy Mitchell (*editors*)
CONDITIONS OF DEMOCRACY IN EUROPE, 1919–39
Systematic Case-Studies

Klaus von Beye
PARLIAMENTARY DEMOCRACY
TRANSITION TO DEMOCRACY IN EASTERN EUROPE

Malcolm M. Feeley and Setsuo Miyazawa (*editors*)
THE JAPANESE ADVERSARY SYSTEM IN CONTEXT
Controversies and Comparisons

Ofter Feldman
THE JAPANESE POLITICAL PERSONALITY

Luigi Graziano
LOBBYING, PLURALISM AND DEMOCRACY

Justin Greenwood and Henry Jacek (*editors*)
ORGANIZED BUSINESS AND THE NEW GLOBAL ORDER

Asha Gupta
BEYOND PRIVATIZATION

Saadia Touval
MEDIATION IN THE YUGOSLAV WARS
The Critical Years, 1990–95

Mino Vianello and Gwen Moore (*editors*)
GENDERING ELITES
Economic and Political Leadership in 27 Industrialised Societies

Advances in Political Science
Series Standing Order ISBN 0–333–71458–X
(*outside North America only*)

You can receive future titles in this series as they are published by placing a standing order. Please contact your bookseller or, in case of difficulty, write to us at the address below with your name and address, the title of the series and the ISBN quoted above.

Customer Services Department, Macmillan Distribution Ltd, Houndmills, Basingstoke, Hampshire RG21 6XS, England

The Japanese Adversary System in Context

Controversies and Comparisons

Edited by

Malcolm M. Feeley
University of California

and

Setsuo Miyazawa
Waseda University

palgrave
macmillan

First published 2002 by
PALGRAVE MACMILLAN
Houndmills, Basingstoke, Hampshire RG21 6XS and
175 Fifth Avenue, New York, N.Y. 10010
Companies and representatives throughout the world

PALGRAVE MACMILLAN is the global academic imprint of the Palgrave Macmillan division of St. Martin's Press, LLC and of Palgrave Macmillan Ltd. Macmillan® is a registered trademark in the United States, United Kingdom and other countries. Palgrave is a registered trademark in the European Union and other countries.

ISBN 0–333–92060–0

This book is printed on paper suitable for recycling and made from fully managed and sustained forest sources.

A catalogue record for this book is available from the British Library.

Library of Congress Cataloging-in-Publication Data

The Japanese adversary system in context: controversies and comparisons/ edited by Malcolm M. Feeley and Setsuo Miyazawa.
p. cm. – (Advances in political science)
Includes bibliographical references and index.
ISBN 0–333–92060–0 (cloth)
1. Adversary system (Law) – Japan. 2. Criminal procedure – Japan. I. Feeley, Malcolm. II. Miyazawa, Setsuo, 1947– III. Advances in political science (Palgrave (Firm))

KNX4616 .J37 2002
345.52'05–dc21

20001050801

10 9 8 7 6 5 4 3 2 1
11 10 09 08 07 06 05 04 03 02

Printed and bound in Great Britain by
Antony Rowe Ltd, Chippenham and Eastbourne

To the memory of
our friend and colleague,
Sho Sato

Contents

List of Figures

List of Tables

Notes on the Contributors

Nobuyoshi Araki is Professor of Law at Rikkyo University, Tokyo. He holds a doctoral degree in law from the University of Tokyo and is President of the Japanese Association of Sociological Criminology.

Malcolm M. Feeley is Claire Sanders Clements Dean's Professor of Law at the University of California at Berkeley. He holds a PhD from the University of Minnesota, and most recently is the author (with Edward Rubin) of *Judicial Policy Making and the Modern State.*

Daniel Foote is Professor of the Sociology of Law at the University of Tokyo. He received a JD from Harvard Law School and was a clerk for Chief Justice Warren Burger of the US Supreme Court. He taught at the University of Washington before moving to Tokyo in 2000.

Roger Hanson is a private consultant in legal research and reform to the ABA, World Bank and individual states. His PhD in political science and philosophy is from the University of Minnesota. He is accessible at www.factory7.com/~rah.

Masahito Inouye is Professor of Law at the University of Tokyo. A graduate of the University of Tokyo, he taught at Boalt Hall as a visiting professor, and has been a member of the Judicial Reform Council of the Japanese government.

David T. Johnson received his PhD from Berkeley in 1996 and has since held a postdoctoral fellowship at Harvard University and a research fellowship from the Abe Foundation. He teaches at the University of Hawaii and is the author of *The Japanese Way of Justice* (2001).

Ann M. Jones is Senior Research Associate at the National Center for State Courts, Denver branch. She holds a PhD from Boston University in educational research, and is coauthor of *Specialization of Domestic Violence Case Management in the Courts: a National Survey* (NCSC, 2000).

Robert A. Kagan is Professor of Political Science and Law at the University of California at Berkeley, and Director of the Center for the Study of Law and Society. He is the author of *Adversarial Legalism*, published by Harvard University Press in 2001.

Richard Leo received his PhD and JD from UC Berkeley in 1994. He is an Associate Professor in the Department of Crime, Law and Society at the University of California at Irvine.

Setsuo Miyazawa holds a doctorate in law from Hokaido University and a PhD in sociology from Yale University, and taught at Kobe University for 17 years before moving to Waseda University in Tokyo in 2000. He has also taught at Harvard, Berkeley, New York University, and at several other American and Canadian universities as a visiting professor of law.

Toshikuni Murai is Professor of Law at Ryukoku University in Kyoto and President of the Japanese Association of Criminal Law. A graduate of Hitotsubashi University in Tokyo, he taught there for many years and was Dean before moving to Ryukoku in 2000.

Masayuki Murayama has a doctoral degree in law from the University of Tokyo and an LLM and MA from the University of California at Berkeley. He is Professor of Law at Chiba University.

Brian J. Ostrom is Principal Research Consultant at the National Center for State Courts, Williamsburg, Virginia. He holds a PhD in economics from the University of Washington, and is the author, with Roger A. Hanson, of *Efficiency, Timeliness and Quality: a New Perspective from Nine State Criminal Trial Courts* (NIJ, 2000).

Satoru Shinomiya is a graduate of Waseda University School of Law and was a visiting scholar at the University of California at Berkeley. He is a member of Chiba Bar Associations, and is Director of Research Office for Judicial Reform at the Japan Federation of Bar Associations.

Takashi Takano is a graduate of Waseda University School of Law and holds an LLM from the Southern Methodist University School of Law. A member of the Saitama Bar Association, he is also a leading member of the Miranda Society in Japan.

Gordon Van Kessel is a former San Francisco prosecutor and Alameda county public defender. He is now Professor of Law at Hastings School of Law, where he teaches criminal law, criminal procedure, and comparative law.

Preface

Like religious institutions, legal systems are usually repositories of tradition. At least in long-established nation-states, today's legal systems are likely to look a lot like those of the last century or the century before; they remain firmly anchored in tradition. If an English or American or German lawyer from the nineteenth century suddenly reappeared in a twenty-first-century courtroom in his own country, he would certainly find much that was bewildering. But after a period of acclimation, the continuities would become apparent. Many features of the process would be familiar.

However, if a Japanese lawyer were to reappear, what he would find would be much less familiar. Since the mid-nineteenth century, the Japanese legal system has undergone two transformations. The Meiji Restoration of 1868 set in motion a period of radical transformation as the newly established government embarked on a crash course to modernize and westernize Japan. All facets of Japanese society were subject to rethinking and change. With regard to law, the new Japanese government turned primarily to Europe (and not to the common-law countries) for inspiration. It embraced Continental jurisprudence, and in so doing brushed aside the Tokugawa legal system. Throughout Japan, for instance, Victorian-era red brick courthouses were built in the early twentieth century that appeared to have been transplanted from England. In addition, the prewar period of military domination of the government imposed its own distinctive concerns on many of these institutions and harnessed them to its own purposes, but ultimately it did not effect a deep transformation of the nature and structure of the Japanese legal system. Postwar American occupation, however, did effect significant changes. What has come to be known as MacArthur's Constitution set about to transform yet again the Japanese legal system. American Occupation forces dismantled emergency provisions adopted by the prewar and wartime military regime. They insisted upon an American-style constitution, complete with an expansive Bill of Rights, and superimposed on this system an Anglo-American style of adversarial structure. While the substantive criminal law remained virtually unchanged, right to counsel, the right against self-incrimination, and the aggressiveness obligatory in the adversarial system all cut against the grain of values implicit in the prewar Japanese legal system.

This series of changes presents enormous challenges for criminal justice scholars. Even attempts to describe practices in Japan are complicated, since a cross-cultural description must not only address the observed reality but also make explicit underlying societal ideals not necessarily shared or understood by potential consumers of the study. And making comparative analyses of Japan with other systems is even more daunting. Should Japanese practice be understood against a background of traditional Japanese culture (whatever this may be)? How should we account for the influences of the original transplanted Continental code? What have been the effects of the more recent embrace of American-style adversarial and constitutional ideals? Or are current practices a consequence of the long-dominant single-party system that unwittingly permits strong bureaucracies to impose their visions of social control upon the population? There is a case to be made for each, and indeed there is an impressive tradition of scholarship on the Japanese legal system that supports each of these perspectives. The dean of sociology of law in contemporary Japan was the late Takeyoshi Kawashima (1963, 1974). In his writings about Japanese civil law, he argued that where Japanese practices differed greatly from those in the West, one could identify the effects of the traditional Japanese culture, which discourages application of universalistic norms of clearly defined rights and duties. This theme has been echoed in the work of criminologist John Braithwaite (1989), who has suggested that Japan's low crime rate, heavy reliance on confessions, and apparent success at rehabilitation are a consequence of its homogeneous population, its "shame culture," and its long-standing practice of extracting expressions of remorse from wrongdoers. David H. Bayley (1976, 1991) and Daniel H. Foote (1992) have presented similar arguments.

Others, including the eminent comparativist David Nelken, have suggested that many of what appear to be distinct features of traditional Japanese culture may in fact reflect features of the inquisitorial system transplanted from Germany to Japan in the late nineteenth century. Still others seek to account for practices (or avoidance of practices) in terms of the failure of Japanese authority to embrace constitutional rights and adversarial norms formally ensconced in the Constitution – that is, in terms of a residual resistance even at the highest levels to internalizing true respect for the rule of law (Upham, 1987).

Some scholars of Japan offer decidedly less culture-specific explanations. Employing rational choice models which assume a sort of universal *homo economus,* Mark Ramseyer (1994; Ramseyer and Rasmusen, 1997) argues that participants in the Japanese legal process are motivated by the same objectives as are citizens in other countries – the desire to minimize costs and maximize benefits – and that their behavior can be accounted for accordingly. For example, in addressing the question of extremely low acquittal rates in criminal cases, Ramseyer and his colleague (Ramseyer and Rasmusen, 2001) present statistical evidence of relationships between judicial decisions and promotions and relocations of judges. Similarly, in a recent book exploring public interest litigation in Japan, Eric Feldman (2000) argues that the pursuit of rights through litigation in Japan and the expectations of the litigants are remarkably similar to what one might find in allegedly hyperlitigious America, despite important structural differences between the two cultures.

What becomes clear is that there is an array of coherent and persuasive perspectives ready to play counterpoint to any given context in which the Japanese legal process might be placed. If one embraces a culture-centric perspective, a critic may claim, "No, the key to the problem is the influence of the inquisitorial transplant." If one adopts this perspective, another critical voice may retort, "Perhaps so, but in fact practices are anchored in traditional norms that preceded this transplantation by centuries." And so forth. Ultimately we might conclude that there is validity to be found in each of these approaches – that each one contributes a true puzzle-piece to a complex whole.

Thus when we suggest, as we have done in the title of the volume, that we are presenting studies that explore *contexts, controversies and comparisons,* we do not mean that we have found a single most powerful perspective. Rather, the essays herein examine facets of the Japanese criminal justice system from multiple perspectives and contexts. If anything, our contributors reveal methodological challenges rather than suggest solutions. This volume offers a wide range of insightful observations and assessments by a stellar grouping of scholars and legal practitioners.

Nine of the 14 essays are written by leading Japanese criminal justice scholars, prominent Japanese criminal defense lawyers, or internationally recognized American experts on the Japanese criminal process. Indeed, the contributors constitute a veritable who's who of experts in the field. Setsuo Miyazawa, formerly a member of the Law Faculty of Kobe University and now at Waseda University in Tokyo, has conducted empirical research on the behavior of Japanese police detectives; he has published widely in Japan, the United States and Europe on police and criminal justice in Japan. Daniel Foote is the preeminent American scholar on Japanese criminal law and is the author of several major studies of the Japanese criminal process. During the period this book was in production, he moved from his longtime home in the School of Law at the University of Washington to Tokyo, where he assumed the chair in the sociology of law at the University of Tokyo Faculty of Law. Masayuki Murayama of Chiba University has conducted empirical research on Japanese patrol officers, and has written widely on the American, English, German, and Japanese criminal justice systems. One of his central interests is the availability of defense counsel to poor people accused of criminal offenses. Satoru Shinomiya practices law in Chiba. He has been a leading proponent of the idea to reintroduce jury trials in Japan, and recently became the head of the Unit of Research on Judicial Reform of the Japan Federation of Bar Associations. Takashi Takano, who received an LLM from Southern Methodist University in Texas and practices in Saitama, is a prominent criminal defense lawyer in Japan. He has been leading the Miranda Society, a group of lawyers advocating for extension of the right to counsel and the right against self-incrimination. David T. Johnson, an assistant professor at the University of Hawaii, has studied in Japan, and received his PhD in the Jurisprudence and Social Policy Program at Berkeley in 1996. He has produced a groundbreaking observational study of Japanese prosecutors, and is the author of an award-winning article on prosecutorial decision-making in Japan. His book on Japanese prosecutors will appear in 2002. Masahito Inouye is professor of criminal procedure at the University of Tokyo. He is the author of numerous books and articles on Japanese law, including a book comparing the criminal process in Japan and the United States. He has also served on numerous government blue-ribbon committees, most recently for two years on the Judicial Reform Council, which presented final proposals to the Prime Minister on June 12 of this year. On the Council, he was particularly involved in the reform of professional legal education and lay participation in criminal trials. Toshikuni Murai, formerly of Hitotsubashi University in Tokyo and now at Ryukoku University in Kyoto, has written extensively on constitutional criminal procedure and juvenile justice in Japan. He is a former dean of Hitotsubashi University Law Faculty and the current President of the Japanese Association of Criminal Law. Nobuyoshi Araki teaches criminal procedure and criminal justice policies at Rikkyo University in Tokyo. He has studied in both the United States and Japan, and has written widely on both the Japanese and American criminal justice and juvenile justice systems. He is the current President of the Japanese Association of Sociological Criminology. Although most of these authors have published other pieces on the Japanese criminal process in English, and most are very well-known to Western scholars of Japanese law, no other single volume in English contains such wealth of analysis of the Japanese criminal justice system.

The remaining contributors to this volume are also well-known scholars of comparative law and politics or specialists on specific issues of the American criminal justice system. Malcolm Feeley, Professor of Law at Berkeley, has published several books on the American criminal process and has lectured extensively in various countries, including Japan. Robert Kagan is Professor of Political Science and Law at Berkeley, and is also the Director of that university's Center for the Study of Law and Society. He is the author of several books on the American legal system, including the recently published volume, *Adversarial Legalism* (2001). Roger Hanson has been Senior Research Associate at the National Center for State Courts, where he and his two colleagues, Brian J. Ostrom and Ann M. Jones, have conducted a series of studies of the quality of counsel offered by various types of public defense systems (in contrast to private counsel) in the United States. Richard Leo received his JD and PhD from Berkeley in the mid-1990s, and is currently Associate Professor in the Crime, Law and Society Program at the University of California at Irvine. He has received several national awards for his research on the consequences of police interrogation. Gordon Van Kessel served for many years as a prosecutor in San Francisco before changing careers to teach criminal law and procedure at the University of California's Hastings School of Law in San Francisco. He has written extensively on criminal law and procedure and comparative law. Much of his work traces changes that he believes will lead to a convergence of the inquisitorial and adversarial systems.

These American scholars offer insights from an Anglo-American perspective; in so doing they offer a valuable perspective from which to view some Japanese practices. Interestingly, the Japanese contributors seem to be explicating, although from different perspectives, various Japanese issues for an English-speaking audience. In contrast, the Anglo-American contributors seem to be writing for their Japanese colleagues, offering various ways to understand similarities and differences between these two systems, and at times cautioning against making unwarranted assumptions about Anglo-American practices. Taken together, these contributions offer a host of perspectives and identify a number of contexts in which to describe, assess, and compare the Japanese criminal justice system.

Although few of the pieces offer sustained methodological discussions of the theory and method of comparative analysis, they are rich in establishing context and offering substantive detail. In a sense many of the contributions offer information that could be the raw material for comparative sociolegal analysis, material that is deeper and more detailed than most other presentations of the Japanese criminal process available in English. Thus this volume should become an invaluable resource for both the interested student of the Japanese criminal process and the dedicated specialist in comparative criminal law and politics.

This volume is decidedly not a book that presents a single integrated framework for comparative analysis. Nor does it purport to be a comprehensive analysis of all major issues in the Japanese criminal process. But it contains a collection of spirited and insightful essays presented by leading scholars and practitioners in Japan who are active and articulate participants in the ongoing and at times raucous debates about the nature and function of the Japanese criminal justice system, as well as a set of observations about the American system for purposes of comparative analysis, that begin to outline bases for sustained comparative study. Indeed, we believe these essays constitute a unique introductory anthology even for scholars outside the field of Japanese legal studies, since many of them crystallize important, contentious, and ongoing policy debates about the nature and future of the criminal justice system in Japan.

This volume had its origins in a conference sponsored by the Sho Sato Japan Fund of the Boalt Hall School of Law at the University of California at Berkeley in 1998. The Fund was established to honor the memory of the late Sho Sato, Professor of Law at Berkeley and the first Japanese-American to hold a professorship at a major American law school. Periodically the Fund sponsors conferences in Berkeley on issues related to Japanese and American legal issues. The contributions to this volume represent the revised, edited, and at times much-changed, versions of the original papers from the 1998 Sho Sato Conference. One note in this vein. The editors standardized the entire volume by following the Western custom of placing first names first, rather than the Japanese custom of last names first. The editors are indebted to the diligence, good nature, and patience of the conference participants and contributors.

The original conference and this volume could not have been completed without the help of a large group of wonderful colleagues, indeed too many to list here. But among those we feel obliged to single out are: Mas Sato, for her unflagging support for the Fund which was established to honor the work of her husband, the late Sho Sato; Professor Harry Scheiber, Director of the Sho Sato Fund at Boalt and the then Associate Dean and Chair of the Jurisprudence and Social Policy PhD Program at Boalt; Professor Robert Kagan, Director of the Center for the Study of Law and Society at Berkeley which cosponsored the Conference; and Professor Herma Hill Kay, then Dean of Boalt Hall, which hosted the conference. As always with Center-sponsored activities, Margo Rodriguez and Rod Watanabe did a marvelous job coordinating complicated travel plans, arranging for housing and expense reimbursements for the participants, and taking care of other countless details in setting up the conference itself. The production of the book was possible only because of e-mail. At times the editors and contributors were in different locations spread over several countries on three continents. The lynchpin which held this enterprise together was Kay Levine, Boalt Hall JD 1993, JSP PhD Candidate, and editor extraordinaire. She kept track of questions and queries, maintained up-to-date files, and above all served as an unerring editor to a group which collectively was in dire need of good editing. Whatever success the volume enjoys owes much to her dedicated work, and whatever defects it contains should be attributed to the editors who no doubt failed to heed enough of her good advice. Many thanks also to Kiara Jordan for her good spirit in typing and retyping some of the essays, as well as her keen editorial contributions, and to Takeshi Akiba for important editorial help at the last minute.

References

Bayley, D. (1976 and 1991) *Forces of Order* (Berkeley: University of California Press).

Braithwaite, J. (1989) *Crime, Shame and Reintegration* (Cambridge: Cambridge University Press).

Feldman, E. (2000) *The Ritual of Rights in Japan: Law, Society, and Health Policy* (New York: Cambridge University Press).

Foote, D. (1992) "The Benevolent Paternalism of Japanese Criminal Justice," *California Law Review*, Vol. 80, p. 317.

Kawashima, T. (1963) "Dispute Resolution in Contemporary Japan," in A.T. von Mehren (ed.), *Law in Japan: the Legal Order in a Changing Society* (Cambridge: Harvard University Press).

Kawashima, T. (1974) "The Legal Consciousness of Contract in Japan," *Law in Japan*, Vol. 7, p. 1.

Ramseyer, M. (1994) "The Puzzling (In)Dependence of Courts: a Comparative Approach," *Journal of Legal Studies*, Vol. 23 (June), p. 721.

Ramseyer, M. and E. Rasmusen (1997) "Judicial Independence in a Civil Regime: the Evidence from Japan," *Journal of Law, Economics and Organizations*, Vol. 13, p. 259.

Ramseyer, M. and E. Rasmusen (2001) "Why is the Japanese Conviction Rate So High?" *Journal of Legal Studies*, Vol. 30, p. 53.
Upham, F. (1987) *Law and Social Change in Japan* (Cambridge: Harvard University Press).

1

Introduction: an Unbalanced Adversary System – Issues, Policies, and Practices in Japan, in Context and in Comparative Perspective

*Setsuo Miyazawa**

Part I The nature of the criminal justice system in Japan

Prewar and postwar criminal justice systems

How do Japanese scholars understand the meaning of adversariness in the Japanese criminal justice system? We must first look to temporal distinctions.

The prewar criminal process can be characterized by the inquisitorial principle (*shokken shugi*), which required active intervention by judges. Under this system, the prosecutor was not merely a party to criminal proceedings, but an overseer of those proceedings. The prosecutor and the judge were not clearly separated. Evidence was collected and interrogations were conducted through the exercise of judicial power. Moreover, the defendant was not clearly recognized as a subject in proceedings. His or her procedural rights were not sufficiently protected (Tamiya, 1994).

After the war, the structure of criminal proceedings was supposed to have changed in accordance with the adversary principle (*tojisha shugi*). Under adversary principles, the judge takes a more neutral and passive role, and the parties (the prosecutor and the defendant) shape the proceedings through their adversary actions. Adversary proceedings have several crucial elements, beginning with the formal separation of the judge and the prosecutor: the prosecutor determines the object of proceedings, while the judge is a passive and impartial adjudicator.

* Malcolm M. Feeley kindly helped me to expand this chapter, while Kay Levine brushed up my English. I am most grateful to them.

Secondly, the parties present and examine evidence, and the defendant's procedural rights receive some degree of protection to counterbalance the power of the government.

Tamiya (1994) has examined the degree to which each of these three crucial adversary elements has been achieved in Japan. He argues that while the first two conditions have been fully realized, Japan has not yet equalized the power of the prosecutor and of the defendant. As a result of policies such as *seimitsu shiho* (judicial proceedings that seek precision in finding truth) (Matsuo, 1979, pp. 15–16) and "benevolent paternalism" (Foote, 1992), the actual powers of the adversaries in the Japanese criminal justice are highly unbalanced, and thus the accused and his or her defense lawyer do not have many chances to act as real adversaries to the police and the prosecutor. While this power imbalance remains intact, Japan cannot achieve meaningful adversariness.

Tamiya contends that the actual administration of criminal justice is still characterized by *shokken shugi* (the inquisitorial principle), under which we expect paternalistic officials to uncover or to determine the truth of each case. In this sense, the adversary system has failed in Japan. Therefore, we must take measures to prevent officials from making errors in this "truth-determining function." One such measure is to strengthen the rights of defense lawyers and defendants. We must also take measures to prevent excessive intervention by officials. One such measure is to honor the right of the accused to remain silent.

Imbalance between the parties

The imbalance between the two sides in criminal proceedings is maintained by four conditions which exist in twenty-first-century Japan. Firstly, the law is structured to benefit the police in conducting investigations (Miyazawa, 1992, Chapter 2). The accused may be detained in a police station for up to 23 days for each count, may be interrogated by investigators without the presence of a defense lawyer, and may not receive the services of a free defense lawyer until after indictment. The accused must defend himself against the efforts of police to obtain a confession; he must survive without the assistance of a lawyer in an environment totally controlled by the police (see, for example, Foote, Chapter 3, Murayama, Chapter 4, and Shinomiya, Chapter 5, this volume).

Moreover, the law is helpful for the prosecutor, in both the investigation and trial stages (Johnson, 1996, pp. 207–20; Johnson, Chapter 9, this volume). The defendant has only a very limited right to compel discovery. The courts frequently allow exceptions to the hearsay rule. Crucial evidence is typically found not in testimony given at the trial, but in dossiers prepared by the police and the prosecutor during the investigation. Furthermore, the courts do not always exclude illegally seized evidence. Following trial, the prosecutor may appeal if the defendant is acquitted, although the defendant is rarely acquitted in Japan (Ramseyer and Nakazato, 1999, pp. 168–75, 178–82).

Thirdly, mainstream judges largely agree with police and prosecutors about the purposes and practices of the criminal justice system (Miyazawa, 1992, pp. 236–8). Judges generally support prosecutors' arguments to maintain the present system and criticize defense lawyers for their reform proposals (Mitsui et al., 1988).

Fourthly, the General Secretariat of the Supreme Court carefully monitors Japanese judges in their performance and can reward or punish judges through assignment and promotion (Miyazawa, 1994; Feeley, Chapter 5, this volume). Ramseyer and Rasmusen (2001) have tested this punishment/reward thesis in the context of criminal cases by employing an econometric analysis. They report, for instance, that granting an acquittal will increase by five years the length of time a judge spends in branch courts, which is considered a punishment.

Taken together, these factors maintain the imbalance between the defense and the prosecution in the criminal justice system. They prevent the parties from becoming real adversaries and allow police and prosecutors to control criminal proceedings.

Efforts to strengthen the position of the accused

Defense lawyers are not resigned to accepting this imbalance. Both the organized bar and individual lawyers are trying to strengthen the position of the accused.

In Japan, practicing attorneys are required to join both a local bar association and the national Japan Federation of Bar Associations (JFBA). Bar associations are taking various steps to improve the rights of the accused. For example, all the local bar associations in Japan now have a duty solicitor scheme, modeled after the British scheme, under which the detained suspect can meet with a volunteer attorney, free of charge (Miyazawa, 1992, p. 239; Johnson, 1996, p. 225; Miyazawa, 1999, p. 23; Murayama, Chapter 4 and Shinomiya, Chapter 7, this volume). Japanese bar associations have also established criminal defense centers in order to provide assistance and guidance to lawyers engaging in criminal defense work (Miyazawa, 1992, p. 240; Johnson, 1996, p. 225; Shinomiya, Chapter 7, this volume). Additionally, the organized bar is attempting to reintroduce jury trials into Japanese criminal courts; jury trials previously existed in Japan between 1928 and 1943 (Shinomiya, Chapter 7, this volume). Finally, the organized bar has sponsored a movement to introduce state-appointed defense lawyers during the investigation stage before indictment (Shinomiya, Chapter 7, this volume).

Individual lawyers are also posing challenges to the present system. The most conspicuous example is the formation of a voluntary organization called *Miranda no Kai* (The Miranda Society) (Miranda no Kai, 1997). Inspired by the *Miranda* rule in the United States, lawyers of this group advise their clients to refuse to submit to interrogation without the presence of a lawyer and to refuse to sign statements taken by investigators without the examination of contents by a lawyer. At trial, they vigorously challenge the admissibility of statements taken in violation of these principles (Takano, Chapter 8, this volume).

There is also a less conspicuous, more individualized challenge to the present system: a lawyer who was denied or limited access to his client can file a civil suit for damages. These plaintiffs have won in a number of cases (Wakamatsu, 1990), although winning in a civil case does not directly affect the outcome of the criminal case.

These reform movements face a fundamental difficulty: under the parliamentary cabinet system in Japan, any legislative changes must be proposed by the Justice Ministry (Miyazawa, 1992, p. 239). Yet the Justice Ministry is the very target of these reforms, and it has a vested interest in maintaining the status quo. The Ministry is therefore unlikely to support any proposal that would diminish its powers.

However, the political environment in Japan has significantly changed since the late 1990s. Both the *Keidanren* (The Federation of Economic Organizations), widely considered the most powerful interest group in Japan, and the ruling Liberal Democratic Party proposed fundamental changes to the judicial system in May and June of 1998. The government established the Judicial Reform Council in July 1999; the Council has 13 members and includes Masahito Inouye (see his Chapter 10, this volume) as its youngest member.

The future looks promising. The agenda issued by the Council on December 21, 1999 (for an official translation, see "The Points at Issue in the Judicial Reform," at http://www.kantei.go.jp/foreign/judiciary/0620reform.html) included the examination of jury trials and the expansion of the public provision of lawyers for indigent suspects and defendants. There is no guarantee, however, that the Council will actually propose these measures when it finishes its two-year term in July 2001. Its 13 members are not necessarily known as reformers, and a few members are clearly committed to the preservation of the present system. It is widely expected that Inouye will play a crucial role on these issues in the Council.

Efforts to strengthen the position of police and prosecutors

On the other side, there are also efforts to strengthen the position of the police and prosecutors. For example, the National Police Agency has sought to secure recognition of police stations as legitimate places for pretrial detention (Odanaka, 1990). Although police stations are widely used as places for pretrial detention, the present law defines them as substitutes for prisons, not as principal places for detention. This effort by the National Police Agency has not yet succeeded, but the legal status of police stations remains an open question.

A more recent and successful example is the enactment of the Law on Interception of Telecommunication for Criminal Investigation, the so-called Wiretapping Law, in August of 1999 (Murai, Chapter 11, this volume). Wiretapping had been illegal in Japan since the end of World War II, even when conducted by police. A serious scandal erupted when it was revealed in 1986 that the house of a Communist Party official was wiretapped, although the police officers involved eventually managed to escape prosecution (Miyazawa, 1986). The new law radically changes the status of wiretapping (for a detailed theoretical and comparative proposal prior to the legislation, see Inouye, 1997); it allows investigators to intercept telecommunications on the basis of a judicially issued warrant when there is sufficient reason to believe that a specified crime will likely be committed through a conspiracy of several people. After the warrant is issued, the fact of wiretapping will not be disclosed to the parties of the wiretapped communication until after the wiretapping is completed. Unlike arrest and search warrants, a wiretapping warrant does not function as a warning to the suspect; its issuance thus reduces the suspect's opportunity to protect himself from investigators (Murai, Chapter 11, this volume).

Additionally, prosecutors have been striving vigorously to curb the activities of aggressive defense lawyers like members of *Miranda no Kai* (The Miranda Society). Top prosecutors constantly criticize such lawyers for interfering with the right of investigators to carry out their responsibilities (Johnson, 1996, pp. 218–20). There have also been more formal proposals to introduce a system to take disciplinary action against defense attorneys who are overly assertive of their clients' rights (see, for instance, Sakai, 1997; Takano, Chapter 8, this volume).

While such efforts have not yet succeeded, prosecutors have significantly more power than the defense bar in the legislative process, since criminal justice bills must be presented by the Justice Ministry. Consequently, efforts to increase the imbalance have a better chance of succeeding than the efforts to restore balance.

Proposals with a mixed character

While the previous two sections have discussed efforts taken by opposing sides, there are some issues which may produce benefits and disadvantages for both sides.

One such issue is the reform of the juvenile justice system. The Japanese juvenile justice system is a classic example of the *parens patriae* ideal. The proceedings are not adversarial: no prosecutor appears in the courtroom, and an attorney may appear not as an advocate for the child, but only as an attendant. A single judge decides even the most serious cases. No proceedings are provided for retrial (Araki, Chapter 13, this volume).

Defense lawyers have long sought to increase defense counsel involvement in the proceedings. Now, however, after a series of widely reported serious juvenile crimes, prosecutors want to increase their own involvement. In response to these two demands, the juvenile justice system will certainly become more adversarial, but it is not clear which side will become stronger.

We have also recently seen proposals to introduce plea bargaining and immunity as legitimate methods of criminal investigation and prosecution in Japan (for instance, Ukawa, 1997). The use of plea bargaining and immunity will have three known impacts: (1) to allow certain suspects to deal directly with investigators; (2) to make investigation and prosecution of certain types of crimes easier; and (3) to make it more difficult for other suspects to defend themselves. It is not clear which side (the prosecution or the defense) will become stronger as a result of these changes. However, because the Justice Ministry expressed its desire to introduce such methods at a recent hearing before the Judicial Reform Council, it is likely that the Ministry expects significant advantages for the prosecution (see also Inouye, Chapter 10, this volume; Johnson, Chapter 9, this volume).

Part II Empirical studies on criminal defense lawyering in Japan

How do attorneys defend their clients in a highly unbalanced adversary system? Empirical research, based on interviews, surveys, and observation, has provided some answers.

Nobuyoshi Araki pioneered the use of empirical studies on criminal defense lawyering in Japan. As part of his comprehensive study on the right to a speedy trial, Araki interviewed 32 lawyers in Tokyo in 1973 (Araki, 1993, Chapter 8). He found that economic factors constrain criminal defense lawyers, for two reasons. Because they cannot maintain their practice by taking only criminal cases, private lawyers must also take a large number of civil cases; they thus cannot devote extensive amounts of time to their criminal clients. Additionally, since civil trials are held intermittently in Japan, the pace of criminal trials is affected by civil practice. In other words, the economic need of lawyers prevents the meaningful exercise of the right to speedy trial by defendants in Japan.

Through a series of questionnaires and interviews, Murayama found that even privately retained attorneys do not engage in aggressive defense work (Murayama, Chapter 4, this volume). They rarely challenge judicial decisions to detain their clients. They do not typically advise their clients to refuse to speak to police and prosecutors. They do not challenge the admissibility of statements introduced by the prosecution in most cases, and they rarely call defense witness on the issue of culpability for the crime itself. Their activities in state-appointed cases are even less vigorous: many lawyers take state-appointed cases in order to keep abreast of criminal defense practices (although by merely taking a few cases each year, it seems unlikely that their skills stay honed).

In exploring the factors that contribute to this state of affairs, Murayama learned that incentives are problematic. Many lawyers think that criminal cases do not contribute financially to their firms, and most contend that compensation in state-appointed cases is worse than in privately retained cases. Because criminal cases often involve people connected to organized crime, many lawyers think that taking criminal cases does not contribute to the development of a respectable clientele and that it may damage the reputation of one's firm.

Work by both Araki and Murayama supports the conventional view of criminal defense lawyering in Japan: the defense practice is not active, not specialized, and incapable of reducing the power imbalance between the suspect and the prosecution. (Contrast these descriptions with those of Hanson and his colleagues concerning criminal defense attorneys in the United States in Chapter 6 of this volume.) If the reality of criminal defense lawyering is such, one may argue that it simply amplifies the existing imbalance.

However, Hiroto Hata departs from Araki and Murayama in both his methods and his conclusions. He observed and interviewed 45 lawyers in Kobe and 16 lawyers in Fukuoka in 1991 in order to find lawyers who specialize in criminal defense work (Hata, 1993, 1994) (see also Johnson, 1996, p. 209). Additionally, he conducted a yearlong observational study of five lawyers in Kobe and Osaka who indicated that they spent 70 percent or more of their time in criminal cases (Hata, 1997, 1998).

His findings are fundamentally different from those of Araki and Murayama. Criminal defense specialists do exist in Japan. Such lawyers comprise two groups: retired prosecutors, and leftist lawyers who started their careers in labor cases and eventually moved to criminal defense work. The latter group is more likely than the former to take private cases and to engage in more sophisticated forms of defense activities. Noncriminal specialists refer difficult cases to them or ask their participation as cocounsel. Their work is highly regarded by both their clients and other lawyers. But even the former prosecutors play a significant role in criminal defense practice: they are willing to take relatively minor cases and relatively more cases than other lawyers do. In either case, while firms of criminal defense specialists are not wealthy, they are financially viable.

If Hata's findings are valid, there is some hope for improving the quality of criminal defense lawyering in Japan, even under the unbalanced adversary system. These improvements will depend on the ability of other Japanese lawyers to understand and to emulate the style of lawyering displayed by the activist group of criminal defense specialists. A particularly attractive possibility may be to form publicly funded criminal defense firms (like public defender offices in the United States) and to transplant the skills of those lawyers to such a setting (see Hanson et al., Chapter 6, this volume).

Part III Looking to the future and lessons from other nations

There appear to be two paths by which Japan can reduce the power imbalance in its criminal justice system. One is to seek legislative reforms, which will change legal rules. In the past, this option has been meaningless, because the criminal legislative process was totally controlled by the Justice Ministry. However, the situation has radically changed with the recent formation and empowerment of the Judicial Reform Council, an entity which has a broad mandate to conduct comprehensive reform. The problem is whether and to what extent the Council will recommend the strengthening of the position of the accused and his lawyers.

The other avenue is to increase the number of specialists in criminal defense. To expand the scope and public funding for criminal legal aid would provide better financial incentives to lawyers interested in criminal defense work. However, these types of expansion require legislative reforms. It remains to be seen how effective the Judicial Reform Council will be in addressing these issues.

In the discussion above I have reviewed the weaknesses of the Japanese adversary process largely on its own terms, that is, by assessing the fit between its stated objectives and actual experiences. But the weaknesses can also be explored in a comparative perspective. Several contributors to this volume provide valuable tools for this type of analysis: these works highlight the range of expectations and practices that people in different cultures bring to bear in understanding their own and others' criminal justice systems.

When specific issues are considered comparatively, Japan's adversary system looks weak. Although the American *Miranda* rule has garnered a lot of interest in Japan and support among Japanese criminal defense lawyers, Leo's analysis suggests that its mixed success in the United States may be a result of distinctive features of American culture that do not transfer easily to Japan (Leo, Chapter 12, this volume). Similarly, the analysis of American public defenders by Hanson et al. (Chapter 6, this volume) describes a system that, while often criticized by American reformers for not being aggressive enough, is by Japanese standards a model of aggressive defense representation. In contrast, Feeley locates some of the features that undermine adversarial proceedings in the Japanese criminal process in the weakness of the bar generally, and not in the failings of criminal defense attorneys themselves (Feeley, Chapter 5, this volume). Bob Kagan (Chapter 2, this volume) similarly argues that the structure of a legal system varies with the nature of the state, but he goes on to warn against emulating the American adversarial model because of its cost and its disruption. Finally, Van Kessel's discussion of the possible convergence of the adversarial and inquisitorial styles offers an excellent overview of the major features and emerging similarities of the Anglo-American and European legal systems. But his article may also indirectly expose another feature of the Japanese system – its roots in the inquisitorial system (Chapter 14, this volume).

The value of such a reorientation in thinking is reinforced by Murayama's contribution (Chapter 4, this volume). His essay illustrates that despite postwar reforms, the Japanese criminal justice system has deep roots in the inquisitorial system. Indeed, these discussions raise the possibility that many of the differences between the Japanese and American legal systems that are usually attributed to differences in "culture" may better be explained by differences between the inquisitorial and adversarial systems. That is, it may not be "cultural" obstacles that separate Japan from a robust American-style adversary system, but rather the historical fact that the Japanese system has its roots in another, earlier, transplanted system based on inquisitorial principles and practices. Moreover, the Japanese elite has succeeded in retaining certain inquisitorial elements of the criminal justice system in spite of the efforts by Japanese reformers since the end of the World War II (for a similar view on other aspects of the Japanese legal system, see Upham, 1987).

Whatever the case, the Japanese criminal justice system in the postwar period has formally embraced the theory of the adversary process and has structured itself accordingly. As a consequence it is fair to ask whether it is achieving the objectives implicit (and often explicit) in this embrace. The answer suggested by most of the articles in this volume is no, or not very well. Some of our authors accept this conclusion without applauding this state of affairs, while others seek to explain it by pointing to culture and structure. Yet others are openly critical of the fact, arguing that the system fails to live up to its ideals. (I fall into this latter group.) Whatever approach ultimately prevails, the contributions in this volume should be of great interest and value to all those seeking a better understanding of the Japanese criminal justice system or comparative criminal procedure.

References

Araki, Nobuyoshi (1993) *Jinsoku na Saiban o Ukeru Kenri* [The Right to Speedy Trial] (Tokyo: Seibundo).

Foote, Daniel H. (1992) "The Benevolent Paternalism of Japanese Criminal Justice," *California Law Review*, Vol. 80, pp. 317–90.

Hata, Hiroto (1993) "Keiji Bengo no Jitsuzo o Motomete" [In Search of the Reality of Criminal Defense Lawyering], *Rokkodai Ronshu*, Vol. 40, No. 1, pp. 120–41.

—— (1994) "Keiji Bengo no Zentai Zo" [A Comprehensive Image of Criminal Defense Lawyering], *Ho Shakaigaku*, No. 46, pp. 217–21.

—— (1997) "Keiji Senmon Bengoshi no Katsudo Sutairu" [Styles of Activities of Criminal Defense Specialists], *Ho Shakaigaku*, No. 49, pp. 213–18.

—— (1998) "Keiji Bengo Katsudo no Jitsuzo to Keiji Bengoshi Ron no Tenkan" [The Reality of Criminal Defense Lawyering and the Transformation of Discussion on Criminal Defense Lawyers], *Kobe Hogaku Zasshi*, Vol. 48, No. 2, pp. 357–412.

Inouye, Masahito (1997) *Sosa Shudan to shite no Tsushin Kaiwa no Boju* [Interception of Telecommunication and Conversation as a Method of Investigation] (Tokyo: Yuhikaku).

Johnson, David T. (1996) "The Japanese Way of Justice", PhD thesis in jurisprudence and social policy, University of California, Berkeley.

Matsuo, Koya (1979) *Keiji Sosho-Ho* [Criminal Procedure], Vol. 1 (Tokyo: Kobundo).

Miranda no Kai (The Miranda Society) (1997) *Miranda no Kai to Bengo Katsudo* [The Miranda Society and Defense Activities] (Tokyo: Gendai Jinbunsha).

Mitsui, Makoto et al. (eds.) (1998) *Keiji Tetsuzuki* [Criminal Proceedings], Vols 1 and 2 (Tokyo: Yuhikaku).

Miyazawa, Setsuo (1986) "Scandal and Hard Reform: Implications of a Wiretapping Case to the Control of Organizational Police Crimes in Japan," *Kobe University Law Journal*, No. 23, pp. 13–27.

—— (1992) *Policing in Japan: a Study on Making Crime* (Albany: SUNY Press).

—— (1994) "Administrative Control of Japanese Judges," in Philip S.C. Lewis (ed.), *Law and Technology in the Pacific Community* (Boulder: Westview).

—— (1999) "Lawyering for the Underrepresented in the Context of Legal, Social, and National Institutions: the Case of Japan," in Louise G. Trubek and Jeremy Cooper (eds), *Educating for Justice around the World: Legal Education, Legal Practice and the Community* (Aldershot: Ashgate).

Odanaka, Toshiki (1990) "The Prison Institution Bill and the Detention Institution Bill," *Law in Japan*, Vol. 23, pp. 72–84.

Ramseyer, J. Mark and Minoru Nakazato (1999) *Japanese Law: an Economic Approach* (Chicago: University of Chicago Press).

Ramseyer, J. Mark and Eric B. Rasmusen (2001) "Why Is the Japanese Conviction Rate So High?" *Journal of Legal Studies*, Vol. 30, pp. 53–88.

Sakai, Toru (1997) "Sho Gaikoku ni okeru Keiji Bengo Katsudo no Ruru" [Rules on Defense Lawyering in Foreign Countries], *Hanrei Taimuzu*, No. 936, pp. 43–55.

Tamiya, Hiroshi (1994) "Keiji Sosho ni okeru Moderu Ron" [Models on Criminal Proceedings], in Koya Matsuo and Kuniji Shibahara (eds), *Keiji Hogaku no Gendai-teki Kadai* [Contemporary Issues of Studies on Criminal Law and Procedure] (Tokyo: Yuhikaku).

Ukawa, Haruhiko (1997) "Shiho Torihiki wo Kangaeru (1)–(17)" [Contemplating Judicial Bargaining], *Hanrei Jiho*, Nos. 1583–4, 1586–7, 1590, 1592–3, 1596, 1598–9, 1601–2, 1604, 1613–14, 1616, 1627.

Upham, Frank K. (1987) *Law and Social Change in Postwar Japan* (Cambridge: Harvard University Press).

Wakamatsu, Yoshiya (1990) *Sekken Kotsu to Keiji Bengo* [Meeting and Communication with Clients and Criminal Defense Lawyering] (Tokyo: Nihon Hyoronsha).

2

Adversarial Legalism and American Criminal Justice

Robert A. Kagan

In Japan, and in some Western European countries, some lawyers and legal scholars are interested in introducing more *adversarialism* into their criminal justice systems. It is natural, in that regard, to look to Great Britain, the United States and other former British colonies for models, for their legal systems are often labeled "adversarial." Yet it is important to note that even in the English-speaking world, criminal justice systems differ significantly. Both in terms of system organization and in terms of decision-making in individual cases, criminal justice in the United States differs substantially not only from countries with a civil law tradition but also from Great Britain and its former colonies.

Before using the American criminal justice system as a model for reform, it is important, this essay argues, to understand (1) the distinctive features of American "adversarial legalism," (2) the particular political system from which it has evolved, and (3) its actual everyday consequences. American adversarial legalism, it will be argued, has features that serve admirably as a barrier against the use of the criminal justice system as a means of political repression, but those same features make the American system inefficient and inconsistent in its handling of ordinary criminal cases. Yet because the American criminal justice system is so distinctive, and operates within a political system so different from Japan's, it should be clear that the introduction of *certain* adversarial elements into the very different Japanese criminal justice system is unlikely to produce American-style adversarial legalism or the unfortunate outcomes it generates.

Part I The concept of adversarial legalism

One way of describing the distinctive aspects of the American criminal justice system is to employ the typology of methods of policy

	DECISION-MAKING STYLE	
ORGANIZATION OF AUTHORITY	INFORMAL <---->	FORMAL
HIERARCHICAL	expert or political judgment	bureaucratic legalism
FRAGMENTED / PARTICIPATORY	negotiation/ mediation	adversarial legalism

Figure 2.1 Modes of policy-making and dispute resolution

implementation and dispute resolution set forth in Figure 2.1. The horizontal dimension refers to legal formality – the extent to which contending parties or interests, as well as legal officials, invoke and insist on conformity to written legal procedures and to preexisting legal rights and duties. At one extreme, a mode of policy elaboration and dispute resolution that is controlled by formal legal rules and procedures – rather than by discretionary judgment, bargaining, and informal processes – can be labeled legalism (Kagan, 1995).

The vertical dimension of Figure 2.1 concerns the extent to which the process is hierarchical – dominated by an official decision-maker, applying authoritative norms or standards – as opposed to participatory. Participatory processes are influenced by disputing parties and their lawyers, by their normative arguments, and by the evidence they deem relevant. Taking each of these dimensions to their extreme form produces four ideal types.

Negotiation/mediation

A process in the lower left quadrant of Figure 2.1 is adversarial in the sense that it is dominated by the contending parties, not by an authoritative governmental decision-maker. But it is informal or nonlegalistic, since neither procedures nor normative standards are dictated by formal law, and the outcome can readily be adjusted to the features of the individual case. In criminal justice, the purest form of this system would be negotiation of a settlement between the complainant and the alleged offender, perhaps abetted by a police officer or by a neighborhood mediation service. Although it is more constrained and guided by legal rules, the plea bargaining between prosecutors and defense counsel that often occurs in the United States would also fit in this quadrant.

Expert/political judgment

The more an official third party (as opposed to the contending interests) controls the process and the standards for decision, and the more authoritative and final the third party's decision is, the more "hierarchical" the process. As suggested by the upper left quadrant in Figure 2.1, hierarchical processes can be legally informal. An example is provided by Tanase's description of how disputes over fault in motor vehicle accidents are typically resolved in Japan: traffic police rush to the scene, question the parties, "hammer out a consensual story as to what happened," and file a detailed report on their findings; those reports are accorded considerable authority (Tanase, 1990, pp. 673–4). Similarly, whenever police have discretion to arrest a defendant or to seek a more informal disposition – restitution, apology, "curbside probation" – we might consider that use of discretion an example of an expert judgment model. Also within this category are juvenile courts, in which judges consult with social workers to devise the best approach for handling a potentially delinquent or troubled child.

Bureaucratic legalism

A policy-implementing or decision-making process characterized by a high degree of hierarchical authority and legal formality (the upper right quadrant of Figure 2.1) resembles an ideal-typical bureaucratic process, as analyzed by Max Weber. Governance by means of bureaucratic legalism emphasizes uniform implementation of centrally devised rules, vertical accountability, and official responsibility for fact-finding. The more hierarchical the system, the more restricted the role for legal representation and influence by affected citizens or contending interests. In contemporary democracies, the pure case of bureaucratic legalism is usually softened in some respects, but it is an ideal systematically pursued, for example, by tax collection agencies. Tending toward this ideal, too, are German and French courts, where bureaucratically recruited and embedded judges – not the parties' lawyers, and not lay juries – dominate both the evidence-gathering and the decision-making process; recruitment and supervision of judges and the decision-making process are oriented toward ensuring uniform and correct application of legal rules.[1]

Adversarial legalism

The lower right quadrant of Figure 2.1 includes policy-implementing and decision processes that are procedurally formalistic but in which hierarchy is weak; parties and their lawyers strongly influence the process. Thus in American criminal adjudication, the introduction of evidence and invocation of legal rules are dominated not by the judge (as in Europe) but by contending parties' lawyers. In contrast to bureaucratic legalism's emphasis on legal correctness, the crucial decision concerning the defendant's guilt or innocence is made not by a professional judge but by lay jurors, whose decisions are not explained in terms of law and are not legally reviewable. Lawyers for the prosecution and defense play a prominent role in choosing the jurors, in recruiting and coaching their own expert witnesses, and in influencing the jury's decision. David Johnson emphasizes that whereas Japanese prosecutors are subject to detailed rules and hierarchical supervision concerning the investigation of facts, the determination of the proper charge, and the recommendation of penalties, individual prosecutors in the US are subject to more cross-cutting pressures from complaining witnesses and defense counsel: they usually make their own judgments, free of review, in formulating the charge and in deciding when or how to reduce the charge in return for a guilty plea (Johnson, 1998). Even in comparison with the British "adversarial system," hierarchical, authoritative imposition of legal rules is relatively weak in the United States (Atiyah and Summers, 1987). Both systems employ trial by jury for serious charges, and British barristers, like US prosecutors and defense counsel, play a prominent role in the trial. But as noted by Graham Hughes in an excellent comparative analysis, the British system imposes more hierarchical constraints on party-driven adversariness. "England may be the cradle of the adversary system," Hughes observes, "but the child it reared never grew to the giant proportions of the sibling who crossed the Atlantic" (Hughes, 1984). Hughes remarks upon the "muted adversariness" of the average British barrister, as compared to the typical American criminal lawyer. The contrast arises not from differences in temperament or culture but from differences in legal rules and institutions.

Hughes provides numerous examples. In the United States, defendants' rights to purge racial and other forms of bias from jury selection have become routinized into a "prolonged jury selection process." In Los Angeles criminal trials in 1984, jury selection averaged five hours. In England, criminal juries usually are impaneled in a matter of minutes. In the United States, defense lawyers' legal objections often generate lengthy in-court wrangles over evidentiary issues. In English criminal trials, lawyers rarely tie up proceedings with objections and disputes about the admission of evidence. In contrast to American judges, British judges in jury trials summarize and comment on the evidence. In American trials, that task is left entirely to the competing lawyers, who may resort to obfuscation and appeals to general values rather than providing a close analysis of the evidence. American prosecutors and defense lawyers engage in "frequently repetitive (as well as pointless and degrading) cross-examination," punctuated by objections and arguments from opposing counsel about the cross-examiner's questioning style. This rarely occurs in English criminal trials, where "judges are forthright and dominating" and opposing counsel are "correspondingly restrained" (Hughes, 1984).

Just as importantly, the American and British criminal justice systems differ sharply in the extent to which adversarial litigation and courts affect the rules of criminal procedure and controls on law enforcement processes. In the UK, as in most countries, these rules are made primarily by legislatures and police bureaucracies. In the US, the rules are made to a significant degree by the courts, through the interpretation of the federal and state constitutions. Court-made rules of criminal procedure, elaborating defendants' constitutional rights, often override those made by legislatures and police departments, and adversarial litigation on such constitutional issues is an everyday phenomenon in both trial and appellate courts. Compared to Great Britain, American courts have instituted a much stricter version of the "exclusionary rule" (illegally obtained evidence, however probative of guilt, cannot be used in court). Moreover, since the enactment of a Parliamentary statute in October of 1994, British judges and juries have been authorized to draw inculpatory inferences from a defendant's refusal to answer questions or to explain his actions, either to the police or in court. American courts, conversely, continue to encourage an adversarial, noncooperative posture on the part of defendants by banning such inferences.

Part II Adversarial legalism and the infrequency of adjudication in the US

A system structured in accordance with the values and tenets of adversarial legalism does not necessarily lead to adversarial legal contestation. Indeed, full-scale adversarial legalism is so costly, cumbersome, and unpleasant that parties and lawyers regularly seek to avoid it. American prosecutors and defense lawyers do not always act in a fiercely adversarial manner. Indeed, overburdened public defenders and poorly compensated private defense counsel often are overly quiescent. More generally, full-scale adversarial adjudication is the exception, rather than the norm, in the United States.

As in other countries, a very large proportion of criminal cases in the US are resolved by the police, entirely or primarily as a result of their investigation and questioning of suspects. Despite strong legal protections for the criminal suspect's right to remain silent, many defendants confess, or are induced to confess, and enter guilty pleas (Leo, 1996). Prosecutors dismiss many cases based on their independent, discretionary assessment of the quality of the evidence provided by the police. In these respects, the "expert judgment" of law enforcement officials is the dominant mode of case disposition in the US. Many other cases in which the evidence of guilt is legally contestable are resolved not by adjudication but by *negotiation* between defense counsel and prosecutor. In Phoenix, Arizona, of 20,000 felony convictions in the 1983–86 period, only 4.3 percent were the result of a jury trial (Lowenthal, 1993, p. 80). Nationwide, more than 90 percent of criminal convictions are obtained by guilty plea, rather than by jury verdict (Boland et al., 1990, pp. 91–7).

On the other hand, the American system of plea negotiation is a direct reaction to, and can only be explained by understanding, the highly adversarial and legalistic *adjudicatory* process. As Albert Alschuler (1986, p. 1825) writes, "During this century, the American jury trial . . . has become one of the most cumbersome and expensive fact-finding mechanisms that humankind has devised." In the mid-1980s, in Oakland, California, homicide trials, which accounted for a third of all criminal trials in the county, averaged 44 hours (excluding jury deliberations) – probably spread over 11 or 12 court days, or more than two weeks (National Center for State Courts, 1988, p. 30). In one California trial of a man charged with murdering two police officers, the defense alone cost the state nearly $1 million, including $255,000 on forensic and legal experts, $100,000 for private investigators, and $50,000 for paralegals; the remainder went for attorneys' fees (Verhovek, 1995). The American jury trial has become so expensive, so difficult for the lawyers to conduct well, and so uncertain as to outcome that most criminal defendants and the professionals involved – prosecutors, defense lawyers, judges – seek to avoid it. So do many potential jurors: in many large cities, 50 percent of citizens called for jury duty fail to appear at the courthouse (Gerlin, 1995).

Defense lawyers in the United States are keenly aware that prosecutors and judges, obligated by law to dispose of criminal cases within a few months, cannot afford to mount many seven-day trials. Hence, whereas Japanese defendants are encouraged to confess and to apologize (Foote, 1991, 1992), American defense lawyers routinely encourage even clearly guilty defendants to maintain a stony silence and to plead not guilty – for the lawyer can then threaten, implicitly or explicitly, to insist on trial unless the prosecutor offers concessions. Prosecutors, in turn, feel compelled to reduce charges (and hence penalties) in order to elicit guilty pleas, thereby avoiding a laborious, schedule-wrecking trial. Judges encourage this aversion to adjudication. Researchers have shown that many judges give defendants who insist on trial harsher sentences than those which they impose on comparable defendants who plead guilty (Brereton and Casper, 1981; Uhlman and Walker, 1979; Lynch, 1994). By emphasizing the "trial penalty" (or, from the prosecutor's standpoint, the guilty-plea discount), defense lawyers pressure at least some defendants who might prefer a trial to plead guilty to a lesser offense.

Ironically, then, the rules and structures of adversarial legalism, because they generate such a cumbersome and costly mode of dispute resolution, produce *too little* adversarial legalism in practice (Stuntz, 1998, p. 24; Alschuler, 1983, p. 935). According to Thomas Weigend (1980, p. 411), a German comparative legal scholar,

> The admirable American preoccupation with safeguarding the individual's procedural rights has backfired. By affording the whole collection of procedural rights to a small minority of defendants, the system deprives the great majority of rights [particularly the right to a meaningful day in court] available to the accused in most civilized countries.

Part III The sources of American adversarial legalism

American adversarial legalism is the product of a particular political history and set of governmental structures. The United States, as a nation, was forged by a revolution against colonial domination. From the start, its political culture was permeated by a spirit of antagonism toward centralized authority and preference for community-based self-government. Both the national constitution and the state constitutions sought to fragment and limit power, and to limit governmental authority through judicially enforceable individual rights. In a study of comparative political culture, Seymour Martin Lipset writes that "America began and continues as the most antistatist, legalistic, and rights-oriented nation" (Lipset, 1996, p. 21).

Organizational fragmentation of criminal justice

The American disposition to fragment power and to subject it to influence by community-level self-government is reflected in the organization of the criminal justice system. Authority over criminal lawmaking, enforcement, and adjudication is scattered over 50 states and their many political subdivisions. In contrast to more hierarchical criminal justice systems in other nations (Damaska, 1975), the United States has no comprehensive nationwide criminal code and no truly national police force or court system. Rather, there are 50 state criminal codes and court systems, plus hundreds of separate municipal ordinances and courts and police departments, plus the criminal laws and courts of the federal government. The authority of the US Attorney General in Washington extends only (and only weakly) to the locally based US attorneys who prosecute federal crimes, and not at all to the hundreds of locally elected district attorneys who prosecute state crimes, or to the thousands of municipal police chiefs and county sheriffs.

In contrast to their counterparts in hierarchical systems, American trial court judges, police chiefs, sheriffs, and prosecutors have not been selected, socialized, and supervised by an overarching governmental bureaucracy which administers entrance exams, provides systematic training, coordinates policy, rewards the diligent and weeds out the incompetent. Rather, American law enforcement officials and judges are elected by local constituencies or appointed by local political leaders. This mode of staffing and supervising the officials of the American criminal justice system emphasizes political preferences for independent judgment and political responsiveness more than carefully honed legal craftsmanship or fidelity to legal rules.

In the adjudicative process, a still more diverse and localistic institution tugs against rule-of-law ideals. Guilt or innocence is determined by legally untrained citizens drawn from the local community, assembled into ad hoc juries to hear a single case, which they decide without having to give reasons. The American jury's unreviewable powers mirror the powers of American police, prosecutors, and judges to make discretionary decisions, particularly decisions to drop or to reduce criminal charges, without meaningful possibility of legal review. The system as a whole seems designed to sacrifice some legal regularity in order to make the criminal process less rigid, more responsive to popular notions of justice.

Accountability through adversarial legalism

In an organizationally fragmented criminal justice system, how is it possible to guard against the injustices that might result from incompetent, corrupt, or underfunded local police, prosecutors, judges, or jailors? There is no national or even state minister of justice with power to review, to discipline, or to dismiss prosecutors who are elected by local constituencies, police chiefs who are appointed by locally elected mayors, or judges elected or appointed for a term. Local democracy seems to trump legal accountability.

But not quite. Support for the rule of law arises from what Mirjan Damaska (1975) calls "coordinate" controls. The coordinate model seeks to achieve legal regularity in a decentralized system through a sequence of "lateral" legal checks. American prosecutors have the authority to reject charges forwarded to them by the police if the prosecutors think the charges are legally unsustainable. Judges have the authority and the obligation to reject charges made by prosecutors for legal inadequacy or for violations of defendants' constitutional rights. Juries can acquit a defendant if they feel that the prosecution's evidence is inadequate or if they think conviction would be "unfair." And there are some hierarchical checks as well, triggered by defendants' appeals to higher courts.

Defense lawyers are the key to this sequential checking system. They carry the burden of invoking the defendant's legal rights, of challenging the validity of a confession, of discovering exculpatory or mitigating evidence, of objecting to the use of improper evidence, of arguing to the jury, and of mounting appeals. Suppose, however, that a criminal suspect does not have a defense attorney, or that his lawyer is inept, lazy, or overburdened. In such cases, the coordinate system's complicated, party-initiated checking mechanisms can easily lie dormant. Earlier in the twentieth century, that was often the case in many cities in the United States. Poor defendants often lacked competent defense counsel or any counsel at all. Even worse, in the American south, where African-Americans were largely prevented from voting until the late 1960s and were the subject of intense racist sentiment, African-American criminal suspects rarely had the benefit of competent defense lawyers and their legal rights were regularly ignored by police, prosecutors, and courts.

But how could reform take place? In the politically decentralized United States, there was no national ministry of justice with the power and mandate to take the lead in changing thousands of local police departments and judges. For liberal reformers in the 1960s, the most promising strategy was to sharpen and to distribute the weapons of adversarial legalism – to arm victims of unprofessional local police and judiciaries with stronger legal rights and lawyers, enabling them to challenge and to resist legally questionable police practices and prosecutions. And the one national institution with a modicum of hierarchical control over the decentralized criminal justice system was the US Supreme Court, which at least arguably had the authority to announce nationwide legal reforms by assertive interpretations of the Constitution and its Bill of Rights.

During the 1960s, committed defense lawyers prodded the Supreme Court to reinterpret the Constitution. Case by case, the "Warren Court" elaborated detailed nationwide rules concerning pretrial detention, interrogation of suspects, jury selection, the conduct of trials, and police searches for evidence. The Constitution, the Supreme Court held, required local judges to exclude evidence obtained by means of illegal searches or interrogations (as defined by the Supreme Court). This "exclusionary rule," it may be noted, sought to discipline local police by means of adversarial lawyering – that is, by defense lawyers' challenges to police and prosecutorial practices in the courtroom – not by hierarchical bureaucratic training and supervision of police, which were remedies beyond the power of the Supreme Court to order.

The US Supreme Court also expanded opportunities for locally convicted defendants to seek collateral review in federal courts, thus enlisting another set of politically autonomous, coordinate bodies that could judge and block decisions by state courts. Most importantly, the Supreme Court held that the Constitution required states and local jurisdictions to provide indigent defendants free defense counsel – before, during, and after trial. Thus a nationwide system of government-subsidized "public defenders," empowered to insist in court that local criminal justice officials comply with the newly elaborated Constitutional rules, became the shock troops of the Court's "due process revolution."

Finally, federal courts expanded opportunities for victims of police misconduct to bring lawsuits for money damages against individual officers and police departments. Between 1961 and 1977, "constitutional" tort suits against government officials in federal courts increased from 296 to over 13,000 annually (Schuck, 1983, pp. 41–51, 200–1). In 1990, lawsuits against the Los Angeles Police Department cost the city about $11.3 million in settlements and verdicts (Skolnick and Fyfe, 1993, p. 202).

In sum, the expanded rights and institutions of adversarial legalism filled an organizational and political void. In a fragmented, locally based criminal justice system, adversarial legalism substituted for the kinds of bureaucratic and professional controls on "malpractice" by police, prosecutors, and judges that other countries employ to maintain the rule of law. Instead of legislatively enacted codes of criminal procedure, the courts – through imaginative interpretation of Constitutional rights – became the primary forum for the elaboration of the rules governing police and other law enforcement practices, while aggressive defense lawyering became a primary mode of elaborating and enforcing those rules.

Part IV The limitations of adversarial legalism

Adversarial legalism is a powerful instrument for protection of criminal defendants' rights. But it is an erratic instrument, one which makes the everyday operations of the American criminal justice system rather inefficient, politically controversial, legally confusing, and unequal (Pizzi, 1999; Van Kessel, 1992).

Inefficiency and injustice

As a method for ensuring legal accountability, adversarial legalism is far more cumbersome, costly, and inefficient than bureaucratic supervision. Inefficiency matters because it impedes the pursuit of justice. As noted earlier, the mechanisms of adversarial legalism have made criminal jury trials so complex and costly that they can only be used in a small proportion of cases. Hence, most defendants do not really get a day in court. Most cases are resolved by negotiated guilty pleas – low-visibility decisions which are not reviewable, explained, or subject to legal rationalization and accountability. Because American prosecutors, confronted with a prohibitively costly and cumbersome trial system, become accustomed to settling cases by bargaining with defense lawyers, David Johnson observes that prosecutors in the US spend less time and effort than Japanese prosecutors probing the facts of the each case and assessing the proper legal disposition. Consequently, Johnson believes, outcomes for similar offenses and offenders in the US are far less uniform – and in that sense, less just – than in Japan (Johnson, 1998).

Political controversy and legal uncertainty

In the United States, the law of criminal procedure is more politicized, volatile, and inconsistent than in other democracies. In other democracies, criminal procedure and limits on police practices are prescribed in legal codes enacted by the national legislature (Bradley, 1993, pp. 95–132). But in the US, once liberal reformers made constitutional litigation a primary strategy for imposing stricter, nationwide standards on local police, the courts (rather than state legislatures) became the forum for elaborating rules of criminal procedure and constraints on law enforcement. Conservative interest groups and politicians therefore turned their attention to the judiciary; they sought to staff the courts with judges who were inclined to reverse or to restrict "liberal" judicial precedents. Liberals fought back, battling to block conservative judicial appointments and to put more liberals on the bench.

The resulting political struggle has made the American judicial selection process more politicized and has, to some extent, politicized the judiciary itself. Moreover, it has contributed to the shifting, confusing, and often inconsistent character of the American law of criminal procedure. In the 1980–84 period, the US Supreme Court decided 35 cases involving the interpretation of the Fourth Amendment's restrictions on searches and seizures. Few were decided unanimously. Seven had no majority opinion at all, as the justices disagreed about what restrictions the Constitution should be read to require (Bradley, 1993, p. 49). Lower court judges, consequently, do not know where they stand. Law professor Craig Bradley, after examining 223 state appellate decisions on search and seizure issues, concluded that in at least a third of the cases, either the trial court judge or the state appellate judges had misunderstood US Supreme Court precedents.[2] Between 1985 and 1990, an increasingly conservative Supreme Court decided 43 Fourth Amendment cases, reversing the court below in 85 percent of the cases that had been decided in the defendant's favor (Bookspan, 1991, p. 475).

Not surprisingly, the police, who have to make snap decisions about searches, chases, and arrests under stressful circumstances, find the law almost hopelessly confusing. Even a judge sitting in the patrol car could not give them clear legal guidance. Two legal scholars asked 547 police officers about the legal propriety of searches undertaken in six fact situations described in cases that had been decided by the Supreme Court. Taking the Court decision as the correct answer, the police officers' mean score was 3.4 out of 6 – only slightly better than the 3.0 one would expect from random guessing. A group of lawyers scored 4.4 on the same test (Heffernan and Lovely, 1991). Because the law is confusing and forever in flux, internal police discipline becomes more problematic. Defense counsel are encouraged to litigate evidentiary questions (Stuntz, 1998, pp. 12–16), using alleged violations of procedural rights as a bargaining chip to get a lighter sentence. This kind of uncertainty is far less prevalent, comparative scholars argue, in nations with more hierarchically organized criminal justice systems, in which the principal restrictions on police behavior are prescribed by comprehensive statutes and regulations (Damaska, 1975, p. 490). And because American adversarial legalism encourages defense lawyers to use the rules of procedure for purposes of delay, bargaining, and obfuscation of the truth, the criminal justice system often appears to the public – as well as to criminal defendants – to be an adversarial game, weakening its political legitimacy.

Inequality

Because lawyers play such a key role in American adversarial legalism, outcomes of pretrial bargaining and jury trials in the United States are far more sensitive to variability in the quality of lawyering than they are in hierarchically organized criminal justice systems. Hence, outcomes in the US are likely to be far more sensitive to variations in the wealth and resources of defendants. In white-collar crime cases, well-paid defense lawyers often get involved early, maneuvering to restrict the prosecution's access to information and negotiating with prosecutors even before the indictment is handed down (Mann, 1985; Penner, 1992, p. 3). When full-scale adversarial defenses are mounted, trials can stretch over a month or more, and jurors are sometimes befuddled by the complexity of evidence and the tactics of defense lawyers. Long before the verdict in the infamous O.J. Simpson case, John Langbein (1995, pp. 32–3) wrote,

> Money is the defining element of our modern American criminal justice system. If Simpson walks, as most lawyers think he will, what will have decided the outcome is not that O.J. is black, but that he is rich. He can afford to buy what F. Lee Bailey, Alan Dershowitz, Johnnie Cochran and the others have to sell: the consultants on jury packing, the obliging experts who will contradict the state's overpowering DNA and related evidence, and the defense lawyer's bag of tricks for sowing doubts, casting aspersions and coaching witnesses.[3]

Adversarial legalism constantly increases the array of legal precedents, arguments, and techniques available to the most competent, best-financed defense counsel. But these weapons are not meaningfully available, in practice, to the overburdened public defender who represents the typically poor defendant. Even the most competent public defender lacks the time and resources for requisite factual investigation, research, and legal argument to raise every plausible claim in each defendant's case (Stuntz, 1998). The poor defendant in the US thus gets fewer legal arguments made on his behalf than the rich defendant, and some poor defendants – particularly those in localities that provide minimal funding for public defenders' offices – get less than others.

Part V Conclusion

Adversarial legalism prods the American decentralized justice system toward the uniform application of legal rights and penalties. It can protect criminal suspects' rights of personal liberty, including their right to refuse to respond to the questions of police and prosecutors. It enables dedicated lawyers and judges to expose and to attack malpractice or legalistic inflexibility by police and by prosecutors, and to employ imaginative constitutional interpretations to make improvements in the justice system. It provides strong barriers against the manipulation of the criminal justice system for political ends by paranoid or ideologically driven governments, should any come into power in the future.

But adversarial legalism does these things at a considerable price. Its inefficiency, costliness, and malleability result in inequality, inconsistency, and hence injustice in ordinary criminal cases. It promotes a cynical, antiauthority, responsibility-avoiding attitude in criminal defendants. By making the public at large somewhat critical of the criminal justice system, it has encouraged the politicization of the judiciary and of the policies that animate the rules of criminal procedure.

Yet "adversarialism" is not the same thing as American adversarial legalism. The American brand of adversarialism arose in the context of a particularly fragmented and decentralized criminal justice and political system, and in a political and legal culture that is particularly suspicious of concentrated, hierarchically organized political and legal authority. Introducing further adversarial elements in a more hierarchically organized, professionalized criminal justice system – one that does not employ jury trials, that does not have a tradition of political selection of judges and prosecutors, and does not have a legal culture that is as suspicious of authority as the United States – would not lead to the same patterns that prevail in the United States.

For example, Antonie Peters offers a fascinating, detailed analysis of several similar criminal cases, focusing on the extent to which Dutch and Japanese investigations and trials are open to the subjective understandings of the accused. He notes that in Holland, defense lawyers are more active and assertive in reconstructing the events and motives surrounding the crime, "suggesting an additional, alternative reconstruction from the perspective of his client" as well as additional legal defenses (Peters, 1992, pp. 285, 288). This suggests that where adversarialism is constrained by hierarchical and professional judicial and prosecutorial norms, it may capture some of the benefits for individual protection and justice that flow from the best aspects of American adversarial legalism, but without incurring its significant costs.

Notes

1. There are some adversarial elements in French and even more in German litigation. Lawyers for the parties provide the judge with documents, lists of witnesses, and suggested lines of inquiry, but it is still a far cry from the lawyer-dominated American pretrial discovery and adjudicatory system (Langbein, 1985; Frase, 1990; Frase and Weigend, 1995).
2. Bradley, a law professor and expert in Fourth Amendment law, examined 223 appeals in nine states involving search and seizure issues in 1980. In 26 percent, the trial judge had misunderstood or misapplied the judicial precedents, and in at least 10 percent the appellate court, in upholding the decision, had interpreted or used Supreme Court precedents incorrectly (Bradley, 1993, pp. 47–8).
3. See also Adler (1994) for an excellent and detailed journalistic account of the successful defense of Imelda Marcos.

References

Adler, S. (1994) *The Jury: Disorder in the Courts* (New York: Doubleday).

Alschuler, A. (1993) "Implementing the Criminal Defendant's Right to Trial: Alternatives to the Plea Bargain System," *University of Chicago Law Review*, Vol. 50, p. 931.

—— 1986 "Mediation with a Mugger: the Shortage of Adjudicative Services and the Need for a Two-Tier Trial System in Civil Cases," *Harvard Law Review*, Vol. 99, p. 1808.

Atiyah, P.S. and R. S. Summers (1987) *Form and Substance in Anglo-American Law: a Comparative Study of Legal Reasoning, Legal Theory, and Legal Institutions* (Oxford: Clarendon Press).

Boland, B. and F. Feeney (1990) *The Prosecution of Felony Arrests, 1987* (Washington, DC: US Department of Justice).

Bookspan, P. (1991) "Reworking the Warrant Requirement: Resuscitating the Fourth Amendment," *Vanderbilt Law Review*, Vol. 44, p. 473.

Bradley, C. (1993) *The Failure of the Due Process Revolution* (Philadelphia: University of Pennsylvania Press).

Brereton, D. and J. Casper (1981) "Does it Pay to Plead Guilty? Differential Sentencing and the Functioning of the Criminal Courts," *Law & Society Review*, Vol. 16, p. 45.

Damaska, M. (1975) "Structures of Authority and Comparative Criminal Procedure," *Yale Law Journal*, Vol. 84, p. 480.

Foote, D. (1991) "Confessions and the Right to Silence in Japan," *Georgia Journal of International & Comparative Law*, Vol. 21, p. 415.

—— (1992) "The Benevolent Paternalism of Japanese Criminal Justice," *California Law Review*, Vol. 80, p. 317.

Frase, R. (1990) "Comparative Criminal Justice as a Guide to American Law Reform: How Do the French Do It, How Can We Find Out, and Why Should We Care?" *California Law Review*, Vol. 78, p. 539.

Frase, R. and T. Weigend (1995), "German Criminal Justice," *Boston College International and Comparative Law Review,* Vol. 18, p. 317.

Gerlin, A. (1995) "Jury-Duty Scofflaws Try Patience of Courts," *Wall Street Journal,* August 9, p. B1.

Heffernan, R. and R. Lovely, (1991) "Evaluating the Fourth Amendment Exclusionary Rule: the Problem of Police Compliance with the Law,"*Michigan Journal of Law Reform,* Vol. 24, p. 537.

Hughes, G. (1984) "English Criminal Justice," *Arizona Law Review,* Vol. 26, p. 507.

Johnson, D. (1998) "The Organization of Prosecution and the Possibility of Order," *Law & Society Review,* Vol. 32, p. 247.

Kagan, R.A. (1995) "Adversarial Legalism and American Government," in Marc Landy and Martin Levin (eds) *The New Politics of Public Policy* (Baltimore: Johns Hopkins University Press).

Langbein, J. (1985) "The German Advantage in Civil Procedure," *University of Chicago Law Review* ,Vol. 52, p. 823.

—— (1995) "Money Talks, Clients Walk," *Newsweek,* April 17, pp. 32–4.

Leo, R. (1996) "Miranda's Revenge: Police Interrogation as a Confidence Game," *Law & Society Review,* Vol. 30, p. 259.

Lipset, S.M. (1996) *American Exceptionalism* (New York: W.W. Norton & Co.).

Lowenthal, G. (1993) "Mandatory Sentencing Laws: Undermining the Effectiveness of Determinate Sentencing Reform," *California Law Review,* Vol. 81, p. 61.

Lynch, D. (1994) "The Impropriety of Plea Agreements: a Tale of Two Counties," *Law & Social Inquiry,* Vol. 19, p. 115.

Mann, K. (1985) *Defending White Collar Crime* (New Haven: Yale University Press).

National Center for State Courts (1998) On *Trial: the Length of Civil and Criminal Trials* (Williamsburg, Va: National Center for State Courts).

Penner, B. (1992) "The Prosecutor and Ex Parte Communications," *National Environmental Enforcement Journal* May, p. 3.

Peters, A. (1992) "Some Comparative Observations on the Criminal Process in Holland and Japan," *Journal of the Japan–Netherlands Institute,* Vol. 4, p. 247.

Pizzi, W.T. (1999) *Trials without Truth* (New York: New York University Press).

Schuck, P. (1983) *Suing Government: Citizen Remedies for Official Wrongs* (New Haven: Yale University Press).

Skolnick, J. and J. Fyfe (1993) *Above the Law: Police and the Excessive Use of Force* (New York: The Free Press).

Stuntz, W. (1998) "The Uneasy Relationship Between Criminal Procedure and Criminal Justice," *Yale Law Journal,* Vol. 107, p. 1.

Tanase, T. (1990) "The Management of Disputes: Automobile Accident Compensation in Japan," *Law & Society Review,* Vol. 24, p. 651.

Uhlman, T. and D. Walker. (1979) "'He Takes Some of My Time, I Take Some of His': An Analysis of Sentencing Patterns in Jury Cases," *Law & Society Review,* Vol. 14, p. 323.

Van Kessel, G. (1992) "Adversary Excesses in the American Criminal Trial," *Notre Dame Law Review,* Vol. 67, p. 403.

Verhovek, S.H. (1995) "Across the U.S., Executions Are Neither Swift Nor Cheap," *New York Times,* February 22, pp. A1, 13.

Weigend, T. (1980) "Continental Cures for American Ailments: European Criminal Procedure as a Model for Law Reform," in (N. Morris and M. Tonry (eds), *Crime and Justice: an Annual Review of Research*, Vol. 2 (Chicago: University of Chicago Press), p. 381.

3
Reflections on Japan's Cooperative Adversary Process

Daniel H. Foote

Part I Introductory comments

Under the influence of the Occupation following World War II, Japan adopted an adversary system that, in structure, is very similar to that of the United States. In practice, however, the adversary system operates in a much less adversarial fashion in Japan than in the United States. Indeed, one leading Japanese scholar has gone so far as to characterize the Japanese version as a "pseudo-adversary system" (Matsuo, 1979, pp. 51, 57).

In introducing the following observations on Japan's adversary process, I begin with a brief anecdote concerning my study of Japanese criminal justice. Over 15 years ago, when I first studied the right to silence in Japan, I was shocked by what I found. I initially read the relevant provisions of Japan's Constitution and Code of Criminal Procedure (see *Kenpo*, art. 38; *Keiso*, arts. 198, 291, 311, 391). On their face, the Constitution and Code provide a right to silence in language that seems nearly as strong as that contained in *Miranda v. Arizona* (1966). Yet when I began to examine the right to silence in more detail, I constantly found myself surprised by the many exceptions to the right to silence that have been recognized in Japan. I also was surprised by the wide range of tools for obtaining confessions that the Japanese criminal justice system continues to provide to police and prosecutors.[1] (In this context, the aspect that surprised me the most was the so-called "duty to submit to questioning" for up to 23 days of custodial interrogation.)

Nevertheless, after further study, I have come to appreciate the continuing importance that is accorded to confessions in Japan, both for evidentiary purposes and as a step in the rehabilitation process.[2] In fact, people may criticize me for overappreciating the role of confessions in

Japan.[3] I still am troubled by both the potential for mistakes that may arise from overreliance on confessions and the intrusion on personal autonomy occasioned by intensive questioning of suspects. Moreover, I continue to find it virtually impossible to reconcile the concept of a "duty to submit to questioning" with the language of the Constitution and the Code of Criminal Procedure. But I have come to see a bright side to the role played by confessions in Japan, as well as a potential dark side.

In any event, in my study of confessions and the right to silence, I had seen so many exceptions and loopholes to the right to silence that I thought nothing I might hear about the right to silence in Japan would shock me anymore. I was wrong.

A few years ago, a Japanese scholar sent me a newspaper clipping about the so-called Miranda League, a group of Japanese lawyers who have advised some clients to refuse to participate in questioning without a lawyer present. In the United States, of course, it is standard practice for defense attorneys to advise their clients in this manner; American suspects and defendants routinely assert the right to silence, which is supposed to automatically terminate all questioning. That is not the case in Japan. Criminal justice authorities have steadfastly refused to allow defense lawyers to attend questioning sessions; questioning may continue even after a suspect has stated that he or she does not wish to speak (hence the concept of a duty to submit to questioning, as distinguished from a duty to answer).

The newspaper clipping described the Miranda League and explained that one of the goals of the League is to introduce into Japan standards similar to those in the United States ("Mado: Miranda no kai," 1996). The clipping's author then reported that some Japanese prosecutors were arguing that it was *illegal* for defense counsel to advise their clients to remain silent. While I thought I had come to appreciate the strength of Japan's tradition of questioning and confessions, I must admit I was shocked by the suggestion that it is illegal to advise a client to assert a constitutional right.

Part II Cooperative stance of defense counsel

Examples

The newspaper clipping concerning the Miranda League led me to reflect further on the relatively cooperative nature of the defense counsel role in Japan. I have observed numerous criminal trials in Japan. From an American perspective, one striking aspect of Japanese trials is the extent to which defense counsel, even in contested cases, consent to the introduction of written statements, prepared by prosecutors, setting forth the statements of witnesses. These statements – which usually are not verbatim transcripts of witnesses' statements, but rather are accounts prepared by the investigators and then signed (or sealed) by the witnesses – are introduced in lieu of live testimony at trial.[4]

In the United States, defense counsel in contested cases insist that witnesses testify in person as a matter of course. By its terms, the Japanese Code of Criminal Procedure provides defense counsel with a similar right to demand the appearance of witnesses (*Keiso*, arts. 320, 321). As an American observer, I kept expecting Japanese defense counsel to demand that more witnesses testify in person. I anticipated that counsel would do so not just to place a greater burden on the prosecution, but because the witness statements often involved facts central to the case and vigorous cross-examination might have revealed faulty memory or discrepancies in the witnesses' accounts. Yet a demand by defense counsel in Japan for the appearance of all witnesses (as in the current trial of Shoko Asahara, guru of Aum Shinrikyo) attracts widespread attention, in part because it is such a rare occurrence. And, in a similar fashion to members of the Miranda League, lawyers who insist upon cross-examining all witnesses are regarded widely as obstructionists and often are accused of engaging in unethical behavior.

David Johnson, in his recent PhD dissertation, provides numerous additional striking examples of this cooperative attitude on the part of Japanese defense counsel (Johnson, 1996). Johnson provides survey results, for example, showing that two-thirds of defense counsel never have advised a client to remain silent, three-quarters never have asked a judge to order discovery, and nearly two-thirds never have objected to a prosecutor's motion to introduce witness statements at trial in lieu of live testimony (ibid., pp. 228–9).

Possible explanations

What accounts for this seemingly very cooperative stance by Japanese defense counsel and for the evident sharp contrast between the Japanese approach and the aggressive American approach to the adversarial system?

(1) Absence of guilty plea system

One possible explanation for the contrast lies in the absence of a guilty plea system in Japan. In the United States, some 90 percent of all criminal convictions are attained through guilty pleas (see e.g. US Department of Justice, Bureau of Justice Statistics, 1998, pp. 397, 422); in those cases, there is no contested trial at all. The Japanese criminal justice system does not recognize guilty pleas as such, nor does it permit conviction based solely upon the defendant's confession (*Kenpo*, art. 38(3); *Keiso*, art. 333). Accordingly, trials must be held, and at least some additional evidence must be introduced, even in the approximately 90 percent of Japanese cases that involve full confessions (Saikosaibansho jimusokyoku, 1998, p. 108, Table 29-4). Not surprisingly, trials in most such uncontested cases tend to be rather brief affairs, and defense attorneys often exhibit a cooperative attitude.[5] Yet the cooperative attitude referred to above is not limited to the full confession cases. That attitude appears to extend to most contested cases as well.

(2) Lack of weapons

A second possible explanation for the contrast between the United States and Japan lies in the prosecutors' dominant position in the Japanese system and the relative lack of weapons available to Japanese defense counsel. In comparison to the United States, the balance of power between the prosecution and defense is tipped to favor the prosecution. For example, the Japanese courts recognize broad exceptions to the right to silence. In addition, although standards have been relaxed somewhat, Japanese lawyers often encounter restrictions on meetings with clients, have only limited rights to compel discovery of evidence held by the prosecutors, and face various exceptions to the hearsay rules. The Japanese Supreme Court has recognized the exclusionary rule, but it remains very limited in scope. Furthermore, indigent suspects in Japan are not entitled to court-appointed counsel; the right to state-assigned counsel takes effect only upon indictment. In these and many other respects, Japanese defense lawyers have far fewer weapons at their disposal than do their American counterparts.

Yet even when Japanese defense counsel do have weapons available, they tend not to use them in an aggressive manner. One example is their evident reluctance to demand that witnesses appear in person and to engage in vigorous cross-examination. Similarly, despite the existence of Supreme Court precedent authorizing courts to order discovery (admittedly subject to many conditions), the survey mentioned earlier reveals that 75 percent of Japanese defense lawyers *never* have asked a judge to order discovery (Johnson, 1996, pp. 228–9). Moreover, those survey results suggest that few Japanese lawyers are actively seeking to expand the weapons they have available. Fully 95 percent, for example, never have asked to attend an interrogation session (ibid.).

(3) Compensation structure

A third possible explanation for the cooperative attitude by Japanese lawyers lies in the compensation structure. Currently, approximately two-thirds of Japanese defendants are represented by court-appointed counsel (ibid., p. 221). Those counsel normally receive fixed fees, which currently stand at the modest level of 65,000 yen (at current exchange rates, approximately $500) for the average case with three trial sessions (ibid., p. 223). Given the low fees and an acquittal rate of less than 1 percent, the defense lawyers may not think it worth the time and trouble to engage in more aggressive tactics. Moreover, they may not want to risk disturbing their relationships with prosecutors and judges.

Still, many of the cases I observed involved counsel who were privately retained by defendants with ample resources. In such cases, the attorney's fee may be commensurate with the degree of success he or she achieves (see e.g. Nagano, 1996, p. 151). The attorney receives additional pay, for example, for obtaining a suspended prosecution, an acquittal, a suspended sentence, or even a sentence that lies below the "normal" range for the crime in question. This fee structure would seem to provide a direct financial incentive for defense lawyers to engage in aggressive tactics if they perceive such tactics as helpful.

(4) Weapons for what?

Both of the preceding points tie to the next possibility – being more aggressive might not help the defense; it instead might backfire. The newspaper clipping referred to earlier regarding the Miranda League provides one example of this possibility ("Mado: Miranda no kai," 1996). According to the clipping's author, prosecutors were perceived to treat clients of the Miranda League attorneys more strictly than other defendants charged with the same crimes. Similarly, a manual on defense tactics, prepared by Japanese criminal lawyers, reports the perception that judges condition bail on whether the suspect has been cooperative or not (Tanji, 1991, pp. 26, 29). In addition, there is a very widely held perception that if a suspect or defendant does not confess, show remorse, and attempt to provide restitution to the victim, he or she will face more severe sanctions than otherwise.[6]

Thus, the answer to why Japanese defense counsel are generally so cooperative, even in contested cases, may simply lie in the view that a cooperative stance is the best way to achieve success, within Japan's existing criminal justice system.

(5) What are defense lawyers' goals?

One may speculate a bit further on the preceding point and consider what it means to "achieve success," from the perspective of Japanese defense counsel. In short, what is the typical Japanese defense lawyer's conception of his or her proper role?

In recent years, various manuals and handbooks on defense tactics and techniques have been published in Japan. For the most part, these manuals and handbooks were prepared by lawyers who are regarded as relatively aggressive, by Japanese standards. Yet even in these materials, one finds a striking acceptance of the search for truth as the dominant objective of the criminal justice system. One manual, for example, in the discussion of the lawyer's initial meeting with a client, advises that it is important to talk to the defendant for a long time and to remove the filter of prosecutor and police questioning in order to get to the actual truth (Ura, 1991, pp. 8, 14). The manual goes on to note that the defendant will often be reluctant to reveal everything, so the lawyer must be prepared to work hard to get the defendant to tell everything that he or she is trying to hide.

This discussion of the initial meeting between defense lawyer and client brought back memories of my first year at Harvard Law School, in 1978. My professor for criminal law was well-known as a criminal defense lawyer. During one class session, he discussed how to conduct an initial meeting with clients. He said that he always gives new clients the same speech. "The truth?" said the professor. "Don't tell me the truth. The truth is the last thing I want to hear. If I hear the truth, it may make it more difficult for me to represent you. What I want to know is what you want the jury to believe. I'll give you a few minutes to think that over. Then we'll talk." This statement appears to represent the predominant view among US criminal defense lawyers today. The contrast to Japan is striking.

The contrast extends beyond simply the attitude toward learning the truth from one's client. In the United States, the criminal defense bar actively pursues a wide range of aims relating to the criminal justice system, beyond simply protecting the innocent against wrongful conviction. One set of aims is protecting the due process rights of suspects and defendants. A related set of aims is protecting the civil liberties and personal autonomy of *all* people. Still a third set of aims relates to equality, with lawyers fighting against bias in the criminal justice system. With respect to all of these aims, the guilt or innocence of the individual is largely irrelevant. Rather, by fighting for and winning dismissals or acquittals on grounds other than reasonable doubt concerning guilt, the lawyers are seeking to deter abuse and undesirable government behavior.

While the goals of protecting civil rights and promoting equality for all represent a characteristic justification for aggressive defense lawyering in the United States, regardless of the guilt or innocence of the defendant, I have found very few signs of such justifications in the manuals and handbooks in Japan. Notably, even the Miranda League, while employing the rhetoric of vindicating the constitutional right to remain silent, explains its concerns largely in terms of the search for truth (which rests on the concern over false confessions).[7]

The manuals contain no reference at all to the "hired gun" or "gunslinger" mentality that is so prevalent in American conceptions of the defense lawyer's role. Furthermore, while Americans contend that the criminal justice system itself is so fundamentally flawed or oppressive that it is appropriate to seek acquittal by any means available, the Japanese make no such claims.

Rather, the discussion of defense tactics contained in the Japanese manuals is heavily grounded in the rhetoric of the search for truth. An early chapter in one of the manuals argues that the "search for truth" should *not* be the *sole* objective of defense lawyers (Ura, 1994, p. 11). Yet even that chapter recognizes that this argument contradicts the accepted, majority view *among Japanese criminal defense attorneys themselves*.

In 1990, the Japan Federation of Bar Associations adopted a new Code of Ethics. Article 9 of that Code bears striking resemblance to the duty of zealous representation set forth in US codes of ethics. The Japanese standard provides: "An attorney shall at all times pursue the most appropriate defense activities in order to protect the best interests and rights of suspects and defendants" (ibid., p. 16). Article 7 of the same Code of Ethics states, however: "An attorney shall not sacrifice the pursuit of truth in seeking to win a case" (ibid.).[8]

One of Japan's leading criminal justice scholars, Professor Koya Matsuo, has suggested combining those two standards (both of which were carried over in identical form from the prior Code of Ethics) in the following manner: "An attorney shall not sacrifice the best interests of his or her client in the pursuit of truth" (Matsuo, 1961, p. 25). This reformulation reflects the possibility that a client's best interests may not be compatible with the truth. Indeed, if acquittal is the only goal, the truth often is antithetical to the client's best interests, as Professor Alan Dershowitz and many others have pointed out in the US context.[9] Accordingly, Matsuo's reformulation of the two standards probably would seem self-evident to virtually every American defense lawyer.

It is far less obvious that the reformulation would seem self-evident to the *typical* Japanese defense attorney. On the contrary, a large proportion of Japanese defense counsel appear to see the search for truth as being entirely compatible with – and perhaps even identical to – their clients' best interests. Many Japanese defense lawyers evidently regard their primary function as being a check on the truth-finding role of the prosecutors. If the lawyers are convinced a client is innocent, they will work very hard to establish that fact. But if they think a defendant is guilty, most Japanese defense counsel appear to believe that it is fair and appropriate for the defendant to be convicted. In those cases the defense lawyers use their greatest efforts to ensure the most favorable disposition for the defendant; they do not try to obtain an acquittal.

Part III Underlying reasons for the cooperative orientation

If the preceding observations regarding Japanese defense lawyers' attitudes toward the search for truth and the proper role of defense lawyers are accurate, they suggest that the adversary process operates in a fundamentally different manner in the United States and in Japan, despite the structural similarities.

The preceding discussion has referred to a number of possible reasons for these differences. Two additional factors bear consideration.

Cooperative culture

The first factor is simply a difference in cultural styles. Roscoe Pound, while commenting on the "sporting theory of justice" over 70 years ago, attributed the adversarialism in the United States to "the Anglo-Saxon bent for contentious procedure and love of a fair fight, and the desire of the pioneer American to see a forensic game of skill in back-woods court houses" (Pound, 1926, pp. 541, 543). To this, one might contrast the communitarianism and cooperativeness widely associated with Japanese culture.

Trust in authority

To my mind, a much more important factor lies in attitudes toward authority. The aggressive adversarial process in the United States is rooted deeply in distrust of authority and fear of abuse of power. As just one example, the enduring strength of the exclusionary rule in the United States reflects a widely held belief that such a weapon is needed in order to deter wrongdoing by police and by other criminal justice officials. Most American defense lawyers firmly believe that police and prosecutors will abuse their authority unless subjected to very strong external checks.[10] In contrast, most defense lawyers in Japan appear to place considerable trust in prosecutors and other criminal justice officials.

Care in screening cases

This trust, in my view, is closely related to two other aspects of the Japanese criminal justice system. The first is the great care that Japanese prosecutors take in screening cases for indictment. In the United States, most prosecutors are not overly concerned if a defendant is acquitted at trial. In their view, no prosecutor can achieve perfection, and it is the role of the court and of the jury, not of the prosecutor, to determine guilt or innocence. Moreover, if prosecutors sought to achieve a perfect conviction record, they would have to forgo prosecuting close cases, with the result that some guilty individuals would go free.

In Japan, however, prosecutors seem intent on achieving a perfect track record of convictions for all cases brought to trial. They come very close to doing so, amassing a conviction rate of over 99 percent. To achieve such a high conviction rate, they must not only engage in intensive investigation of cases, they presumably must forgo prosecution in a significant number of close cases. The vast majority of Japanese defense lawyers appear to believe that prosecutors truly do engage in careful screening of cases. Indeed, according to a major survey conducted by the Japan Federation of Bar Associations, 58 percent of the lawyers who responded said they had *never* felt a prosecutor's decision to charge a suspect was inappropriate, and over 96 percent had felt that way only three or fewer times in their entire careers (Johnson, 1996, p. 228). The approval ratings were even higher with respect to prosecutors' decisions not to charge suspects (ibid.).[11] Just as defense lawyers view their own primary mission as the search for truth, so too they trust that prosecutors are committed to the search for truth.

Rehabilitative ethos

I believe a second reason for the trust placed in prosecutors and other criminal justice officials lies in the fundamental orientation of the Japanese criminal justice system toward rehabilitation and the reintegration of offenders into society.[12] In sharp contrast to the punitive orientation in the United States today, the basic ethos of the Japanese criminal justice system throughout most of the twentieth century has been that of specific prevention, with a heavy emphasis upon reform of offenders. With the exception of certain categories of crimes (such as brutal crimes, where deep public sentiment is involved, and drug crimes, where issues of general deterrence come into play), authorities usually opt for the lowest level of punishment likely to assure the offender's successful return to society. This may consist simply of an apology and restitution, with the matter disposed of entirely at the police level. It may consist of suspension of prosecution or a suspended sentence. Given the recognition that imprisonment often leads to a hardening of criminal tendencies, actual imprisonment is viewed as a last resort. Even for those sentenced to imprisonment, sentences are very light in comparative terms.

It seems likely that this orientation toward rehabilitation has helped maintain defense lawyers' trust in the criminal justice system and their willingness to counsel clients to confess. Additionally, Japanese criminal defense lawyers often aid in the disposition process, arranging restitution and apology and taking other steps to assist the offender in his efforts to reintegrate into society.

Contrary views

Of course, not all criminal defense lawyers or other observers share the same degree of trust in the criminal justice authorities. Indeed, the sharp contrast in views between the members of the Miranda League and other harsh critics of the Japanese criminal justice system,[13] on the one hand, and those who praise the system, on the other, seems to rest largely on a difference in the degree of trust in the authorities. Although most defense lawyers undoubtedly would agree that Japan should expand its discovery provisions or establish other mechanisms to provide greater external checks on the criminal justice authorities, on the whole defense lawyers in Japan place far more trust in the authorities than do their American counterparts.

Part IV Concluding comments

Is the nature of Japan's adversary process changing? Today one can identify various developments that might point to a more aggressive adversary system. These include the introduction of the so-called duty solicitor system, in which lawyers voluntarily represent indigent suspects during the preindictment investigation stage, and the advent of the Miranda League. At least in the near future, though, these developments are not likely to alter the fundamental structure or ethos of the

Japanese criminal justice system. Notably, in sharp contrast to the manner in which defense counsel in the United States routinely advise suspects to assert the right to silence, even the Miranda League accepts the basic principle of questioning. The goal of that League is not to eliminate questioning, but rather to use the right to silence to achieve greater openness in the questioning process.

Thus, in the final analysis, despite the strong structural similarities to the United States, Japan offers a very different model of how an adversary process may function. In short, the Japanese system remains a cooperative "adversary" system.

Notes

1. For an examination of the right to silence in Japan, including a discussion of the various exceptions and the tools used to obtain confessions, see Foote (1991).
2. For a discussion of some of the positive aspects, see Foote (1991, pp. 484–5; 1992, pp. 337, 379).
3. One example is particularly memorable. I completed "Right to Silence" (Foote, 1991) prior to "Benevolent Paternalism" (Foote, 1992). However, as a result of the vagaries of the law review publication process, I received reprints of the latter article first and sent them out at that time. A few months later, I sent out reprints of "Right to Silence." Soon thereafter, I received a note from one of Japan's leading criminal justice scholars, indicating that he was glad to see I had abandoned the benevolent paternalism view. I have not abandoned that view, nor have I abandoned my concerns regarding the right to silence. Rather, I continue to view these as two sides of the same system. Indeed, I endeavored to include both sides in "Benevolent Paternalism," seeking to highlight many of my concerns within my discussion of the paternalistic aspects of the Japanese criminal justice system. In subsequent discussions, however, I have been struck by the extent to which many readers, both in the United States and in Japan, seem to regard that article as reflecting unconditional praise for the Japanese system.
4. For discussions of the witness statements, see for example Hiratani (1988, p. 879).
5. A further area for inquiry is the attitude of defense counsel in pretrial negotiations with prosecutors concerning these "uncontested" cases. While Japanese analogues to plea bargaining do exist, as noted by David Johnson (Chapter 9 of this volume), by all accounts "plea bargaining, Japan-style" is a far less explicitly adversarial affair than in the United States.
6. John Haley has explored this aspect of the Japanese criminal justice system in detail in his writings (see e.g. 1989, p. 195).
7. See for example "Kinkyu taidan: Sosa bogai ka seito na bengo katsudo ka, Miranda no kai no bengo katsudo to sosa," 1995, pp. 16, 17–19 (comments of attorney Takashi Takano).

8. Ibid. A third article, Article 54, contains a somewhat more specific admonition. It provides: "An attorney shall not abet false evidence or false statements and shall not submit false evidence."
9. In 1982, Dershowitz went so far as to assert the following propositions regarding the US criminal justice system. "Rule I: Almost all criminal defendants are, in fact, guilty. Rule II: All criminal defense lawyers, prosecutors and judges understand and believe Rule I" (Dershowitz, 1982, p. xxi).
10. In this connection, just as Dershowitz offered two propositions concerning the guilt of most defendants, he also offered two propositions regarding abuse of authority: "Rule IV: Almost all [police officers] lie about search-and-seizure issues." And Rule V: "All prosecutors, judges, and defense attorneys are aware of Rule IV" (Dershowitz, 1982, pp. xxi–xxii).
11. About two-thirds of the respondents said they never had considered a non-charge decision to be inappropriate, and over 98 percent said they had felt that way three or fewer times in their careers.
12. This orientation is one of the central themes developed in "Benevolent Paternalism" (Foote, 1992).
13. The critics include a leading academic, Professor Ryuichi Hirano, who has characterized the Japanese criminal justice system as "diseased" and even "hopeless" (Hirano, 1985, p. 407).

References

Dershowitz, Alan M. (1982) *The Best Defense* (New York: Random House).

Foote, Daniel H. (1991) "Confessions and the Right to Silence in Japan," *Georgia Journal of International and Comparative Law,* Vol. 21, p. 415.

—— (1992) "The Benevolent Paternalism of Japanese Criminal Justice," *California Law Review,* Vol. 80, p. 317.

Haley, John O. (1989) "Confession, Repentance and Absolution," in Martin Wright and Burt Galaway (eds), *Mediation and Criminal Justice: Victims, Offenders and Communities* (London; Newbury Park: Sage Publications).

Hirano, Ryuichi (1985) "Genko keijisosho no shindan" [Diagnosis of Current Criminal Procedure], in Hiraba Yasuhara et al. (eds), *4 Dando Shigemitsu hakase koki shukuga ronbunshu* [Collection of Works to Commemorate the Seventieth Birthday of Dr. Shigemitsu Dando, Vol. 4] (Tokyo: Yuhikaku) (translated in *Law in Japan,* Vol. 22, (1989), p. 129).

Hiratani, Masahiro (1988) "Kyojutsu chosho no yakuwari – saibankan no tachiba kara" [The Role of Witness Statements from the Judicial Perspective], in Makoto Mitsui, Yoshifusa Nakayama, Kazuo Kawakami, and Masayoshi Tamura (eds), *Keiji tetsuzuki* (ge) [*Criminal Procedure,* Vol. 2] (Tokyo: Chikuma Shobo).

Johnson, David Ted (1996) "The Japanese Way of Justice: Prosecuting Crime in Japan," PhD dissertation, University of California at Berkeley.

Keiji sosho ho [Code of Criminal Procedure], Law No. 131 of 1948 [referenced as *Keiso*].

Kenpo [Constitution] (Japan) [referenced as *Kenpo*].

"Kinkyu taidan: Sosa bogai ka seito na bengo katsudo ka, Miranda no kai no bengo katsudo to sosa" [Urgent Dialogue: Interference with Investigations or

Appropriate Defense Activity? The Miranda League Defense Activities and Investigations] (1995) *Kikan keiji bengo*, Autumn.

"Mado: Miranda no kai" [Window: The Miranda League] (1996) *Asahi Shimbun*, August 14 (evening edition).

Matsuo, Koya (1961) "Bengonin no chii" [The Position of Defense Counsel], in *Sogo hanrei kenkyu sosho; Keijisoshoho (11)* [Comprehensive Precedent Research Report: Criminal Procedure (11)] (Tokyo: Yuhikaku).

—— (1979) "Tojishashugi to bengo" [The Adversary System and Criminal Defense], in *Keiji saiban no riron: Kamo Yoshisuke Sensei koki shukuga ronshu* [Theoretical Bases of the Criminal Trial: Essays in Honor of Professor Yoshisuke Kamo] (Tokyo: Nihon Hyoronsha).

Miranda v. Arizona, 384 US, 1966, 436.

Nagano, Yoshitaka (ed.) (1996), *Bengoshi no nedan* [The Price of Lawyers] (Tokyo: Asahi News Shop).

Pound, Roscoe (1926) "The Canons of Procedural Reform," *American Bar Association Journal*, Vol. 12, p. 541.

Saikosaibansho jimusokyoku [General Secretariat, Supreme Court (of Japan)], (1998) *Heisei 9 nen, Shiho tokei nenpo, 2 Keijihen* [Annual Report of Judicial Statistics for 1997, Vol. 2, Criminal Cases] (Tokyo: Supreme Court of Japan).

Tanji, Hatsuhiko (1991) "Hoshaku seikyu" [Demand for Bail], in Rokuro Kitayama (general ed.), Hatsuhiko Tanji, Isao Ura, and Osamu Watanabe (eds), *Jitsumu keiji bengo* [Criminal Defense Practice] (Tokyo: Sanseido).

Ura, Isao (1991) "Jizen junbi" [Prior Preparation], in Rokuro Kitayama (general ed.), Hatsuhiko Tanji, Isao Ura, and Osamu Watanabe (eds), *Jitsumu keiji bengo* [Criminal Defense Practice] (Tokyo: Sanseido).

—— (1994) "Bengonin ni shinjitsu gimu wa aru ka" [Do Defense Lawyers Bear a Duty to the Truth?], in Tetsuo Takezawa, Yasuo Watanabe, and Toshikuni Murai (eds), *Keiji bengo no gijutsu (jo)* [Criminal Defense Skills, Vol. 1] (Tokyo: Daiichi hoki shuppan).

US Department of Justice, Bureau of Justice Statistics (1998), *Sourcebook of Criminal Justice Statistics, 1997* (Washington: US Government Printing Office).

4

The Role of the Defense Lawyer in the Japanese Criminal Process

Masayuki Murayama

Part I Introduction

Following World War II, Japanese criminal procedure was strongly influenced by American criminal procedure. The new Constitution guarantees the fundamental right of the people to be protected against the arbitrary exercise of the state power. In particular, the legal rights of the accused have been enhanced by the postwar Constitution. A judicial warrant is required to arrest or to detain a suspect (*Kenpo* [Constitution], art. 33). The arrested or detained suspect and every defendant has the right to retain counsel and the indigent defendant has the right to counsel provided by the state (*Kenpo*, arts 34 and 37, para. 3). The Constitution also provides the right against self-incrimination (*Kenpo,* art. 38, para. 1) and gives the defendant the right to cross-examine witnesses (*Kenpo*, art. 37, para. 2).

The new law of criminal procedure has changed the system of prosecution. The investigating judge has been abolished; the prosecutor has consolidated the power of crime investigation and prosecution. The police have become an independent crime investigation agency, not subject to direct supervision by the prosecutors. Both the police and the prosecutor have to obtain judicial warrants to make arrest or search and seizure, except for flagrant crimes.

On the surface, these changes appear to signal that Japanese criminal procedure has undergone a structural change, from the inquisitorial to the adversarial model.[1] However, subsequent developments in criminal justice practice indicate that the Japanese criminal justice process is not as adversarial as the American model. While the criminal procedure has incorporated adversariness, particularly in the trial stage, the basic organizational structures of the judiciary, the prosecutors and the police have not radically changed, and their institutional values remain relatively unaffected.[2]

In the traditional Japanese criminal justice process, defense lawyers were often invisible. Traditionally, criminal defense work was considered to be very significant for lawyers, as the professional ideal of the Japanese lawyer was to protect human rights against the arbitrary exercise of state power. However, despite the postwar changes, the invisibility of Japanese defense lawyers continues. In this essay, I will examine the role of the modern defense lawyer in Japanese criminal practice, by looking at the history of criminal defense work and, in particular, at current defense practices in ordinary cases.

The description of recent defense practice and lawyers' attitudes is based on my questionnaire and interview research in Tokyo, Sapporo and Aomori conducted from 1991 to 1993.[3] More details of the research are found in the Appendix to this chapter.

Part II The historical development of criminal defense work

The law of criminal procedure before and after the war

(a) The prewar period[4]

Before World War II, the right to counsel was very limited. The accused could retain a defense lawyer only after indictment. Once prosecution began, the defendant could retain a lawyer during the pretrial investigation conducted by the investigating judge. However, the defense lawyer generally could not be present at the judge's interrogation of either the defendant or the witnesses. The defense lawyer also could not see the evidence and investigation documents without the permission of the investigating judge. Apparently, the defense lawyer was expected to defend the accused only at the trial stage, while his participation at the pretrial stage was supplementary at best.

If the prescribed minimum penalty was one year or more of imprisonment, the judge could not conduct the trial unless the defendant had legal representation. In such a case, the judge was obligated to appoint a defense lawyer if the defendant had not retained one or if the retained lawyer was not present at trial. Therefore, in heavy penalty cases, the right to have defense counsel was guaranteed to the defendant by compulsory appointment.

Certain defendants received additional protection. If the defendant was younger than 20 or older than 69, was female, was incapable of hearing or speaking, had limited mental capacity, or if the judge otherwise considered it necessary to have the defendant represented by a lawyer, the judge could appoint a defense lawyer. However, the judge had to first consider the prosecutor's opinion and could only appoint a lawyer when the defendant had not retained a lawyer or when a retained lawyer was not present at trial (Ono, 1933, pp. 126–8).

(b) The expansion of the right to counsel after the war

After World War II, the right to defense counsel was expanded in two ways. At first, although the system of compulsory and discretionary appointment of defense counsel was maintained,[5] all indigent defendants could now ask the court to appoint defense lawyers, even those who did not face one or more years' imprisonment. This expansion of the right to counsel was based on the Constitutional guarantee noted above. Therefore, unless he or she specifically rejects court-appointed counsel, the indigent defendant can seek the assistance of a defense lawyer.

Secondly, the accused can now retain a defense lawyer even before indictment. Pursuant to Article 34 of the Constitution, the law of criminal procedure requires the police to notify the arrested suspect of the right to counsel. The law also provides for free communication between the defense lawyer and the detained suspect, although in serious cases, particularly when the accused does not admit his guilt, the prosecutor or the police can limit the attorney–client communications.[6]

This expansion of the right to counsel corresponds to changes in the structure of pretrial and trial procedure. At trial, the prosecutor and the defense attorney are expected to take the initiative in submitting evidence, although a judge can ex officio examine evidence. The judge has become more or less a passive third party who renders judgment based on the evidence and arguments submitted by the adversaries during trial. To that extent, the trial process has become adversarial.[7]

However, the change in the structure of the pretrial procedure has been more equivocal. First, pretrial defense work was totally new to lawyers. They had no professional expertise in this field, and retrospectively it seems that there was not much professional incentive to develop an adversary form of active defense practice except in political cases.[8] Second, the law and judicial interpretations thereof did not always favor the active assertion of rights.[9] This also discouraged lawyers from conducting and developing active defense practices.

(c) Two faces of the postwar criminal procedure

Although the law of criminal procedure seems to have adopted the adversarial procedure, at least on the surface, crucial provisions have allowed inquisitorial processes to survive and to develop in the postwar period (Hirano, 1989, pp. 131–5).

Regarding the pretrial stage, the law is silent on whether a detained accused has an obligation to endure interrogation. The Supreme Court has never held that an accused in custody need not submit to interrogation, while the prosecutors and the police have interpreted the law as imposing such an obligation upon the accused. The law also does not give the accused the right to have a lawyer present during interrogation. Moreover, the prosecutor can limit the communication between the accused in custody and his or her defense lawyer in order to further the crime investigation. These indicators show that the accused remains the primary source of incriminating evidence, and that defense lawyers are discouraged from intervening in the interrogation process. In other words, obtaining evidence from the detained accused is the core part of the police and prosecutor's crime investigation.

At trial, any of the investigation documents, including written statements by witnesses, can be admitted into evidence if both parties agree. However, even if a defense lawyer opposes the introduction of a written statement of a witness, the judge can apply an exception to the hearsay rule, which makes admissible a statement of a witness made to the prosecutor during interrogation.

To treat the accused as the source of incriminating evidence contradicts the ideal of the adversary system.[10] The above exception to the hearsay rule might infringe on the Constitutional right to cross-examination.[11] However, if we understand the modern prosecutor's role to resemble that of the traditional investigating judge, those practices are not necessarily inconsistent. If the prosecutor acts not as an adversary of the defense during the pretrial stage, but rather as a neutral judicial figure who collects evidence, there would be little reason to distrust the even-handed nature of his or her investigation. Moreover, the defense lawyer is not expected to work as an adversary, but to make sure that the prosecutor does not overlook any evidence so that "the truth" will be found at trial (Roxin, 1995, pp. 113–14).

In sum, the law of criminal procedure contains equivocal provisions that allow the conflicting principles of the adversarial and inquisitorial systems to stand as more or less valid interpretations. The developments of legal practices over time have determined which principles gain primacy.

The growth of the court-appointed counsel system

After the war, the court-appointed counsel system was created pursuant to the Constitutional guarantee of the right to counsel. The court-appointed counsel system existed before the war, but lawyers participated as a public service and received no fees. Under the postwar system, the court pays the fees of the defense lawyer. However, as the fee for court-appointed counsel is much smaller than that for retained counsel, lawyers still consider the work to be public service without much financial benefit.

Originally, only indigent defendants were eligible for court-appointed counsel. However, as the court did not check the income of any defendant who applied for court-appointed counsel, the system was extended to cover defendants who wanted to have a defense lawyer but might not be indigent.[12] As a result, the percentage of defendants receiving court-appointed counsel gradually increased. In 1970, the portion of defendants with court-appointed counsel was 50 percent, while those with retained counsel constituted 47 percent of the defendant pool (Saiko Saibansho Jimusokyoku [Supreme Court, General Secretariat] ed., 1971, p. 204, Table 37). In 1997, the former increased to 71 percent, while the latter decreased to 27 percent (Saiko Saibansho Jimusokyoku ed., 1998, p. 157, Table 31-3).

The large increase in court-appointed counsel cases brought about two interrelated problems. First, a growing number of lawyers began to feel that they were forced to work for nonindigent defendants for fees much lower than those paid by other defendants.[13] Second, the work of court-appointed counsel in confession cases became formalized as routine work.

Because many lawyers consider the fees paid for court-appointed work insufficient compensation for their time,[14] they tend to view court-appointed work as a liability, rather than as an opportunity. Therefore, how the public service should be shared among lawyers is a significant issue for bar associations. All bar associations have formally declared that court-appointed counsel work should be shared by as many lawyers as possible. This policy presumes that every lawyer should be able to handle criminal cases, since criminal defense has been the most significant work for the Japanese legal profession. Thus, the policy of the bar associations is closely linked with the political morality of the legal profession.[15]

However, the actual distribution of court-appointed counsel cases varies among the bar associations, depending on the size of an association and the general situation of lawyers. In a small bar association like Aomori, virtually all the members are assigned to court-appointed counsel cases. In a medium-sized bar association like Sapporo, court-appointed counsel cases are assigned to only those lawyers who have volunteered for the work. In Tokyo, those who have volunteered to work as court-appointed counsel can choose which cases to defend. Volunteers can even refuse to take any case in Tokyo.[16] In the 1990 fiscal year, while 29 percent of the lawyers in Tokyo volunteered for court-appointed counsel work, only 65 percent of them (19 percent of all the Tokyo lawyers) actually took at least one court-appointed counsel case.[17]

Where court-appointed counsel work is not evenly divided, lawyers who take court-appointed counsel cases tend to fall into two groups: the young and inexperienced or the very old and nearly retired. Young lawyers will take court-appointed work because they hope to gain experience, in order to establish their own law offices in the future.[18] However, young lawyers tend to "graduate" from court-appointed counsel work as they become busier, particularly with civil cases.[19] Lawyers nearing retirement, who are no longer active in civil cases, may take court-appointed counsel cases just to keep busy, although the courts sometimes criticize them for incompetence.

Despite the formal policy of the bar associations, it is obvious that only a small fraction of lawyers work on court-appointed counsel cases in Tokyo. In fact, even those lawyers who take court-appointed counsel cases do not always support the policy. In my interview research in Tokyo, only 44 percent of the respondents supported the policy.[20] However, the bar associations have maintained the policy, due both to its strong association with the professional ideal and to the internal politics of the bar associations.

The "duty lawyer" movement

In the 1980s, active members of Japan's criminal defense bar recognized two emerging problems : an increase in the number of court-appointed counsel cases and the tendency for lawyers to decline requests for criminal representation. These lawyers devised an innovative scheme of defending suspects, built upon the basic principles underlying the court-appointed counsel system. The "duty lawyer" plan started in the small bar association of Oita, Kyushu, in 1990 and spread very quickly throughout the country. By 1992, all the bar associations had adopted this model and began to provide legal advice for suspects.[21] The bar associations hoped that the new scheme would both activate criminal defense work, including court-appointed counsel work, and expand opportunities for retained counsel work.[22]

According to this "duty lawyer" scheme, a suspect arrested or detained can meet a lawyer once free of charge.[23] At the end of the meeting, the suspect must decide whether to retain the lawyer. When a suspect needs a defense lawyer but cannot afford the fees, he or she can apply for legal aid to pay for pretrial defense.

The "duty lawyer" scheme was the first attempt at innovation by the bar associations without the help of the state.[24] Its symbolic effects in this regard are significant. By creating this plan to assist suspects, private lawyers demonstrated that the traditional ideal of the Japanese legal profession was very much alive among core members of the bar associations, and it showed that lawyers could change the practice of law by themselves without relying on legislation. Although the burden imposed by the "duty lawyer" scheme has been increasing, members of the judiciary and the bar seem to have accepted it as a workable solution, and as an important first step in the implementation of a pretrial public defense system.

However, as the number of suspects who want to meet "duty lawyers" grows,[25] problems have emerged which are somewhat similar to those associated with the court-appointed counsel system (Takenouchi, 1998, p. 24). One problem is that fewer lawyers are volunteering to be duty lawyers than to be court-appointed counsel. This disparity may be caused in part by the bar associations' insistence that duty lawyers, unlike court-appointed counsel volunteers, cannot refuse to take cases once they volunteer.[26] Another problem is that, despite the increasing number of requests for duty lawyers, the percentage of cases in which duty lawyers are retained has been decreasing rapidly.[27] In contrast, the percentage of legal aid cases has been increasing rapidly.[28] The decrease of the former percentage might be partly related to the increase of the latter, as many suspects who employ duty lawyers have no ability to retain a lawyer for additional services.[29]

Part III Criminal defense practice

A general outline of criminal defense work

The point at which a suspect retains a defense lawyer varies from case to case. At the earliest, a suspect might contact a lawyer when he is asked by the police to come to a police station for voluntary questioning. Most suspects do not retain a lawyer before arrest; a suspect or family member typically calls a lawyer or a bar association during arrest or pretrial detention. However, the majority of suspects go through the pretrial stage without defense lawyers.

Within 72 hours of the arrest, the prosecutor must apply to the court for the detention of the arrestee. Upon the prosecutor's request, the judge must conduct a hearing to decide whether the arrestee should be detained. According to the 1997 data on duty lawyers, only about 18 percent of the suspects who met duty lawyers had contacted the bar associations immediately after arrest. In contrast, 82 percent asked for counsel on the day of the detention hearing or later, undoubtedly because information about the availability of a duty lawyer first became available at the detention hearing (Nihon Bengoshi Rengokai Keiji Bengo Center [The Japanese Federation of the Bar Associations, The Criminal Defense Center], 1998, p. 5).

A defense lawyer who meets a detained suspect will familiarize himself with the client's story and will inform the accused of his or her rights. Although the accused has the right to remain silent, a defense lawyer does not always advise a suspect to be silent; the lawyer might instead advise him or her to tell nothing but the truth.[30] In fact, most suspects confess to the police during arrest or detention.[31]

Although bail is not available for suspects, the law provides several means to challenge detention. However, it is extremely rare for a defense lawyer to use any of those means.[32]

The main goal of pretrial defense work is twofold: to make the prosecutor dismiss the charge or to get a summary conviction. Summary conviction is more desirable than trial because in the case of summary conviction the court is limited to imposing a fine, but no imprisonment. To achieve this purpose, a defense lawyer will try to find exonerating factors or to create mitigating circumstances.[33] The payment of civil compensation to a victim is considered to be one of the most important mitigating factors (Dando, 1970, pp. 525–6; Mitsui, 1974, pp. 1712–22). If a defense lawyer finds exonerating evidence, or if the accused agrees to pay compensation to the victim, counsel will call or write to the prosecutor, asking him not to prosecute his client.

Once the defendant has been indicted and requests legal assistance, the court appoints defense counsel. In 1997, lawyers, including retained lawyers, defended 97 percent of the defendants whose cases went to trial. The main purpose of the defense attorney at trial is to secure as light a sentence as possible, preferably a suspended sentence.[34] If the accused has not paid any compensation to the victim, the attorney will try to convince the accused to make payment. If possible, the defense lawyer will obtain a letter from the victim recommending that the court impose a lenient punishment on the defendant. The defense lawyer will also try to convince relatives and superiors at the defendant's workplace to serve as character witnesses, and will make arrangements for the re-socialization or rehabilitation of the defendant.

Despite the availability of bail, most defendants remain in custody.[35] Whether a defense lawyer will apply for bail might depend on the possibility of obtaining a suspended sentense.[36] If the defence lawyer believes that it will be possible to obtain a suspended sentense, he may recommend that his client stay in jail, as the judge might consider that the defendant was "punished" severely enough by this detention.

Comparison of court-appointed counsel and retained counsel practices

As we saw above, the majority of defendants are represented by court-appointed counsel. However, there are some crucial differences in the way court-appointed counsel and retained counsel handle their cases.

First of all, a court-appointed attorney often reads crime investigation documents before meeting his or her client. However, lawyers practising in criminal law believe that a defense lawyer should listen to the client's story before reading the police version of events. They stress that a defense lawyer who does not conduct this initial client meeting will likely find it difficult to take the client's point of view.[37]

Secondly, in Tokyo and Sapporo, bail is not often sought in court-appointed counsel cases, but it is asked for in more than half of the retained counsel cases.[38] Lawyers attributed this difference to the following factors: (1) a defendant with court-appointed counsel more often has a previous criminal record than a defendant with retained counsel;[39] (2) the former is more likely to be unemployed than the latter;[40] and (3) since the former is indigent, he cannot afford bail.[41] However, it is questionable whether the difference in bail application can be completely explained by these three factors.[42]

Thirdly, court-appointed counsel negotiate for the payment of compensation less frequently than do retained counsel.[43] Negotiation for the payment of civil damages is an important part of criminal defense work, since judges consider the payment of damages to a victim to be a mitigating circumstance. However, some lawyers say that the work of court-appointed counsel is limited to criminal defense and that negotiation for civil damage is outside the scope of criminal defense. Other lawyers contend that they cannot afford to spend time on negotiations, because the fee for court-appointed counsel is too low for them to do so.

At trial, retained counsel are more likely than court-appointed counsel to dispute charges. They tend to dispute facts presented by the prosecutor more often than court-appointed counsel[44] and are less likely to stipulate to the introduction of investigation documents for evidentiary purposes.[45] Retained lawyers sometimes offer an alternative perspective on the facts to get a mitigated sentence; they believe that to simply argue for mitigating circumstances, is insufficient to convince the judge to consider different interpretations of the alleged facts.[46]

There are several reasons why court-appointed counsel are much less zealous in the representation of their clients than retained counsel. First of all, there is widespread dissatisfaction with the fee system for court-appointed counsel, as already noted. The fee for an average case in the district court, for up to three trial sessions, was about ¥80,000 (US$727, US$1 = ¥110) in 1998.[47] However, the dissatisfaction is not always with the amount of the fee for an average case, but with the more or less fixed fee scale. Many lawyers complain that even when they spend a lot of time and energy for defense work, the fees do not increase proportionately. They complain that the harder they work, the more they lose financially.

Secondly, certain stereotypes exist concerning the type of defendant who asks the court to appoint defense counsel. Since the defendant has already confessed to the prosecutor, there is little room left for a defense lawyer to dispute alleged facts. Because the defendant is unemployed, lacks a stable residence, and has a previous criminal record, a defense lawyer is quite limited in what he can argue for mitigating circumstances. However, such a stereotypical image does not correspond to reality. In 1997, court-appointed counsel defended 73 percent of the defendants who confessed, but court-appointed counsel also defended 50 percent of those who did not confess.[48] Although Tokyo defendants with court-appointed counsel more often had previous criminal records and were unemployed (compared to those with retained counsel), the differences were not as clear-cut as the stereotype would indicate. It seems that the stereotypical image of the court-appointed counsel case is the Japanese version of what David Sudnow once called 'normal crimes' (Sudnow, 1965). Presumption of guilt based on the stereotype probably explains why a court-appointed attorney usually reads prosecution documents before meeting a defendant.[49]

Moreover, an accused might choose to be represented by court-appointed counsel when he believes that the quality of defense work would not change the outcome of his trial. For instance, a repeat offender who believes that a judge will impose imprisonment without suspension might decide not to hire a defense lawyer, even if he could afford to pay the fee.[50] Such cases might intensify the stereotypical image of court-appointed counsel cases among defense lawyers.

As we have seen above , retained counsel tend to work more actively for their clients. However, it would be wrong to conclude that retained counsel's work centers on asserting an alternative interpretation of the alleged facts. Even though retained counsel tends to dispute the charge more often than court-appointed counsel, retained counsel's work still focuses on mitigating circumstances to obtain lenient sentences.[51]

It is rather rare even for retained counsel to challenge the charge and argue for a different legal construction of the alleged facts. Although the core part of the defense lawyer's wok is to challenge the prosecutor's interpretation of the alleged facts by presenting an alternative legal construction, this is rarely done in criminal cases.[52] An essential elements of profesional legal skills is the intrepretation of the law and its application to the facts. This is what makes legal work interesting and intelectually challenging to many lawyers. However, typical defense work consists of negotiation with a victim, and preparing witnesses, if any, for the purposes of obtaining a mitigated sentence. It is, therefore, not really surprising that lawyers often says that criminal work is not interesting at all.

Impact of the "duty lawyer" scheme

In 1996, about 20 percent of suspects arrested or detained had legal advice from "duty lawyers." However, only 26 percent of the suspects who met "duty lawyers" retained lawyers in the same year. In other words, about 5 percent of all arrestees and detainees retained lawyers under the "duty lawyer" scheme (Nihon Bengoshi Rengokai, Hokkaido Bengoshikai Rengokai and Sapporo Bengoshikai [The Japan Federation of the Bar Associations, the Hokkaido Federation of the Bar Associations and the Sapporo Bar Association], 1997, pp. 1–14). About half of those suspects received criminal legal aid (Horitsu Fujo Kyokai [The Legal Aid Association], 1997, p. 64).

The "duty lawyer" scheme has probably had a larger impact on criminal defense work as a whole.[53] First of all, the "duty lawyer" scheme might have increased the number of nonprosecutions and the number of summary convictions. At the same time, even if a suspect is eventually prosecuted, a lawyer appointed early could generate an effective defense, as he or she will know the evidence much better than a lawyer retained or appointed after prosecution begins.

However, it is doubtful that the "duty lawyer" scheme will change the basic structure of the criminal justice process by making the present practice more adversarial, unless the defense practice itself drastically changes. As shown above, the defense attorney predominantly focuses on finding and presenting mitigating circumstances. Certainly it seems likely that such concerns guide pretrial defense work as well.

In the present practice, there seem to be two types of pretrial defense strategies: adversarial and adaptive. Lawyers who adopt the adversarial type of defense practice try to pursue an aggressive defense against the police and the prosecutor. They advise the accused to be silent, to challenge custody decisions, and to dispute alleged facts or legal constructions presented by the prosecutors. There is a small group of lawyers in the Tokyo metropolitan area who have adopted the adversarial practice; they call themselves the Miranda Association. These lawyers insist that the police and prosecutors allow them to be present at interrogations and warn the prosecutors that, without counsel present, their clients will not say anything. However, their defense activities have antagonized the prosecutors, and judges have criticized their activities as overreaching.[54]

In contrast, lawyers who utilize the adaptive type of defense practice try to avoid an outright challenge to the police and prosecution. They do not advise the accused to remain silent when questioned by the police and prosecutors, because they believe that the accused would not be able to remain silent during aggressive interrogations. They rarely challenge custody decisions, because they think that it would not lead to any significant benefits for their clients but only annoy prosecutors and judges. Adaptive defense lawyers believe that exercising the right to silence and challenging custody decisions would irritate the prosecutors, which would adversely affect their clients. For instance, the prosecutor may "punish" the defense by prosecuting the accused who might well be dismissed if the accused did not not exercise any of the rights. Most lawyers believe that such a result would be contrary to the interests of their clients and that they should not run the risk of getting their clients "punished" more severely. Therefore, adaptive defense lawyers mainly try to prevent the police from conducting illegal interrogations so that the accused can talk to the police voluntarily.

Defense lawyers of the adaptive type try to negotiate with victims for civil damages and to make arrangements for the rehabilitation of the accused. The prosecutors and judges welcome such defense activities. In this way, defense lawyers ask the prosecutor to suspend prosecution and the judge to give the defendant a lighter or suspended sentence.

Although such defense work can profit each individual accused, it will not change the structure of the criminal justice process overall.

Given the institutional traditions of the Japanese criminal justice administration, the adoption of the adversarial defense strategy means working against the routine assumptions shared by judges, prosecutors, and even many lawyers themselves. Thus, lawyers would need strong incentives to break through the routine practice of the criminal justice administration. As the present time, these incentives generally do not exist.

Part IV Conclusion

The role of the defense lawyer in the Japanese criminal justice process

As we saw above, once an accused has confessed to the police or to the prosecutor, the defense lawyer tends to look for and to present mitigating circumstances. In so doing, the defense lawyer accepts the legal construction of guilt alleged by the prosecutor and tries to get a lenient disposition from the prosecutor or the judge. Even when the defense lawyer emphasizes the procedural rights of the accused, it is done not for the purpose of challenging the legality of the crime investigation, but rather to secure the integrity of crime investigation as a fact-finding process.

In these cases, the defense lawyer is not a true adversary of the prosecutor, but is instead a supplementary "caretaker" for the accused throughout the criminal justice process. Defense lawyers help their clients to tell the police the truth, in order to obtain the best prospect of lenient treatment. However, in acting as a caretaker, the defense lawyer really provides a supplementary service to the prosecution, since both the prosecutor and the judge are supposed to consider all the circumstances of the accused when they make decisions. Only when the prosecutor or the judge fails to do so, could the work of the defense lawyer/caretaker become significant.

Lawyers often say that any lawyer can do criminal defense work. Such a statement reflects the political morality of their professional ideal: every lawyer should be able to do criminal defense work. But it also reflects the reality of criminal defense work: because it requires little skill or creativity, criminal defense work is something that every lawyer is capable of doing.[55]

If we take the professional expertise of the legal profession seriously, it is the legal construction of "the truth" which the lawyer is expected to challenge. As counsel for the accused, the defense lawyer presents a legal construction of facts, made from the defendant's point of view, as a challenge to the legal construction offered by the prosecutor. In this way, the defense lawyer can work as an adversary to the prosecutor. However, this is rarely the case with the defense lawyer.

The future prospect of the criminal defense bar

Even if the "duty lawyer" scheme is extended, we cannot expect the role of the defense lawyer to change until either the crime investigation procedure or the structure of the legal profession changes drastically.

One reason which prevents the defense lawyer from pursuing a more active defense is that the accused is interrogated by the police almost freely and very often a detailed confession is extracted during his detention. If the interrogation of the accused can occur only in the presence of the defense lawyer, it is much less likely that the police could obtain a detailed confession. However, in order to allow the presence of the defense lawyer during the interrogation, the police would have to change the way of conducting crime investigation. It is also difficult to imagine that the judiciary and the prosecutors would give up the idea, in near future, that the accused is the primary source of incriminating information.

Another reason preventing the defense lawyer from conducting active defense work is the lack of expertise among defense lawyers. Defense councel's focus on mitigating circumstances requires little specialized skill or experience. In order to challenge the legality of crime investigation quickly and to present an effective argument challenging the allegations, the defense lawyer needs specialized skill and experience.[56] However' at present, the development of a specialized criminal defense bar is difficult to conceive, because it is against the basic policy of the bar associations as well as the widely shared professional orientation among Japanese lawyers.[57]

Part V Appendix: research and data

The following research was conducted in Tokyo in 1991 and 1992 and was repeated in Sapporo and Aomori in 1993. The purpose of the research was twofold: to explore the way in which criminal defense work is organized as part of the general practice of law and to understand the present defense practice in the context of lawyering as a whole. The latter point of view was considered significant because the overwhelming majority of Japanese lawyers are generalists, and little specialization exists in criminal defense work.

Socioeconomic conditions affecting lawyering differed from one area to the next. Tokyo Metropolis is the business and political center of Japan, home to 11.8 million residents and 6494 lawyers; 46 percent of Japanese lawyers were registered with three Tokyo bar associations in 1990. Sapporo is one of the largest cities in Japan; it is the business and political center of Hokkaido, the northern island, with 1.7 million residents, and 244 lawyers registered with the Sapporo bar association in 1992. Aomori is the central city of Aomori Prefecture, but the city has only 0.3 million residents. There were only 43 lawyers registered with the Aomori bar association, including two branch offices out of the city of Aomori.

Survey in Tokyo in 1991 (Tokyo Survey)

A random selection of 1000 lawyers was made from the directory of the Japanese Bar Federation in 1990. A 12-page questionnaire was mailed to the 1000 lawyers in May 1991; 502 responded by the end of June. In the questionnaire, the lawyers were asked how they handled criminal clients whom they had defended in 1990, and to state opinions and attitudes concerning criminal defense work. Effective responses were 476, after excluding responses with inconsistent answers or answers omitted because of sickness or retirement.

When the group of the respondents is compared with the general population of Tokyo lawyers, two differences emerge. First, there is a disparity based on age: lawyers aged 80 and above are underrepresented in the survey group relative to the general population, mainly because answers from sick or retired survey participants were excluded. Lawyers who were registered as practitioners for more than 35 years and up to 45 years are also underrepresented in the survey group for the same reason. Otherwise, there is no statistically significant difference in age or in the years of practice between the two groups.

The second difference concerns criminal defense practice experience. While 19 percent of lawyers in the general population worked as court-appointed counsel in the fiscal year 1990, the percentage of survey respondents who did so during the same period is 32 percent.[58] Although the questionnaire asked a wide range of questions, its focus was obviously on criminal defense practice. Therefore, lawyers who work for criminal defense are overrepresented in the respondents' group.

Interview in Tokyo in 1991 and 92 (Tokyo Interview)

A random selection of 103 lawyers was made among 1227 lawyers who worked as court-appointed counsel in the fiscal year 1990. A letter to request an interview was sent out in September 1991, and an appointment for interview was sought by telephone later; 75 lawyers agreed to be interviewed. Each interview lasted from 45 minutes to two hours. The author conducted all the interviews. Respondents were asked about the organization of their law office and the overall distribution of their cases including civil cases and criminal defense work. The main purpose of the interview was to obtain more detailed information about respondents' work and to hear their views and attitudes concerning criminal defense work. Although the interview was conducted with a written format, much time was spent on particular matters when respondents were willing to talk about them.

Questionnaire in Tokyo in 1991 and 92 (Tokyo Questionnaire)

At the end of the interview (Tokyo Interview), the 75 lawyers were asked to fill out a questionnaire and to send it back by mail. The questionnaire asked for information about each individual case on which respondents worked during the first six months of 1991 (when the interview was conducted in 1991) or during the last six months of 1991 (when the interview was conducted in 1992). It inquired about their defense activities, the outcome of each case, and the amount of the fee; 60 lawyers (82 percent of the interviewees and 58 percent of the original sample) returned the questionnaires. Data from 241 cases were collected.

Questionnaire in Sapporo 1993 (Sapporo Questionnaire)

In November of 1993, a questionnaire was mailed to all of the 244 lawyers registered in Sapporo. The questionnaire asked for a general description of the respondents' caseload and for information about their defense activities in criminal cases on which they worked as court-appointed and retained counsel during the previous 12 months. Of the 99 lawyers who responded, we received 95 effective responses, which was 39 percent of the population. There is no statistically significant difference between the respondents' group and the population in terms of age. Data from 56 court-appointed counsel cases and 45 retained counsel cases, 101 cases in total, were collected.

Questionnaire in Aomori in 1993 (Aomori Questionnaire)

In September of 1993, a questionnaire almost identical to that used in Sapporo was mailed to 35 of the 43 lawyers registered in Aomori; an interview was conducted with the remaining eight. There were 18 responses to the questionnaire. At the end of each interview, the interviewee was asked to fill out a questionnaire about the latest cases on which he or she had worked during the previous 12 months, and to send it back by mail. Seven interviewees among the eight mailed back the questionnaire. In total, 25 lawyers responded to the questionnaire, yielding 23 effective responses, which was 53 percent of the population of Aomori lawyers. All of the lawyers aged 50–59 responded, while lawyers in their sixties and seventies were underrepresented in the respondents' group. Data from 18 court-appointed counsel cases and 11 retained counsel cases, 29 cases in total, were collected.

Interview in Sapporo and Aomori in 1993 (Sapporo Interview; Aomori Interview)

I interviewed eight lawyers in Aomori in September of 1993 and ten in Sapporo in November of 1993. In Aomori, nine lawyers were randomly chosen and all of them agreed to be interviewed. However, one interview could not be completed because of the participant's schedule. In Sapporo, ten lawyers were randomly chosen and seven agreed to be interviewed. Because the number of initial interviewees was small for the size of the bar, I interviewed three other lawyers who were considered by other lawyers to take many criminal cases.

As in Tokyo, the main purpose of the interview was to obtain more detailed information about respondents' work and to discern their views and attitudes about criminal defense work. The interviews lasted from a little less than one hour to two hours.

Notes

1. In this article, the term "adversary procedure" is used in its American sense. It is not the same as the accusatorial procedure, which was adopted in the prewar Japanese laws of criminal procedure and was based on the European Continental model. On this point, see Damaška (1983) and Fuller (1961).
2. The judiciary became independent of the executive branch but kept its hierarchical civil servant system, placing the Supreme Court at the top. The prosecutors succeeded in increasing their resources, as the position of prosecutor's clerk was created after the war. Though the police were initially decentralized after the war, the centralized police system was restored in the 1950s. The prewar institutional traditions were not clearly severed after the war. For instance, both the judiciary and the prosecutors seem to share the European civil law ideal of criminal procedure, "the objective pursuit of truth."

The criminal process that has emerged since the 1970s is somewhat similar to that of prewar Japan: prosecutors exercise a wide range of discretionary power not to prosecute, but once prosecuted, the conviction rate is extremely high. The police and the prosecutors dominate the pretrial stage with limited judicial supervision over crime investigation. It would be safe to say that the pretrial procedure has remained inquisitorial, while the American adversary model has had more impact on the trial procedure.

This does not mean that the Japanese trial process has become similar to its American counterpart. For a critical view of the characteristics of the criminal procedure, see Hirano (1989). For a historical perspective on these characteristics, see Matsuo (1994). For analyses of statistics on characteristics of the Japanese criminal justice administration in the postwar period, see Matsuo (1991) and Murayama (1992a). For a comparison between the prewar (1920s) and postwar period (1980s), see Murayama (1998, pp. 30–5).

3. I am grateful to the bar associations in Tokyo, Sapporo and Aomori, and to the Japanese Legal Aid Association, for their kind help. I am especially grateful to the lawyers who spent time answering my questions, some of which were not pleasant to them. The research was funded by the Grant-in-Aid for Scientific Research from the Ministry of Education in 1991 and 1993.
4. The law of criminal procedure was changed twice during the period from the Meiji Restoration to World War II. The first Western-style law of criminal procedure was drafted by a French lawyer, Boisonade, and promulgated in 1880. The law was changed in 1890 and again in 1922 under the increasing influence of German law. The description in the text concerns the 1922 code of criminal procedure.
5. The postwar law of criminal procedure brought two principal changes. A judge cannot begin a trial without a defense lawyer when the defendant faces more than three years' imprisonment. Female defendants no longer receive special treatment regarding discretionary appointment of counsel.
6. When necessary for crime investigation, the prosecutor, the prosecutor's clerk or the police can limit the time and the duration of a meeting between a defense lawyer and the accused (Keiji Shusutto [Code of Criminal Procedure], art. 39, para. 3). Apparently this has been a serious obstacle to the effective assistance of counsel.
7. Compared to French and German judges, Japanese judges allow parties to take a more active role in a trial. In this sense, the form of trial procedure is more adversarial in Japan than in France or in Germany.
8. Criminal charges stemming from labor disputes and student movements often have been defended vigorously by politically motivated lawyers. Though such cases might give the impression that Japanese lawyers maintain an active defense practice, they are only one part of the total picture.
9. For example, where to draw the line between compulsory and voluntary investigation is left to interpretation by the judiciary. The judiciary has been reluctant to establish clear rules to restrain criminal investigation (see Murayama, 1992a, pp. 237–9).
10. The privilege against self-incrimination is considered a basic principle of the American adversary system (Damaška, 1983, p. 25).
11. Academics were critical of the exception until the 1970s, but the criticisms disappeared as the practice became firmly rooted.

12. This expansion does not mean that more defendants have begun to obtain free defense counsel. The court often orders a guilty defendant to pay a part or all of the trial costs, including the cost of court-appointed counsel. In this way, non-indigent defendants have to pay the cost of court-appointed counsel, but probably save on attorneys' fees as compared to those charged by retained counsel.
13. For instance, a lawyer who represented a defendant charged with the possession of toluene was paid ¥56,500 (US$514, US$1=Y110) by the Tokyo district court in 1989. The lawyer estimated that he would have been paid about ¥150,000 (US$1364) if he had worked on the case as retained counsel. In another case involving the forgery of a document, the court paid this lawyer ¥64,319 (US$585) in 1990; he estimated that he would have been paid about ¥300,000 (US$2727) if he had worked as retained counsel.
14. Most lawyers believe that the fee paid to court-appointed counsel is too small. On this point, lawyers in Tokyo, Sapporo and Aomori agree. However, there are a few who do not consider the fee too small. One group of lawyers thinks that the fee is sufficient, given that the cases are simple. However, this group of lawyers does not consider the fee system appropriate for complex and difficult cases. Other lawyers do not expect a large payment for court-appointed work, because they think that representation of indigent defendants is a public service which lawyers should perform, even free of charge.
15. The traditional self-image of the Japanese lawyer is very different from that of the American lawyer. The historical development of the Japanese bar, since the prewar period, can be characterized by a deep cleavage between judges and prosecutors on the one hand and private attorneys on the other. Private attorneys referred to judges and prosecutors as "lawyers in the government" and to themselves as "lawyers in the field." They defined themselves as the protectors of human rights against the arbitrary exercise of state power. This professional ideal long dominated the Japanese bar associations of private attorneys even after World War II, and it has often been invoked to oppose changes to the status quo, such as increasing the number of lawyers and opening up the legal market to foreign lawyers. Japanese lawyers might appear to oppose those changes to protect their self-interest, but it would be wrong to infer that their opposition came from pure economic self-interest. Opposition was stronger in bar associations outside of Tokyo, although the outside associations would be much less affected by those changes.
16. In a small or even medium-sized bar association, personal networks tend to remain strong among members, as they usually know each other personally. Such bar associations can enforce their policy through the personal networks. However, in the large bar associations in Tokyo, it is impossible for attorneys to rely on such informal "coercion." At the same time, an average fee per case, particularly per civil case, varies among bar associations. An average fee tends to be smaller in rural cities than in urban centers. Thus, appointed counsel work could be financially less unfovorable in rural areas than in urban centers.
17. Lawyers who volunteered only for summary court cases are not included in the above statistics. The data were obtained from the three bar associations in Tokyo (Murayama, 1992b, pp. 311–12).

18. Most Japanese lawyers seem to desire sole practice. Even in Tokyo, it was estimated that in 1990 more than 40 percent of the lawyers practiced alone and more than 30 percent worked in offices with two to three lawyers. Most of the latter group did not share income, but only costs; nearly 70 percent of the lawyers were virtually sole practitioners in Tokyo. The percentage of sole practitioners was even larger outside of Tokyo (Murayama, 1994, pp. 216–18). The image of the legal profession as a free and independent occupation has been widely shared in Japan. According to my survey of the Tokyo lawyers, 80 percent of the respondents chose as a reason for becoming a lawyer "the lawyer is free and independent." Such a self-image may help Japanese lawyers maintain nonspecialized sole practice.
19. According to my survey in Tokyo, lawyers who volunteered for, but did not take, any court-appointed cases most often explained that they were too busy for court-appointed work.
20. In contrast, 50 percent of the respondents supported the idea of specialization, although 6 percent answered that specialization was desirable but impossible. Four percent of the respondents manifested ambivalence, stating that lawyers should be generalists but that specialization was desirable for clients.
21. Although the Japanese learned a great deal from the British system of duty solicitors, the Japanese "duty lawyer" scheme was generated as a response to requests from suspects for a lawyer referral service.
22. The increase in court-appointed counsel cases meant that an increasing number of suspects go through the pretrial stage without defense counsel. The duty lawyer scheme was expected to help the accused to retain defense lawyers from the pretrial stage onwards.
23. At least one lawyer is "on-call" every day. When a lawyer receives a phone call from a suspect, he or she is expected to meet the suspect within 48 hours.
24. Since state subsidies were not provided for the duty lawyer scheme or for criminal legal aid, the former was financed by the bar associations themselves and the latter depended upon donations from the bar associations and upon the redemption money paid by the accused. This financial situation has not changed. An accused donates redemption money to create a mitigating factor for encouraging lenient disposition by the prosecutor or the judge.
25. The number of applications received by the bar associations has grown rapidly, from 5654 in 1992 to 22,910 in 1997 (Nihon Bengoshi Rengokai Keiji Bengo Center News [The Japan Federation of the Bar Associations, The Criminal Defense Center News], No. 7, 1993, p. 36, Table 3 and No. 18, 1998, p. 5).
26. In Tokyo, a particular volunteer is assigned to a particular day; he or she cannot refuse to work as "duty lawyer" on that day. Once a "duty lawyer" meets a suspect, he or she is expected to take the case when a suspect wants the lawyer to assist with a defense.
27. The percentage decreased from 47 in 1992 to 26 in 1996 (Takenouchi, 1998, p. 28).
28. The percentage increased from 12 in 1992 to 49 in 1996 (ibid.). The total expense incurred by the legal aid association for criminal legal aid increased from ¥76,164,731 to 204,759,689 during the same period (Horitsu Fujo Kyokai [The Legal Aid Association], 1998, p. 13). This expense exacerbated the financial difficulty.

29. "Duty lawyers" might try to avoid taking cases in bar associations where the burden falls heavily on a small number of lawyers (Takenouchi, 1998, p. 28).
30. According to my interview research in Tokyo, 46 percent of lawyers usually did not explain the right to remain silent to defendants, mainly because they believed it insignificant after the accused had already been charged. When the other lawyers advised their clients of the right to remain silent, 44 percent told defendants that they did not have to tell what they did not want to tell, while 38 percent told defendants that they should not tell what was not true; 18 percent told defendants that they did not have to tell what was against their interests. Apparently, lawyers allow defendants to decide whether they will talk and what they will say.
31. In 1997, 92 percent of defendants confessed at the first instance (Saikosai Jimusokyoku [Supreme Court, General Secretariat], 1998, p. 157, Table 31-3). However, prosecutors must have dismissed charges on many suspects who confessed and whose offenses were not serious. Therefore, it is probably safe to assume that the percentage of cases with a confession in the pretrial stage is higher than 92.
32. For instance, defense attorneys submitted an application to disclose the reason for detention in less than 1 percent of detention cases in 1997 (Saikosai Jimusokyoku [Supreme Court, General Secretariat], 1998, pp. 16–17, Table 22, p. 20, Table 24).
33. Article 248 of the Code of Criminal Procedure specifies three factors which the prosecutor must consider when deciding whether to suspend prosecution: (1) the character, age and environment of the offender, (2) the circumstances and gravity of the offense, and (3) the circumstances following the offense. The last factor includes repentance expressed by the offender, civil settlement with the injured party, and a change in the public's attitude toward the offender (Dando, 1970, pp. 522–6).
34. The majority of prison sentences handed out at the trial level were suspended in 1997: 63 percent at the district court level and 66 percent at the summary court level (Saiko Saibansho Jimusokyoku [Supreme Court, General Secretariat], 1998, p. 214, Table 34-2, p. 236, Table 34-6).
35. Seventy-nine percent of the defendants in the district courts and 91 percent of those in the summary courts were detained in 1997 (Saiko Saibansho Jimusokyoku [Supreme Court, General Secretariat], 1998, p. 188, Table 33-1, p. 190, Table 33-2).
36. The probability of release on bail is not high. Only 17 percent of the detained defendants at the district court level and 9 percent of those at the summary court level were released during trial in 1997 (Saiko Saibansho Jimusokyoku [Supreme Court, General Secretariat], 1998, pp. 188–9, Table 33-1, pp. 190–1, Table 33-2).
37. According to the Tokyo Questionnaire, the court-appointed counsel read prosecution documents before meeting the clients in 76 percent of their cases, whereas the retained counsel did so in none of their cases. Lawyers in the Tokyo Interview explained that many retained attorneys begin to work on a case in the pretrial stage, while court-appointed counsel do not begin to work until the trial stage. By saying this, Tokyo lawyers indicated that court-appointed counsel could understand alleged facts more easily through reading prosecution documents. Similar differences, which were statistically

significant at the 0.05 level, were also found among respondents in the Sapporo and Aomori Questionnaires. Hereafter, the significance level is 0.05, unless noted otherwise.

38. According to the Tokyo Questionnaire, court-appointed counsel apply for bail in only 2 percent of their cases, whereas the retained counsel do so in 57 percent of theirs. Among respondents to the Sapporo Questionnaire, the former percentage was 7, while the latter was 74. No statistically significant difference was found in the Aomori Questionnaire respondents.
39. This correlation existed in Tokyo and Aomori. Among the Tokyo Questionnaire respondents, the percentage of clients with a previous record in court-appointed counsel and retained counsel cases was 68 and 52 respectively. Among Aomori Questionnaire respondents, the former was 71 percent and the latter 38 percent (significant at the 0.1 level). However, in Sapporo, the percentage of clients with a previous record was higher in retained counsel cases than in court-appointed ones (73 v. 55 percent, significant at the 0.1 level).
40. Such correlation was found in Tokyo and Sapporo. According to the Tokyo Questionnaire, 48 percent of the clients represented by court-appointed counsel did not have a job, compared to 32 percent represented by retained counsel. In Sapporo, the former percentage was 47, while the latter was 23. However, no significant correlation between the type of defense counsel and employment was found in Aomori.
41. However, defendents assisted by appointed counsel are no longer always indigent. If the third explanation is taken seriously, it implies that those who can pay have the chance to "buy" freedom. Such a practice would discriminate against the indigent accused.
42. Another relevant factor increases the frequency of bail applications for defendants who hire attorneys. In retained counsel cases, the money that the defendant prepares for bail becomes a kind of surety for the payment of the lawyer's fee.
43. According to the Tokyo Questionnaire, court-appointed counsel work for civil compensation in 36 percent of their cases, while the retained counsel do so in 73 percent. Such a difference was also found in the Sapporo and Aomori Questionnaires: 36 and 67 per cent in Sapporo and 20 and 75 per cent in Aomori. All the differences were significant.
44. Among Tokyo Questionnaire respondents, the court-appointed attorneys disputed at least part of the alleged facts in 16 percent of their cases, while retained counsel did so in 30 percent of theirs. In Sapporo, the percentages were 5 and 35 respectively. There was no significant difference found in Aomori.
45. According to the Tokyo Questionnaire, court-appointed counsel object to the introduction of prosecution documents in 17 percent of their cases, while the retained counsel do so in 33 percent of theirs. In Sapporo, the former was 18 percent, whereas the latter was 41 percent. There was no significant difference in Aomori.
46. Some lawyers interviewed in Tokyo mentioned this kind of practice as a defense "technique." According to them, such a technique was sometimes employed in negligence cases, because what would constitute "negligence" was often not clear, and thus became susceptible to alternative interpretations.

47. The defense work for an average case entails holding one or two meetings with a defendant who is usually in custody, reading prosecution documents, and attending one or two trial sessions. This is a case in which a defendant admits his guilt. Nonconfession cases could demand much more work.
48. Among the defendants who retained counsel in 1997, the percentage of those who did not confess was 14. Among defendants with court-appointed counsel, 4 percent did not confess (Saikosai Jimusokyoku [Supreme Court, General Secretariat], 1998, p. 157, Table 31-3). Such a difference may have left a stronger impression upon defense lawyers.
49. In some cases, court-appointed counsel do not even meet their clients before trial, although the number of such cases would be small.
50. Several lawyers interviewed in Tokyo and Sapporo gave this explanation. According to some lawyers in Tokyo, the police sometimes tell the accused that it would be sufficient for the accused to have court-appointed counsel, suggesting that their fate would not be different with a private lawyer.
51. According to the Tokyo Questionnaire, retained counsel disputed at least a part of the alleged facts in 30 percent of their cases, but called at least one witness on this issue only in 21 percent of their cases. In contrast, retained counsel called at least one witness for mitigating circumstances in 82 percent of their cases.
52. This role of a defense lawyer is an essential element of the adversarial system (Fuller, 1961, p. 32). However, even in a Continental-type non-adversarial system, if we take the moral and human nature of criminal process seriously, it is important to understand the subjective meaning of the alleged conduct for the accused. On this point in a comparison of the Japanese and Dutch criminal processes, see Peters (1992, p. 247).
53. In Sapporo, defense lawyers who were retained in the pretrial stage were more active in defense work than those who were either retained or appointed only for trial (Murayama, 1996, pp. 192–4).
54. For their efforts and difficulties, see Takano, Chapter 8 in this volume.
55. It is true that criminal defense work is an essential obligation of private attorneys, because only they can work as defense counsel. However, this fact should not lead one to conclude that every lawyer should be able to do criminal defense work. Whether any lawyer can provide effective assistance is a wholly separate inquiry.
56. Specialization itself might promote the defense lawyer to the role of adversary to the prosecution by encouraging more active practice.
57. An attempt to set up a legal office specializing in criminal defense work just started recently. However, this office is designed to send young lawyers to geographic regions with few lawyers, so that the "duty lawyer" scheme can effectively cover all areas of Japan. Though this attempt also envisions producing specialized defense lawyers, it is not clear at present what effects it would have on the emergence of a specialized criminal bar.

    The gradual expansion of the lawyer population has been planned and implemented since the early 1990s. If the number of lawyers increases rapidly, it might create pressure toward specialization, which might in turn help a specialized criminal bar to emerge.
58. As the number of lawyers who accept criminal retainers is not known, comparison between the two groups on this point is impossible. Among the

respondents, 41 percent did not take any criminal cases, 10 percent took only court-appointed counsel cases, 27 percent only retained counsel cases, and 22 percent took both court-appointed and retained counsel cases.

References

Damaška, M. (1983) "Adversary System," in S.H. Kadish (ed.), 1 *The Encyclopedia of Crime and Justice* 24 (New York: The Free Press).

Dando, S. (1970) "System of Discretionary Prosecution in Japan," *American Journal of Comparative Law,* Vol. 18, p. 518.

Fuller, L.L. (1961) "The Adversary System," in H.J. Berman (ed.), *Talks on American Law* (New York: Vintage Books), Ch. 3.

Hirano, R. (1989) "Diagnosis of the Current Code of Criminal Procedure," (D.H. Foote trans.), *Law in Japan,* Vol. 22 p. 129.

Horitsu Fujo Kyokai [The Legal Aid Association] (1997) *Heisei 8 Nendo Jigyo Hokokusho* [Annual Report for the Fiscal Year of 1996] (Tokyo: Horitsu Fujo Kyokai).

—— (1998) *Heisei 9 Nendo Jigyo Hokokusho* [Annual Report for the Fiscal Year of 1997] (Tokyo: Horitsu Fujo Kyokai).

Matsuo, K. (1991) "Keiji Saiban no Keinen Henka" [Annual Changes in Criminal Trial], in *Hirano Ryuichi Sensei Koki Shukuga Ronbunshu* [Festschrift for the 70th Birthday of Professor Hirano Ryuichi] (Tokyo: Yuhikaku), p. 371.

—— (1994) "Keiji Soshoho no Nihonteki Tokushoku – Iwayuru Moderu Ron tomo Kanren shite" [Characteristics of the Japanese Criminal Procedure Law – In Relation with So-called Model Theory], *Hoso Jiho,* Vol. 46, p. 1249.

Mitsui, M. (1974) "Kensatsukan no Kiso Yuyo Sairyo – Sono Rekishiteki oyobi Jisshoteki Kenkyu" [The Discretion of the Prosecutor to Suspend Prosecution – a Historical and Empirical Study]" (Pt 4), *Hogaku Kyokai Zasshi,* Vol. 91, p. 1693.

Murayama, M. (1992a) "Postwar Trends in the Administration of Japanese Criminal Justice: Lenient but Intolerant or Something Else?" *Journal of the Japan–Netherlands Institute,* Vol. 4, p. 221.

—— (1992b) "Keiji Kokusen Bengo no Jisshouteki Kenkyu" [An Empirical Study of Court-Appointed Criminal Defense]," in Horitsu Fujo Kyokai [Legal Aid Association] (ed.) *Rigal Eido no Kihon Mondai* [Basic Problems of Legal Aid] (Tokyo: Daiichi Hoki), p. 307.

—— (1994) "Horitsuka to Seigi no Jitsugen" [Lawyers and the Realization of Justice], in T. Tanase (ed.), *Gendai Hoshakaigaku Nyumon* [Introduction to the Modern Sociology of Law] (Kyoto: Horitsu Bunkasha), Ch. 4.

—— (1996) "Horitsu Gyomu no Shakai Soshiki to Keiji Bengo – Sapporo Aomori Chosa kara – "[The Social Organization of Lawyering and Criminal Defense Work – Sapporo and Aomori Survey –], *Chiba Daigaku Hogaku Ronshu* [Chiba Journal of Law & Politics], January, p. 161.

—— (1998) "Nihongata Keiji Shiho Katei no Tokucho – Hikakuteki Kanten kara –" [Characteristics of the Japanese Criminal Justice Process – from a Comparative Point of View –], in *Matsuo Koya Sensei Koki Shukuga Ronbunshu* [Festschrift for the 70th Birthday of Professor Matsuo Koya], Vol. 2 (Tokyo: Yuhikaku), p. 25.

Nihon Bengoshi Rengokai Keiji Bengo Center (1993, 1998) *Nichibenren Keiji Bengo Center News* [News From the Criminal Defense Center, the Japan

Federation of the Bar Associations], Nos 7 and 18 (Tokyo: Nihon Bengoshi Rengokai Keiji Bengo Center).

Nihon Bengoshi Rengokai, Hokkaido Bengoshikai Rengokai, Sapporo Bengoshikai [The Japan Federation of the Bar Associations, the Hokkaido Federation of the Bar Associations and the Sapporo Bar Association] (1997) *Dai 6 Kai Kokusen Bengo Symposium Kicho Hokokusho* [Main Report for the 6th Symposium on the Court-Appointed Counsel] (Tokyo: Nihon Bengoshi Rengokai).

Ono, S. (1933) *Keiji Sosho Ho Kogi* [Lecture on the Law of Criminal Procedure], rev. 3rd edn (Tokyo: Yuhikaku).

Peters, A. (1992) "Some Comparative Observations on the Criminal Process in Holland and Japan," *Journal of the Japan–Netherlands Institute*, Vol. 4, p. 247.

Roxin, C. (1995) *Strafverfahrensrecht*, 24th edn (Munich: C.H. Beck).

Saiko Saibansho Jimusokyoku [Supreme Court, General Secretariat] (ed.) (1971) *Showa 45 Nen Shiho Tokei Nenpo, Keiji Hen* [Annual Report of Judicial Statistics for 1970, Criminal Cases] (Tokyo: Hosokai).

Saiko Saibansho Jimusokyoku [Supreme Court, General Secretariat] (ed.) (1998) *Heisei 9 Nen Shiho Tokei Nenpo, Keiji Hen* [Annual Report of Judicial Statistics for 1997, Criminal Cases] (Tokyo: Hosokai).

Sudnow, D. (1965) "Normal Crimes: Sociological Features of the Penal Code in the Public Defender's Office," *Social Problems*, Vol. 12, p. 255.

Takenouchi, A. (1998) "Toban Bengoshi Seido no Totatsuten to Kadai" [Achievements and Problems of the Duty Lawyer Scheme], *Jiyu to Seigi*, Vol. 49, p. 24.

5
The Bench, The Bar, and the State: Judicial Independence in Japan and the United States

Malcolm M. Feeley

Introduction

In his book, *Courts: a Comparative and Political Analysis*, Martin Shapiro (1981) develops a blunt and powerful theory about the relationship of law to politics. Everywhere and always, he argues, courts are creatures of the state. He maintains that, although they resolve disputes in particular cases, courts are state agents of social control which serve the interests of the ruling regime. Judicial independence is a myth. At some level his argument is undoubtedly correct; courts are institutions of government and it is difficult to imagine how, in any polity, this "least dangerous branch" could consistently act contrary to the wishes of other more powerful governmental institutions.

Yet Shapiro's insight is incomplete. It fails to appreciate obvious and important differences; in its bold form it admits to no variation of degrees or kind. Both the conception of the state and the conception of law and courts need to be deconstructed in order to identify and explore important variations in the nature and forms of relationships between the legal system and the state.

This chapter outlines a framework for developing a more nuanced appreciation of the relationship of courts to politics, and to the legal system and the state more generally. Its objective is to identify and explore variation among types of states and types of legal systems, and following this to illustrate the value of judicial independence by assessing its character and impact in the United States and in Japan. In so doing it reveals important differences among states and legal systems and courts, and in turn identifies conditions under which courts may have varying degrees of independence. More generally, it seeks to identify those conditions under which legal systems enjoy varying degrees of autonomy from the state.

The discussion proceeds as follows: Part I explores two well-known concepts of the state. Part II presents two types of legal systems. Part III uses these distinctions to examine the legal and political systems in the United States and Japan. Part IV considers the relationship of the bench and the bar. A brief conclusion follows.

Part I Two types of state

I begin with the well-known distinction between two conceptions of the state, the weak reactive state and the strong activist state. This simple distinction has powerful implications for understanding the nature of the state, governmental institutions, and political culture. It also yields important implications for understanding varying degrees of autonomy of law and legal systems. One of the few who has been concerned with this connection between the nature of the state and its legal system is Yale Law School professor Mirjan Damaska (1986), who has elaborated the distinctions between strong and weak states, and then shown how each type of state implies quite different and distinct types of legal systems and institutions as well. This chapter builds on his insights, showing how judicial independence may be but one aspect of a broader issue of "legal autonomy," and that in turn autonomy is largely a consequence of the nature of the state.

The weak or reactive state

Liberal theory and culture embrace the ideals of a limited or weak state and a robust civil society apart from the state (Selznick, 1969; Nonet and Selznick, 1978). Indeed, a primary function of the state is to assure the maintenance of a robust civil society. The state itself has no "mission," no interests apart from those of its individual citizens; its central task is to coordinate the aggregation of these interests. Classical political theory (Hayek, 1994; Buchanan and Tullock, 1965) represents one extreme version of this view. It envisions a "procedural" state, which does little more than provide a stable polity and legal system through which individuals can pursue private wants through the market and other mechanisms of exchange. Modern positive pluralist theorists espouse variations on this view. Without a guiding philosophy – or more important, without a felt need to formulate one – the state reacts to "interests." Indeed, public policies can be understood to result from the clash of various conflicting and competing interests (Dahl, 1961; Lowi, 1979). Government provides the forum in which this clash takes place, but remains largely neutral in the process.

Although his view has been sharply criticized as not being descriptive of any Western liberal political system, nevertheless various versions of pluralism continue to dominate theories of liberal democracies.

The strong, activist state

In sharp contrast, the activist state is grounded in a belief that the state has strong, independent, self-referential interests. The state, and perhaps it alone, represents the national interest in its collective and historical (past, present, and future) sense. Unlike the reactive state which views society as little more than the sum of its parts, the activist state subordinates the interests of individuals to the collective whole, which is understood as something much more than the sum of individual interests. The state embodies the nation – a people, a language, a tradition, a culture, a vision. Although what voters, legislatures, and other elected officials want is important, they are understood as temporal caretakers of a tradition in an ongoing enterprise. The state embodies more than their fleeting concerns; it encompasses a tradition. Thus in contrast to the reactive state, the activist state is animated by a mission. Politics is understood not so much as the resolution of conflicts among competing groups, but the unfolding of a destiny.

Part II Two conceptions of law and legal systems

These contrasting ideas about weak and strong states have parallels in differing ideas about law and the legal system, "weak" and "strong" notions of law. For instance, these distinctions help account for the oft noted difference between "negative" rights (i.e. "freedom from") in the weak state, and "positive" rights (i.e. "right to") in the strong state. However, this tradition of reflecting on different types of law has not attempted to tie systematically different types of law to different conceptions of the state. For example, commentators as varied as Marx (Collins, 1982), Pashukanis (1978), and Weber (1978), have all linked modern Western law to the rise of modern forms of industrial capitalism, but they have not systematically anchored these discussions of law to discussions of the state. Similarly in *Law and Society in Transition*, Nonet and Selznick (1978) have developed an important typology of law and examined the sources of the legitimacy of each. Law and legal systems, they argue, follow something of an evolutionary pattern, from repressive, to autonomous, and as legal systems "mature," to responsive law. The maintenance of order is the central concern of repressive law. Once order is established, the goal of autonomous law is independence.

And finally responsive law seeks to counter the bureaucratic proceduralism of autonomous law by infusing law with purpose and competence, and in so doing reuniting law with politics. The task of responsive law is not to impose order, but to realize aspirations. Competence and purpose shape responsive law. Yet despite the obvious implications their theory has for the politics, they do not focus on the relation of law to the state. Instead they concentrate on the "internal" dynamics of law, which generate their own impetus for evolution.

One of the few contemporary theorists who has systematically explored the relationship between the nature of state authority and the law and the legal system is Mirjan Damaska. In his important book, *The Faces of Justice and State Authority* (1986), he shows how differing conceptions of law and different institutional arrangements in the law – "the faces of justice" – are both nested in and reflect differences in the conceptions of the state and its institutional structures. Implicit in the idea of the liberal, "reactive state," he argues, is a distinct vision of law, the legal process, and set of legal institutions. Similarly, the activist state is associated with an implicit but distinct idea about law and the legal process. The discussion below is informed by Damaska's work. However, he is something of an idealist and emphasizes political and legal ideals and values; in contrast I am concerned with concrete institutional arrangements. Consequently my discussion also draws on the important recent work of Halliday (1989) and Halliday and Karpik (1997), which examines a feature of the legal process largely neglected by both Shapiro and Damaska: the role of lawyers and the legal profession in the construction and maintenance of liberal societies. My discussion below builds on and expands on their insights, and uses it to help distinguish the importance of law and the legal system in the United States and Japan.

Below, I outline two models of law, autonomous law and bureaucratic law. They are distinguished from each other by at least three features: their sources, their missions, and their relationships to the legal profession. These two models are only briefly sketched out here as ideal types, but I hope that they are elaborated clearly enough to make the distinction clear, and to be useful in the subsequent section which shows how the legal systems of the United States and Japan represent examples of each type.

Autonomous law

One conception of law – sometimes characterized variously as an anthropological or a "bottom-up" perspective – holds that law is an emergent institution. According to this view, law develops from social practice, as people seek rules by which to govern themselves and to resolve their conflicts. This view of law has fostered the theory of legal pluralism, a school of sociolegal thought that acknowledges the existence of multiple legal systems, as various subcommunities articulate their own norms and develop their own institutions for conflict management. This view of law is compatible with some schools of legal history as well. It resonates with classical discussions of customary *Volkrecht* in nineteenth-century Germany and with traditional accounts of the development of the common law.

This bottom-up view of law, however, is more than a historical anachronism or restricted to exotic subgroups. It is well-represented in modern legal thought. Perhaps the most articulate proponent of this perspective is Lon Fuller (1964). For him, the paradigmatic form of law is contract, an arrangement reached through mutual exchange secured by private agreement. More recently such a view of law independent of political sovereignty has been developed by Neil MacCormick (1999) to account for the continuation of the rule of law in the United Kingdom despite steady political devaluation. Here the legal system becomes a public institution designed to facilitate the realization of private wants. Although judges are obviously agents of the state, and although law is enforced by state officials, its substantive core or essential features are nevertheless understood as something separate and apart from the state.

Contract is not the only way this idea is expressed. Both the common law and natural law traditions locate sources of law outside of and independent of the state. The common law – and more recently various theories of legal pluralism – locates law in the emergent norms of separate and distinct communities that the state may or may not recognize (Milgrom et al., 1990, Hadfield, 2001). One consequence of this view is that it justifies active judicial interpretation and lawmaking, since the judge owes his or her allegiance to the law and not the state. Various natural rights traditions also locate the sources of many forms of law outside the framework of the state, as transcendental or "inalienable" rights attaching to individuals independent of the state. Indeed, liberal legal theory conceives of the state as a compact arrived at through contract which restrains the power of the state and accords power to individuals. As such, law is connected to the state, but is understood as a protector and facilitator of individual rights and not as an authoritative expression of a "general will." In this understanding, although law is part of the state and a bridge and indispensable link between the state and civil society, it is not state-centered. Rather, law is firmly rooted in civil society. It may be in the state, but it is also of civil society.

In this conception of law, it is important to ask where judges and the members of the legal profession – the bench and the bar – are located on this bridge between the state and civil society. Everywhere it is argued that judges are, or should be, "independent," and that their central job is to interpret the law in a disinterested manner and resolve conflicts fairly. But what are the nature and sources of this independence? Independence from what? What institutional arrangements exist to assure it? And when they resolve conflicts how is judges' behavior different from that of other government officials? In even the most centrally controlled hierarchies, bureaucrats can be neutral, fair, and even-handed. In some real sense, they can even be simultaneously independent and also serve the interests of hierarchy.

Autonomous law implies a particular type of independence. It means more than merely applying rules in a neutral, even-handed, and disinterested manner. These are important and necessary conditions for autonomous law. But an autonomous legal system must also have institutions that are rooted in, flourish in, and draw their sustenance from civil society, not predominantly from the state. It requires to some considerable extent that law be "outside" the state. This view of autonomy implies that law has a distinct base, constitutes a separate sphere of activity, and operates at some distance from the state.

Of course law in modern societies can never be wholly autonomous or completely severed from the state; it is, after all, a bridge between civil society and the state. And in modern societies law is sustained by the state, and in turn the legitimacy of the state is sustained by the rule of law. But the distinctive feature of autonomous law is that it is firmly anchored in civil society as well. Indeed, autonomous law is distinct from the state and vigorous to the extent that it is nurtured by institutional arrangements that insulate it from the state and have independent foundations in civil society. It is beyond the scope of this chapter to provide a detailed enumeration of these factors. But illustrations can be suggested and contrasted with its opposite – bureaucratic law.

What are some of the distinguishing features of autonomous law? Obviously, as suggested above, autonomy requires "independent" judges, who do not cave in to the dictates of power or blindly follow state directives when rendering decisions. But as I also suggested, if these are the only criteria for independence, then judges can look a lot like bureaucrats in a state that conforms to the Austinian model of sovereignty. A more robust idea of independence must locate law and the sources of law outside of such an idea of state sovereignty. Autonomous law is an institution set apart in various ways from the state. If so, there must be indications that it has an institutional base apart from the state.

The classical liberal tradition addresses these issues. Various versions of liberal theory locate ultimate sources of law not in the state but in some form of natural law. Rights are prior to and independent of the state. While natural law once located sources of law in religious authority, modern versions are likely to base it on theories of human dignity and autonomy. More concretely, the common law tradition locates law in "custom" which also emerged prior to and independent of recognized political authority.

Another concrete manifestation of legal autonomy is found in an independent and powerful legal profession. Two indicators of this institutional autonomy are a robust and self-generating legal profession, and a judiciary with close and continuing ties to the profession. In particular, an autonomous legal system is likely to be conditioned on: (1) a robust bar which controls legal training, selects its own members, has authority to discipline violators of its professional norms, has a voice in shaping the law, participates actively in the selection of judges, and is a "spokesperson" or institutional manifestation of the legal system; and (2) a judiciary whose identity is firmly anchored in an association with the legal profession itself.

Of course, each of the several distinct features of these two institutional arrangements is likely to vary widely. Not all of these factors are likely to be equally developed in all autonomous legal systems. But enough of these features (as well as other institutional arrangements) must be present to assure that the legal system has institutional roots outside the state. In short, if a legal system is to be autonomous, it must have ample and strong institutional bases outside of and independent of the state. It must be anchored in civil society (Halliday and Karpik, 1997).

Bureaucratic law

This idea of autonomous law will become clearer when contrasted with another type of law, bureaucratic law. Under this arrangement, law is an instrument of the state, an instrument through which the state realizes its own vision of society. It is an institution for "creating citizens." In this conception of the legal system, law is also a bridge between the state and the multiplicity of institutions and activities in society. But rather than being a link that connects these two realms, influence flows primarily in one direction, from the state through the legal system to society. Law is understood as an instrument of governance. It must be disciplined and harnessed to the service of the state, or as in Marxism, a dominant group that in turn controls the state.

Bureaucratic law does not mean that the rule of law has been abandoned. Bureaucracy is or can be consistent with the rule of law. Once promulgated by the sovereign, bureaucratic law can be even-handed, consistently applied, solicitous of individual rights. Judges can be neutral and even-handed, and in a very real sense independent in that law can force the state to abide by its own rules. Thus parties to disputes in court can have the opportunity to offer proofs and arguments. Yet law, if it is harnessed to the mission of the state, is also bureaucratic in that its source is the state and its purposes are shaped by the concerns of the state.

If the distinguishing features of bureaucratic law are not found in the lack of even-handed and independent judges, where then are they found? Consider the two features of autonomous law, identified above: a robust bar, and a bench closely identified with it. Bureaucratic law is more likely to be distinguished by the absence or the weakness of such arrangements. Harnessed to its state-directed mission, bureaucratic law is likely to act jealously, curbing competitors for its allegiance, and opposing groups which might question its goals, seek to subvert its mission, or simply reshape its form and content. In a bureaucratic legal system, judges and courts are likely to be separated from and distanced from the legal profession, and distinguished, relatively speaking, by weak ties to civil society and strong ties to the state. For instance, under bureaucratic legal regimes, the state rather than the bar is likely to maintain control of the content of legal education, define conditions for entry into the legal profession, and take the lead in law reform. Similarly, as is the case in some countries, the state could blend prosecutorial and judicial functions that might have the effect of drawing judges into the orbit of the executive rather than assuring that prosecutors have judicial-like independence when mounting prosecutions. In some regimes, lawyers have been annexed to the state and the legal profession has been maintained as a semistate organization, subject to strict governmental regulation or abolished altogether (Rueschemeyer 1997, pp. 207–13). But even when permitted, the organized bar is likely to be small and weak, to have little influence in determining legal training and entry into the legal profession, and to have a minimal role in influencing judicial selection and the shaping of the law. In fact members of the legal profession may not, on balance, be accorded elite status in society. Similarly, judges in bureaucratic legal systems are not likely to identify strongly with the bar. Bureaucratic legal systems are likely to recruit as judges young lawyers whose professional identities and loyalties have not yet been shaped by legal practice. Judges in well-developed bureaucratic legal systems are understood by the public, by the state, by lawyers, and by themselves to be a group apart from lawyers. They are judges not lawyers, and certainly not lawyers who happen to become judges.

If I am correct in all this, the sources of robust judicial autonomy are likely to be found not in formal structural features of a professional judiciary or in a merit-based selection process, but in the relationship of the bench to the bar and indeed in the bar itself. An autonomous legal system must be firmly anchored in civil society, as well as in the state. For this reason, there is affinity between the weak, reactive state and autonomous law, and between the strong, activist state and bureaucratic law. These connections, in the context of the United States and Japan, are explored below.

Part III Law and the state: the bench and the bar in the United States and Japan

So far we have identified two types of state, the weak, reactive state, and the strong, activist policy-making state. We have also identified two types of law and legal systems, autonomous and conflict-resolving legal systems, and purposive bureaucratic legal systems. The affinity between the weak state and the conflict-resolving legal system on the one hand, and the strong state and bureaucratic law on the other, is obvious and powerful. Strong or activist states use law as an instrument to promote their visions for society. Law is bent to the will of the state, and in turn is an instrument for extending the state's will. Thus conceiving of law as an instrument of its control, the state will resist development of institutions that undermine its efforts. Weak states which are understood as brokers for private interests will make fewer claims on law and on judges. Indeed, reactive states permit and are open to influences by legal institutions with firm roots in civil society and insulated from state control.

A comprehensive analysis of the legal system and its connection with the state would require a lengthy analysis of a great number of institutions – the bar, legal education, influences in lawmaking, the role of lawyers in politics, and the like (Halliday and Karpik, 1997; Karpik, 1999). However, one can glimpse the differences by examining a single institutional arrangement in two quite different but nevertheless modern and stable democratic political systems. Below I contrast selected characteristics of the judiciaries and their relationships to the bar in the United States and Japan. The differences are striking. No doubt examination of other institutions would amplify these differences, but the comparison below is enough to illustrate my thesis.

The judiciary in the United States

On the surface, the judiciaries of the United States and Japan are polar opposites. American judges are amateurs, recruited from the ranks of practicing lawyers, and typically have backgrounds in local politics. Recruited in middle or late-middle age after a career in public service or law practice, they are elected or appointed to serve on the bench for only a few years before final retirement. Throughout their brief careers, American judges are likely to serve only on one court, the one to which they are initially appointed. Although a judicial appointment sets a person apart, once selected for the bench American judges do maintain their ties to the organized bar. American judges receive no specialized training or possess any distinct qualifications other than a degree in law, a desire to be a judge, and sufficient connections and resources to mount a vigorous campaign for the bench. As a condition for selection, they do not have to undergo any specialized preparation, and once selected, they receive little if any training before they ascend to the bench. They do not start in less demanding or inferior positions and then work themselves up a judicial ladder. Indeed, most American judges have few prospects for advancement; most will sit on only one bench, the one to which they are initially assigned (Jacob, 1997). Even in the largest state jurisdictions, judges are likely to receive only a handful of different assignments within the "unified" court on which they sit. They may begin their careers with an initial assignment in one of the lower-prestige and very busy divisions (juvenile, small claims, misdemeanor, arraignment, etc.) and then be moved up to a higher-status or slower-paced division which handles trials, major criminal offenses or larger civil controversies. But even here, it is not likely there will be a change of position, title or salary; only a switch across a hall or up a floor or two, from one division to another within the same court. Despite its great prestige, there is even less mobility within the federal judiciary. Almost all federal district court judges are likely to sit in the same courtroom and hear the same sorts of cases throughout their entire tenure on the bench.

Of course there is a judicial hierarchy; most state judicial systems and the federal judicial system are divided into three levels, trial courts, intermediate appellate courts, and supreme courts. But the pyramid is nearly flat; the vast majority of judges are trial court judges. Furthermore, judges from upper-level courts need not be and usually are not recruited from lower courts. In short, the overwhelming majority – perhaps as high as 98 percent – of American judges begin and end their judicial careers sitting in the same courthouse and indeed often on the same bench (Jacob, 1997).

The fragmentation and decentralization of the American governmental system are paralleled in its judiciary. Although the American federal judiciary is national in scope, there are no "national" searches for its benches. Federal trial courts are organized by local districts – closely paralleling local units of government – and appointments to these courts are invariably filled by those who live in and have professional ties in these districts. Even for the United States Supreme Court, there is an informal but well-understood norm that different regions of the country must be represented, and thus retiring justices are likely to be replaced by someone from the same area. State courts are even more locally based. Trial courts are in fact organized – and often financed – at the county level, and judges for those courts are always recruited from the local area. Although graduates of the nation's most prestigious law schools are overrepresented among the nation's judiciary (and especially among the more prestigious federal courts and state appellate courts), typically judges are recruited from those who were raised, educated, and have practiced law in the area in which they sit.

More generally, in the United States, there is no tradition of strong judicial administration which engages substantial numbers of judges to oversee docket management, train new judges, and the like. In contrast to the judiciary in most other large industrialized countries, virtually all American judges are "sitting judges." Although there may be a handful of judges temporarily assigned to administrative duties, their numbers are exceedingly small. Chief judges, even in the nation's busiest courts, are likely to hear cases; at best they may be relieved of some portion of their caseload. And even though the Chief Justice of the United States has a number of distinct responsibilities, he carries a full caseload as well. Although there are a number of judicial administration and training institutions in the United States, they are not staffed, even at the top, by members of the judiciary, and operate at arm's length from any judicial system. The Federal Judicial Center has, at times, been directed by a federal judge on leave, but this is the rare exception. At the National Center for State Courts (NCSC), a national clearinghouse and training center for state court judges, the founding director was a state judge who took a year's leave of absence from his bench, but since then, no other full-time positions have been held by sitting judges. The only judges on the staff of the Federal Judicial Center, the NCSC, or still another state judicial training institution, the National Judicial College, are retired judges who are pursuing second (or third) careers. These institutions do, however, rely on judges to serve as short-term instructors, but even here these judges are likely to be either retirees or volunteers who serve a few weeks of the year, often doing so during their vacations. Similarly, judges on state judicial council-sponsored sentencing guideline commissions and various other law-reform commissions are rarely released from their duties of deciding cases, and never is this a long-term or permanent assignment. Even those judges appointed to the United States Sentencing Commission, a unique institution whose commissioners consist of judges, as well as legislative and executive appointees with limited terms, continue to hear at least some case on their home benches. In short, virtually all judges in the United States are "sitting" judges.

There is of course something of a weak judicial bureaucracy; the federal judiciary and each state judicial system has an administrative office of the courts which compiles judicial statistics, assesses trends in caseloads, and makes recommendations for additional judicial staff and facilities. But as important as these functions are, they are basically administrative, and have little if any policy impact on the judiciary. Furthermore, they are staffed exclusively by nonjudges. Because it is so weak, this administrative bureaucracy cannot be an effective means by which the state seeks to extend control over the judiciary, although its weakness may prevent the state from trying to do so.

Nominally the judiciary is hierarchical, with higher-level courts supervising lower courts through the appeals process. In fact, however, each trial court judge in the United States is something of a solo practitioner, sitting alone to dispense individual justice. Even though appellate court judges sit in panels, they work in isolation. Furthermore, so few cases are appealed that at best appellate review is only a very weak and tenuous form of supervision (Feeley, 1983). And although state supreme courts or their chief justices may possess various formal supervisory powers over lower courts, these powers are more nominal than real. Similarly, although local courts all have "presiding" or "chief" judges, such positions are either honorific or are restricted to performance of routine administrative duties. Indeed, most such positions are filled by rotation or seniority and are regarded as temporary administrative chores by those who hold them.

There is no ministry of justice in the United States, at either the national or state level, nor is there any strong judicial hierarchy (Feeley, 1983). Although the United States Supreme Court and the 50 state supreme courts exercise some oversight responsibilities for the "inferior" courts under them, this control does not amount to much. Apart from appellate review, what little oversight powers they are granted by statute or state constitutions are likely to be restricted to intervention in the face of a crisis or ritualistic formalities. Indeed, even problems of judicial misconduct are not likely to be handled within a judicially supervised process; almost all states have special independent misconduct commissions, but they are not part of any hierarchical supervisory body. Instead they are likely to be independent boards, whose members consist of representatives of the judiciary, as well as the bar, and the public. In the event that a federal judge is charged with misconduct, there is little that can be done other than for the chief judge to stop assigning cases to the judge in question until matters are clarified, or for the Congress to institute impeachment proceedings.

One important measure of the weakness of the American judicial hierarchy and of state control of the judiciary may be the degree to which judges continue to be active in and consider themselves part of the legal profession. Many judges continue to maintain membership in the bar, pay dues, attend meetings, serve on committees, subscribe to publications, and the like. Indeed, the American Bar Association and its state equivalents even offer a number of specialized publications and programs earmarked for sitting judges. Continued association with the organized legal profession is more than nominal. State court judges regularly sit on bar association committees, take part in the bar's educational and training programs, and write for its publications. Prudence dictates the need for some reserve on the part of judges in some of these activities, but on the whole American state court judges regard themselves as part of the larger legal profession and are viewed as such by other members of the profession.

Conversely, one indicator of the strength of the American bar in shaping the law and drawing judges into its orbit separate from the state is the importance of the American Law Institute (ALI). Established at the outset of the twentieth century, the ALI is a private, membership organization comprised of distinguished lawyers, judges, and legal academics. Established early in the twentieth century by a coalition of progressive Midwestern lawyers and legal scholars and lawyers for the East Coast Establishment, it has as its aim "nonpolitical" law reform. Funded by individual donations and foundation grants, ALI appoints committees to review specialized areas of the law, and charges them with drafting proposals to rationalize the law or to develop model codes. Over the years the ALI has worked on innumerable drafts of statutes and model codes in virtually all areas of the law. A committee comprised of distinguished practitioners, legal scholars and jurists may work on successive drafts of a work product for years before it is finally approved by the ALI assembly, the full membership of the Institute.

ALI reports and recommendations – both in draft and final form – are extremely important in the American legal system. Courts routinely refer to them in interpreting the law, and state legislatures routinely adopt entire model codes constructed by the ALI. Without a doubt ALI, a private organization formed and maintained by the legal profession and with active participation by the judiciary, is one of the most important sources of new law and law reform in the United States. And it is wholly independent of the government.

This discussion may resolve the paradox identified earlier in this discussion. Although American judges are selected in an overtly political process – and in some states through partisan election – the American judicial and legal process is in fact independent and largely autonomous of the state. The resolution of this paradox rests on the fact that the American judiciary is radically decentralized and firmly attached to institutions in civil society, and as such cannot easily be harnessed to the service of the state. And of course as I have also argued, politics in the United States is radically decentralized, so that the state is both weak and reactive.

The judiciary in Japan

The judiciary in Japan stands in marked contrast to the American judiciary. Paralleling its governmental structure generally, the Japanese judiciary is professionalized, centralized, and hierarchical. The vast majority of judges are graduates of one of a handful of the country's most competitive and prestigious universities (Miyazawa, 1991). They are informally identified and invited to apply for a judicial position at the outset of their legal training, indeed before finishing it. Each year roughly 25,000–30,000 law school graduates take the national bar examination. Many who take this exam have devoted as many as three or more years after graduation from law school to prepare for it. In recent years, roughly 3 percent, or 1000 people, of those who take the exam are selected for the legal trainee program. This is not because of failure to achieve some minimally acceptable score on the examination, but because the government specifies in advance the number of trainees it will "pass."

In order to qualify as a lawyer, all those passing this exam must then attend a two-year course at the national Legal Research and Training Institute (LRTI), a judge-staffed division of the Supreme Court Secretariat, the administrative and training arm of the Supreme Court. At the Institute, trainees attend lectures and gain practical experience through clinical assignments in various public and private law offices. Towards the end of their two-year stay, these trainees must select among three career options: private practice, the judiciary, or the public prosecutor's office (there is some fluidity between judges and prosecutors, but none between these two and private practice). About 25 percent of the trainees select a judicial career. Virtually all those who select this option are accepted, although it comes at the end of an informal process in which some students at the Institute are heavily recruited by the judiciary and others are actively discouraged from seeking such a position. Although each person applying for a judicial position must be formally approved by the Cabinet, career judges serving in the Supreme Court Secretariat actually make the selection. Judges are routinely reappointed by the Secretariat for successive ten-year terms until mandatory retirement at age 65, or until they retire in their late fifties or early sixties to pursue second careers in politics or private practice (Miyazawa, 1991; Ramseyer and Rasmusen, 1997).

In contrast to the American judiciary, even within a single state or within the federal system, the Japanese judiciary is organized in a classic bureaucratic structure. The Supreme Court Secretariat is responsible for staffing the judiciary, and routinely transfers judges to postings around the country. Formally such transfers serve two functions: firstly, they assure that the most onerous duties and the least prestigious posting will be assigned to new judges, and frequent rotation assures that new judges will receive a wide variety of experience. Each judge is then expected to work his or her way up to more responsibility, although some younger judges, most typically graduates of two or three of the most prestigious law schools who also had among the highest scores on the bar examination, are placed on a fast track for promotion (Miyazawa and Otsuka, 1997). Secondly, judges are allocated to areas proportionate to demand for their services. As a routine part of its job, the Secretariat monitors the decision-making and productivity of all judges, and advancement flows accordingly. Formally, it is a system of meritocracy. One measure of the strength of this judicial bureaucracy is its size. In Japan nearly one-half of all active judges are assigned to tasks other than hearing cases; they staff the judicial bureaucracy, serve as instructors in the legal training program, and occasionally are on leave to help staff national prosecutors' offices and serve in other governmental capacities (Miyazawa 1991).

Part IV The bench and the state

By examining the formal structures of these judicial systems in Japan and the United States, one might conclude that Japanese judges are more independent than their American counterparts. After all they are selected and promoted on the basis of a rigorous competitive examination, in sharp contrast to judges in the United States whose selection depends almost entirely upon political sponsorship. Yet almost all scholarly work asserts the opposite, or at least has argued that Japanese judges are timid and responsive to governmental directives, at least when compared to their American counterparts. The argument is a familiar one to political scientists; despite formal guarantees in Japan designed to assure independence, single-party control, a strong state, and a powerful bureaucratic structure overcome the independence built into the Constitution. With but two brief interludes, since the war and the beginning of American Occupation in the mid-1940s, Japan has been governed by a single political party, the Liberal Democratic Party (Ramseyer and Rasmusen, 1997). Furthermore, Japan's governmental structure is administered by powerful and prestigious bureaucracies which recruit bright and talented graduates from the top universities, and propel them into positions of power at relatively young ages. Retiring in their mid- to late fifties, some of them begin second careers in politics and business. This process has been described as an "iron triangle," a set of relationships which bind party, bureaucracy, and business together in a powerful alliance. Dominated by leaders with ties to a handful of prestigious universities, this group constitutes a meritocratic "power elite." Many commentators use this idea of an iron triangle to explain three enduring features of postwar politics in Japan: the continuation of one-party domination of Japanese politics, the relative unimportance of the Diet, Japan's parliament, and the close and smooth relationship between business and government.

A modified version of the iron triangle accounts for the lack of judicial independence: a highly bureaucratized judicial system which closely supervises the actions of sitting judges has links with retired judges, who have begun new careers in politics including election to the Diet as representatives of the dominant Liberal Democratic Party. This tight-knit relationship assures that sitting judges are not likely to do anything that embarrasses the government. It also assures that the most compliant judges are promoted to supervisory positions in the Judicial Council. Similarly the principle of seniority assures that those judges appointed to the Supreme Court have long histories of "safe" decisions (Miyazawa, 1991), and are so near mandatory retirement at the time of their appointment that they are not likely to serve on the high court long enough to have an opportunity to have a distinct impact even if they tried. Conversely, younger judges sitting on trial courts who rule against the government or make controversial rulings are likely to find themselves transferred to remote outposts or assigned onerous duties (Ramseyer, 1994; Miyazawa, 1991). Most will conform; those who do not are likely to get the message and retire or not seek reappointment after the ten-year term is up. In contrast, judges who "go along" can expect more attractive postings (i.e. closer to their homes) and more regular promotions.

The judiciary is bureaucratized in more ways than recruitment and promotion. Judges routinely find their actions scrutinized by their superiors. They may even receive unsolicited advice from senior judges on how to rule in pending cases. And because the work of both prosecutors and judges falls within the responsibility of the Ministry of Justice, there are continuing connections between government lawyers and judges. Occasionally prosecutors will shift careers and accept an assignment as a judge or will take a leave of absence to accept a temporary assignment as a prosecutor. This strong and continuing connection between judges and prosecutors also facilitates occasional *ex parte* communications between judges and prosecutors in current criminal cases, much to the chagrin of defense attorneys who do not enjoy such camaraderie with the judges. In short, the nominally independent judiciary is subjected to the classic twin features of effective political control – a strong political party, and a strong bureaucracy – and as such the judiciary becomes an instrument of social control for the ruling regime.

I am certainly not the first to make such an claim. Over the years, numerous scholars have commented on the weakness of the Japanese judiciary, and others have tried to place the weaknesses of the Japanese judiciary in comparative context (Miyazawa and Otsuka, 1997; Ramseyer, 1994; O'Brien and Oskoshi, 1996). In perhaps the most penetrating analysis on this issue, Mark Ramseyer has linked the lack of judicial independence of Japanese judges and the relative independence of American federal judges to the tradition of single-party rule in Japan and the competitive two-party system in the United States. Drawing on a model of judicial independence first developed by William Landes and Richard Posner (1975), and a model of political control of administrative institutions more generally (McCubbins et al., 1987), Ramseyer (1994) argues that political systems with competitive parties are more likely to produce independent judiciaries than systems dominated by a single party. He argues that all governing parties have an incentive to extend their grip on the institutions of social control by capturing the judiciary and molding it to fit their own goals, but that in regimes with competitive party systems they resist this impulse. Knowing that occasionally they will be voted out of power and not control the levers of governmental power and not wanting a politicized judiciary to be used against them at these times, rational party leaders will recognize the long-term advantage of not politicizing the judiciary and of preserving its independence. In contrast, such concerns are not so salient in political systems with single dominant parties. In the absence of competition, they are less concerned about what might happen to them if they were voted out of power. Consequently, they are more willing to convert the powers of the judiciary to their own, partisan purposes.

Ramseyer uses this theory to account for the lack of judicial independence in Japan and its presence in the United States. With only two very brief exceptions, Japan has been ruled continuously by the same party – the Liberal Democratic Party – since the end of World War II. Consequently, he argues, the party has developed deep and continuing connections within both the judiciary and the public service more generally. One consequence is a judiciary which if it does not do the direct bidding of the party, at least does nothing to hinder the power of the government it controls. In contrast, Ramseyer continues, a competitive party system in the United States leads to a federal judiciary that is relatively free of political influence.

This is an elegant and powerful model. But it is incomplete. It ignores the possibility of influences of competition within a single dominant party, and it ignores the influences of other types of factors. For instance, it does not deal with the possibility that even within a single dominant party, there may be distinct factions whose agendas differ substantially from one another. These factions may want to preserve their prerogatives in much the same way that distinct parties in a competitive electoral system do, and as such they may see the long-term advantages of an independent judiciary. More generally, the single variable – party – explanation for judicial independence is too simple; it neglects the role of the bar in shaping the judiciary. In the discussion of the American and Japanese legal system in Part III, above, we noted that the organized American bar was influential in lawmaking and law reform, and that the American judiciary identified with and was active in the bar. In contrast, the small Japanese bar, while well-organized, extremely civic-minded, and active, has limited impact on law reform and lawmaking and is almost wholly isolated from the judiciary.

The earlier discussion linked the issue of judicial independence to factors much broader than single-party versus multi-party governments. It suggested that judicial independence is more likely in countries with a tradition of weak states and an autonomous legal system. Although these factors may be associated with single versus multi-party systems, both the nature of the political culture and legal culture identify broader and I think more basic issues than a focus on party alone does. The distinction between reactive and activist states is important for the judicial function because the activist state has a ready-made rationale for harnessing the legal system, including the judiciary, to a collective mission while the former does not. Similarly, a country with an autonomous legal system rooted in civil society is less likely to have its judiciary harnessed to a state-defined mission.

Recall that I identified a large, active, and independent bar as the cornerstone of an autonomous legal system. It may, as well, be a feature of a vibrant civil society in a weak state. This factor distinguishes the United States from Japan. The American bar is large, powerful, independent, and closely associated with the judiciary. Indeed, the bar plays a major role in judicial selection. Although it may not be able to pick and choose judges, in many jurisdictions bar association approval is required to make a candidate credible. Furthermore, once on the bench continued association with the bar is the norm and not the exception.

The United States may be an extreme example of both a weak state and a system with autonomous law. Japan certainly does not represent anything approaching the extreme opposite, but there is no doubt that its political system is both more centrally organized and its institutions of government more tightly controlled (Feldman, 2000). Similarly, although it has a robust, liberal, and activist bar, this bar is tiny in comparison to the American bar and the size of the legal profession in virtually all other advanced industrial societies. Furthermore, the Japanese bar is excluded from exercising much power over shaping the legal profession, selecting judges, and in law reform. The state and not the bar establishes requirements for entry into the legal profession. The state and not the bar oversees legal education, formulates and administers the bar examination, specifies the numbers to be admitted, oversees specialized training of successful candidates, and indeed absorbs half or more of all lawyers. Once career choices have been made, judges (and government lawyers more generally) and lawyers are virtually cut off from contact with each other. Judges and lawyers are distinct and different professions each with its own professional identity and parallel career tracks remain separate and do not intersect.

Conclusion

We have now come full circle. We began this chapter reflecting on Professor Shapiro's claim that courts are not independent, but are agents of the state, and criticized it for ignoring important variations and differences. We then outlined two theories of the state and two theories of law and legal systems to suggest there is considerable variation in both the nature of the state and the nature of the legal systems, and to argue that there are important connections between them. We then reviewed claims about the independence of the Japanese and American courts in light of these theories. One of our conclusions is that despite the fact that the American judiciary is highly politicized and the career judiciary in Japan is selected on the basis of merit and competitive examination, the American judiciary is more independent than its Japanese counterpart. This conclusion is not self-evident, but once considered in light of the judiciary's relationship to the bar, the nature of the legal system, and perhaps most importantly, the nature of the state in the two countries, it is understandable. A strong state produces weak legal systems, and a weak state may be a necessary condition for an autonomous legal system.

This brief discussion hardly disposes of the issues. Indeed, it is meant to introduce them and to open up discussion. I have not done justice to the comparison of Japan and the United States, let alone introduced complexities that would be revealed by consideration of still more countries. Italy, for instance, has a conception of a strong state but notoriously weak political parties and in practice a weak state. And although it is recognized by consensus as having an independent judiciary, it has a career judiciary and a weak bar with no formal connections to the judiciary. It may be that Italy is an outlier, that the independence of its judiciary is tenuous and likely to be short-lived, or that a more complicated theory would anchor independence in a more contingent set of factors. Indeed, the idea of independence may be up for grabs (Larkins, 1996). Still, this essay seems to me to be a step in the right direction. It seeks to bring a long-neglected institution – the bar – to the table, and in so doing suggest that it is profitable to explore the role of the bar and its relationship to the bench in the exploration of judicial independence. I am confident that I have shown the importance of judicial independence as a general factor in accounting for differences in two settings. It remains to be seen if the argument can be generalized.

References

Buchanan, James and Gordon Tullock (1965) *The Calculus of Consent: Logical Foundations of Constitutional Democracy* (Ann Arbor: University of Michigan Press).

Collins, Hugh (1982) *Marxism and Law* (Oxford: Oxford University Press).

Damaska, Mirjan (1986) *The Faces of Justice and State Authority* (New Haven: Yale University Press).

Dahl, Robert (1961) *Who Governs* (New Haven: Yale University Press).

Feeley, Malcolm M. (1983) *Court Reform on Trial: Why Simple Solutions Fail* (New York: Basic Books).

Feldman, Eric (2000) *The Ritual of Rights in Japan: Law, Society, and Health Policy* (New York: Cambridge University Press).

Fuller, Lon (1964) *The Morality of Law* (New Haven: Yale University Press).

Hadfield, Gilian (2000) "Privatizing Commercial Law," *Regulation*, Spring, p. 40.

Halliday, Terence C. (1989) "Legal Professions and the State: Neocorporatist Variations on the Pluralist Theme of Liberal Democracies," in Richard Abel and Philip S.C. Lewis (eds), *Lawyers in Society: Comparative Theories* (Berkeley, University of California Press).

Halliday, Terence C. and Lucien Karpik (eds) (1997) *Lawyers and the Rise of Western Political Liberalism* (Oxford: Clarendon Press).

Hayek, Fredrich A. (1994) *The Road to Serfdom*, 15th edn (Chicago, University of Chicago Press).

Jacob, Herbert (1997) "The Governance of Trial Court Judges," *Law and Society Review*, Vol. 31, pp. 3–30.

Karpik, Lucien (1999) *French Lawyers: a Study of Collective Action, 1974–1994* (Oxford: Clarendon Press).

Landes, William and Richard Posner (1975) "The Independent Judiciary in an Interest Group Perspective," *Journal of Law and Economics*, Vol. 18, pp. 887–901.

Larkins, Christopher M. (1996) "Judicial Independence and Democratization: a Theoretical and Conceptual Analysis," *American Journal of Comparative Law*, Vol. 44, pp. 605–26.

Lowi, Theodore (1979) *The End of Liberalism*, 2nd edn (New York: W.W. Norton).

MacCormick, Neil (1999) *Questioning Sovereignty* (Oxford: Oxford University Press).

McCubbins, Matthew, Robert Noll, and Barry Weingast (1987) "Administrative Procedures as Instruments of Political Control," *Journal of Law, Economics, and Organization*, Vol. 3, pp. 243–77.

Milgrom, P., D. North and B. Weingast (1990) "The Role of Institutions in the Revival of Trade: the Medieval Law Merchant, Private Judges and the Champagne Fairs," *Economic and Politics*, Vol. 2, p. 1.

Miyazawa, Setsuo (1991) "Administrative Control of Japanese Judges," in Philip S.C. Lewis (ed.), *Law and Technology in the Pacific Community* (Boulder: Westview Press).

Miyazawa, Setsuo and Hiroshi Otsuka (1997) "Legal Education and the Reproduction of the Elite in Japan," paper prepared for the conference on "New Challenge for the Rule of Law: Lawyers, Internationalization, and the Social Construction of Legal Rules," University of California at Santa Barbara, November 7–9, 1997.

Nonet, Philippe and Philip Selznick (1978) *Law and Society in Transition: Towards Responsive Law* (New York: Harper and Row).

O'Brien, David M. and Yasuo Oskoshi (1996) *To Dream of Dreams: Religious Freedom and Constitutional Politics in Postwar Japa*n (Honolulu: University Press of Hawaii).

Pashukanis, Evgeny, B. (1987 [1927]) *Law and Marxism: a General Theory* (London: Ink Links).

Ramseyer, Mark (1994) "The Puzzling (In)Dependence of Courts: a Comparative Approach," *Journal of Legal Studies*, Vol. 23 (June), pp. 721–47.

Ramseyer, Mark and Eric Rasmusen (1997) "Judicial Indepedence in a Civil Law Regime: the Evidence from Japan," *Journal of Law, Economics, and Organization*, Vol. 13, pp. 259–76.

Rueschemeyer, Dietrich (1997) "State, Capitalism, and the Organization of Legal Counsel: Examining an Extreme Case – the Prussian Bar, 1700–1914," in Terence Halliday and Lucien Karpik (eds), *Lawyers and the Rise of Western Political Liberalism* (Oxford: Clarendon Press), pp. 207–28.

Selznick, Philip (1969) *Law, Society and Industrial Justice* (New York: Russell Sage Foundation).

Shapiro, Martin (1981) *Courts: a Comparative and Political Analysis* (Chicago: University of Chicago Press).

Weber, Max (1978) *Economy and Society* (Berkeley: University of California Press).

6

Effective Adversaries for the Poor

Roger A. Hanson, Brian J. Ostrom, and Ann M. Jones

Part I Introduction

Most criminal cases in the United States are resolved in the nation's state trial courts. Two and a half million felony cases (homicide, rape, robbery, burglary, drug sale, and illegal weapons possession) were filed in the nation's 3500 state trial courts in 1996, in addition to more than 11 million driving while intoxicated/driving under the influence (of alcohol) (DWI/DUI) and misdemeanors. In contrast, there were fewer than 50,000 criminal cases, including both felonies and misdemeanors, filed in the federal district courts in 1996 (Ostrom and Kauder, 1997). Almost all felonies provide for the possible incarceration of the defendants in prison or jail for at least one year.

Courts appoint defense attorneys to represent criminal defendants who lack the resources to hire private attorneys, in accordance with US Supreme Court decisions (*Gideon v. Wainright*, 1963, 335; *Argersinger v. Hamlin*, 1972, p. 25; *Scott v. Illinois*, 1979, p. 367). Compensation for this legal service comes from state or local government budgets. In some instances, the appointed attorneys are full-time employees of a public defender's office. In other instances, attorneys who are in private practice are assigned by the court to represent a particular individual defendant. Assigned attorneys are paid on an hourly or flat fee basis. Finally, some private attorneys contract with a state or local government to accept a designated number of appointments in return for a lump sum of money.[1]

There is perhaps no issue in the American criminal justice system more controversial than the quality of court-appointed attorneys. This chapter will present and analyze evidence on the performance of criminal defense attorneys. Are publicly appointed attorneys doing a deficient job, as their critics assert? Compared to privately retained attorneys, are publicly appointed attorneys effective or ineffective advocates for the accused?

This chapter examines performance-related data gathered by the National Center for State Courts from 11 state trial courts in 8 states (Baltimore City, Maryland; Baltimore County, Maryland; Des Moines, Iowa; Fort Worth, Texas; Omaha, Nebraska; Riverside, California; St Petersburg, Florida; San Jose, California; Seattle Washington; Spokane, Washington; and Tucson, Arizona). The communities range from medium to large population centers. Des Moines is the smallest, with a population of 349,560 in 1995, and Seattle is the largest, with 1,595,243 residents.

The data from these 11 courts confirm findings from prior investigations.[2] They demonstrate that, in key respects, publicly appointed attorneys do reasonably well when compared to privately retained attorneys. Hence, the American experience with court-appointed counsel may be relevant to Japan, where the role of criminal defense attorneys in strengthening the rights of the accused is a live issue.

Part II Previous criticism of publicly appointed attorneys

What provokes strong criticism of publicly appointed attorneys? Basically, five factors have been said to distinguish the quality of publicly appointed attorneys from the quality of privately retained counsel. Relative to privately retained counsel:

1. Publicly appointed criminal defense attorneys are inadequately compensated. Public defenders have low salaries, assigned attorneys receive substandard fees, and contract attorneys receive too little money for the number of cases that they agree to take (Klein and Spangenberg, 1993). As a result, publicly appointed attorneys have little financial incentive to work as hard as necessary to represent their clients.
2. Publicly appointed attorneys are often unprepared because they have too much work. Public defender caseloads are too large. Assigned attorneys have a financial incentive to allocate as little time as possible to their appointed cases, and contract attorneys must ration their work time to avoid going over budget (ibid.). Why? Because the total payment for criminal defense work is maximized by squeezing more cases into the workday. In addition, the assigned and contract attorneys can make more money working for paying clients on other cases.

3. Publicly appointed attorneys frequently lack the experience and training to represent defendants, especially in cases in which the defendant is accused of a very serious crime. The inadequate compensation makes it difficult to attract qualified and talented attorneys (ibid.).
4. Publicly appointed attorneys are not vigorous advocates for the rights of the accused, due to the minimal compensation and maximum workload. They prefer to plea-bargain cases to limit the number of court appearances and to avoid trials, which tie up scarce resources (see e.g. McConville and Mirsky, 1986–87, p. 581; Mounts and Wilson, 1986, pp. 193–201).
5. Publicly appointed attorneys also ineffectively represent the rights of the accused because they are co-opted by the rest of the courthouse community. Judges and prosecutors, it is argued, have certain expectations about how criminal cases should be processed; publicly appointed attorneys are coerced into making their practices conform to the court's objective of efficiency.[3]

In sum, the critics assert that the institutional constraints and personal limitations of publicly appointed attorneys ensure that their performance is substandard relative to that of their privately retained counterparts. As a result, for many if not most indigent criminal defendants, the constitutional right to representation is meaningless.

Part III A method to test the effectiveness of publicly appointed attorneys

There are at least two basic ways to assess the effectiveness of criminal defense attorneys. One is to document whether lawyers satisfy the requirements and guidelines governing attorney preparation. Do attorneys meet with clients, contact witnesses, conduct research, review presentence investigation reports, and so forth? The American Bar Association and others have articulated the need for guidelines concerning "the duty to investigate," "attorney competence," and "ensuring effectiveness."[4] However, no objective performance measures have yet been introduced.

A second approach is to determine whether attorneys achieve relatively favorable outcomes, such as acquittals, dismissals, charge reductions, and noncustodial sentences for their clients. Do appointed attorneys achieve a greater, a lesser, or the same proportion of favorable outcomes as do privately retained attorneys? (see e.g. Hermann et al., 1977; Willison, 1984, pp. 87–101; Hanson et al., 1992).

While there is merit in both approaches, the first one lacks the means to measure objectively what attorneys accomplish. It therefore precludes us from comparing the work and performance of publicly appointed attorneys and privately retained counsel. We have adopted the second method in our current research to evaluate publicly appointed attorneys, to make several important comparisons that describe the landscape of criminal defense representation and the quality of performance of publicly appointed attorneys. Basically, three areas of analysis are covered in the remaining chapter.

First, we examine the 11 courts in terms of their caseload composition and type of defense representation system. Do all courts handle the same types of cases? What is the most common type of publicly appointed attorney? Do publicly appointed attorneys handle different kinds of cases than do privately retained attorneys?

Second, are the clients of publicly appointed attorneys different from or similar to the clients of privately retained attorneys? A comparison of the defendants in terms of prior record and bail status will indicate whether even the best publicly appointed attorneys might find it difficult to gain favorable outcomes for their clients.

Third, and finally, the research objective is to compare outcomes gained by publicly appointed attorneys for their clients with those secured by privately retained attorneys for their clients. Are publicly appointed attorneys more or less likely to obtain acquittals, charge reductions, or noncustodial sentences for their clients? Answers to these questions will help determine whether the criticisms commonly levied against publicly appointed attorneys are valid.

Part IV Comparing courts and their defense representation systems

For purposes of analysis, felonies are broken down into four basic categories:

1. Crimes against the person (homicide, rape, robbery, kidnapping);
2. Burglary/theft;
3. Drug sale/possession;
4. Other types of felonies (illegal weapons possession, driving while intoxicated).

Interestingly, there is a striking similarity in the felony caseload composition among the 11 courts, as shown in Table 6.1. Overall, most felonies are either drug sale/possession (33 percent) or burglary/theft (32 percent).

Table 6.1 What kinds of felony cases were resolved in each of the courts?

	Baltimore City	*Baltimore County*	*Des Moines*	*Fort Worth*	*Omaha*	*Riverside*	*San Jose*	*St Petersburg*	*Seattle*	*Spokane*	*Tucson*	*All courts*
Crimes against the person (%)	29	46	16	26	18	19	16	19	25	21	28	23
Burglary/theft (%)	11	25	40	36	31	31	31	39	35	47	29	32
Drug sale/ possession (%)	54	23	27	28	26	41	40	33	33	23	27	33
Other felonies (%)	6	6	17	10	25	9	13	9	7	9	16	12
All case types (%)	100	100	100	100	100	100	100	100	100	100	100	100
(No.)	(432)	(275)	(370)	(376)	(466)	(465)	(461)	(494)	(488)	(458)	(433)	(4718)

Crimes against the person account for the largest share of felony cases only in Baltimore County (46 percent). The "other types of felonies" do not represent the largest share of the caseload in any of the courts.

There are similarities in the nature of criminal defense representation in the 11 communities. Public defenders are the largest category in every court except for Fort Worth, and privately retained attorneys are present in at least 7 percent of every court's caseload, as shown in Table 6.2. The relatively large number of privately retained attorneys in Fort Worth stems from court policy: in many Texas communities, defendants are not released on bond unless they retain an attorney.[5] Assigned attorneys and contract attorneys are lumped together because we could not differentiate them in the data collection process. However, even this combined category is the smallest in six individual courts (Baltimore City, Baltimore County, Omaha, San Jose, St Petersburg, and Spokane) and for all courts combined (14 percent).

The kinds of cases handled by the different types of criminal defense attorneys are also similar, as shown in Table 6.3. There is a relationship between the types of felonies and the types of defense attorneys, but it is a relatively weak one. Burglary/theft cases represent the largest share of public defenders' workload composition (35 percent). These cases constitute a smaller portion of the workload breakdown of other types of appointed attorneys (30 percent) and of privately retained attorneys (26 percent). The largest segment of the workload of other types of appointed attorneys and privately retained attorneys consists of cases involving drug sale and/or possession. Cases involving crimes against the person represent a greater portion of privately retained attorneys' workload than public defenders' workload. The crimes against the person cases handled by privately retained attorneys are mainly in the area of sexual offenses (22 percent) and attempted murder (19 percent).[6]

Defendant characteristics

Several factors beyond the relative capabilities of attorneys make it more difficult for indigent defendants than for those who possess resources to gain favorable outcomes. First, for any given crime, a poor defendant is more likely to be detained than a defendant with money; money allows a defendant both to post a bond and to hire a private attorney. A defendant who remains in detention pretrial will have less of an opportunity to assist in the preparation of his or her case. As shown in Figure 6.1, publicly appointed attorneys more likely represent clients who are not released on bail. Also, Table 6.4 illustrates that this trend exists regardless of indictment charge.

Table 6.2 What kinds of attorneys handle felony defenses in each of the courts?

	Baltimore City	*Baltimore County*	*Des Moines*	*Fort Worth*	*Omaha*	*Riverside*	*San Jose*	*St Petersburg*	*Seattle*	*Spokane*	*Tucson*	*All courts*
Public defenders (%)	70	51	50	0	68	75	61	75	83	85	65	64
Assigned and contract attorneys (%)	2	2	36	42	8	14	13	7	10	5	22	14
Privately retained attorneys (%)	28	47	14	58	24	11	26	18	7	10	13	22
All types of criminal defense attorneys (%)	100	100	100	100	100	100	100	100	100	100	100	100
(No.)	(432)	(275)	(370)	(376)	(466)	(465)	(461)	(494)	(488)	(458)	(433)	(4718)

Table 6.3 What kinds of cases do different types of criminal defense attorneys handle?

	Public defenders	*Assigned and contract attorneys*	*Privately retained attorneys*	*Totals*
Crimes against the person (%)	20	27	29	23
(No.)	(615)	(179)	(295)	(1092)
Burglary/theft (%)	35	30	26	32
(No.)	(1061)	(199)	(274)	(1539)
Drug sale/possession (%)	33	33	32	33
(No.)	(992)	(217)	(333)	(1544)
Other felonies (%)	12	10	13	12
(No.)	(354)	(65)	(134)	(554)
Total (%)	100	100	100	100
(No.)	(3022)	(660)	(1036)	(4729)

Chi-square = 49.99; significance level < 0.0005.

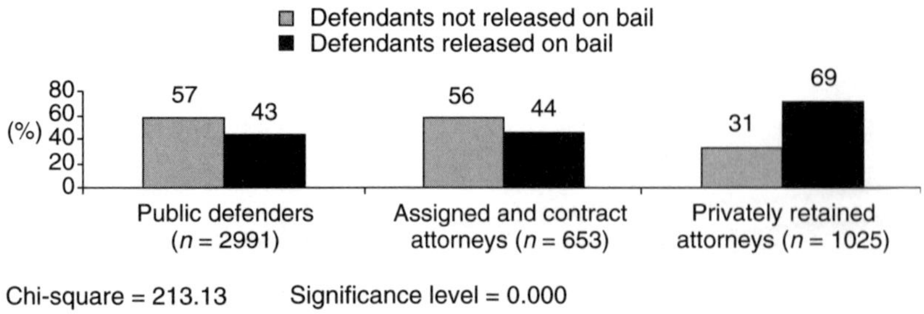

Figure 6.1 What is the bail status of criminal defendants?

Second, poor defendants are more likely to have at least one prior felony conviction. A prior record likely will influence plea negotiations and the likelihood of receiving a prison sentence. As shown in Figure 6.2, this handicap occurs more frequently among clients represented by publicly appointed attorneys.[7] As seen with bail status, a similar trend in relationship exists between type of defense attorney and the prior felony record of the client, regardless of the offense with which the defendant is charged. As illustrated in Table 6.5, for each of the offense categories, appointed attorneys are more likely than privately retained defense attorneys to have clients with prior felony convictions.

Table 6.4 What is the bail status of criminal defendants by indictment charge?

	Public defenders		*Assigned and contract attorneys*		*Privately retained attorneys*		*Totals*	
	Released	*Detained*	*Released*	*Detained*	*Released*	*Detained*	*Released*	*Detained*
Crimes against the person (%)	33	67	41	59	69	31	44	56
(No.)	(201)	(403)	(72)	(103)	(200)	(92)	(473)	(598)
Burglary/theft (%)	47	53	43	57	70	30	51	49
(No.)	(492)	(558)	(85)	(113)	(189)	(81)	(766)	(752)
Drug sale/possession (%)	44	56	47	53	67	33	49	51
(No.)	(431)	(555)	(101)	(114)	(221)	(108)	(753)	(777)
Other types of felonies (%)	43	57	48	52	70	30	50	50
(No.)	(151)	(200)	(31)	(34)	(94)	(40)	(276)	(274)

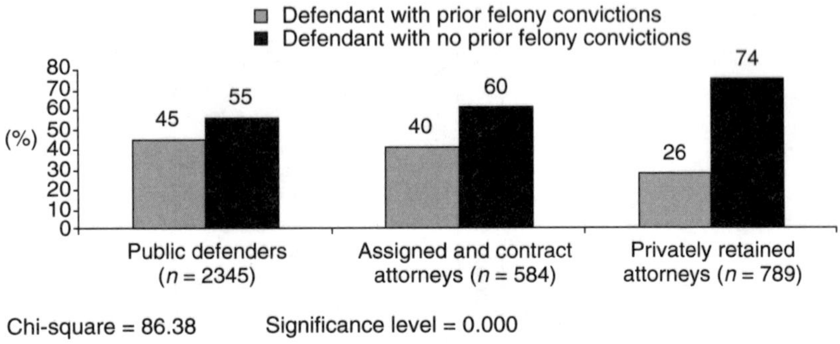

Figure 6.2 Are publicly appointed attorneys more or less likely to represent defendants with prior record (for example, at least one prior felony conviction)?

Overall, it is apparent that appointed and privately retained defense attorneys are serving different populations. Public defenders and other appointed attorneys are more likely to defend clients who are not released on bail and who have prior felony convictions. The public defenders and other appointed attorneys tend to represent defendants whose charges are more "serious" in nature. For example, the percentage of defendants for whom bench warrants are issued is greater for clients with public defenders (22 percent) and other assigned attorneys (27 percent) than for defendants represented by privately retained counsel (13 percent).

Part V Case outcomes

Criminal cases can be resolved in several ways; certain outcomes are more preferable from the defense perspective. From the perspective of the criminal defendant, "winning big" means having the case dismissed or being acquitted at trial. A second category consists of "winning little," wherein the defendant's charges at conviction are reduced from those at indictment. Such charge reductions typically do not eliminate punishment, but they may substantially reduce the "degree of exposure" faced by the convicted offender. Finally, if found guilty by plea or at trial, convicted offenders usually prefer not to receive a sentence of incarceration in prison. The sections below examine the relative success of publicly appointed attorneys and privately retained counsel in achieving these outcomes.

Table 6.5 Given the indictment charge, are publicly appointed attorneys more or less likely to represent defendants with prior records (for example, at least one prior felony conviction)?

	Public defenders		*Assigned and contract attorneys*		*Privately retained attorneys*		*Totals*	
	Prior record	*No record*	*Prior record*	*No record*	*Prior record*	*No record*	*Prior record*	*No record*
Crimes against the person (%)	39	61	36	64	23	77	34	66
(No.)	(180)	(279)	(57)	(103)	(51)	(169)	(288)	(551)
Burglary/theft (%)	48	52	44	56	24	76	43	57
(No.)	(401)	(440)	(80)	(100)	(53)	(164)	(534)	(704)
Drug sale/possession (%)	45	55	39	61	29	71	41	59
(No.)	(366)	(442)	(72)	(115)	(73)	(182)	(511)	(739)
Other types of felonies (%)	48	52	40	60	33	67	43	57
(No.)	(114)	(123)	(23)	(34)	(32)	(65)	(169)	(222)

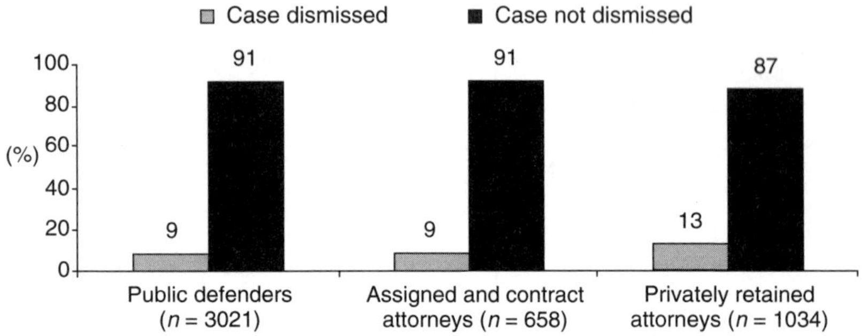

Chi-square = 13.9 Significance level = 0.001

Figure 6.3 What is the dismissal rate for defense attorneys?

Dismissed cases

The most favorable outcome for a defendant is the dismissal of the case. Overall, as illustrated in Figure 6.3, privately retained counsel have a slightly higher dismissal rate than publicly appointed counsel, but the difference is quite small in practice. Specifically, 9 percent of the cases handled by public defenders or other appointed counsel were dismissed, while privately retained attorneys had a slightly higher dismissal rate (13 percent). Since specific characteristics may play a role in dismissal rates, what is the dismissal rate for different types of offenses? As seen in Table 6.6, privately retained attorneys secure a slightly higher dismissal rate for each of the offense categories. When compared to appointed counsel, privately retained attorneys were especially effective in gaining dismissal of cases in the drug sale/possession and "other types of felonies" (weapons possession, driving while intoxicated) categories.

Charge reductions

Because most defendants are convicted, an important outcome sought by most defendants is a reduction in the seriousness of charge at conviction. If the offense at conviction is a less serious offense than the one with which the defendant was initially charged, this outcome is favorable to the defendant. The performance question is, therefore, are the charge reduction rates for publicly appointed attorneys significantly different from those of privately retained attorneys?

The similar performance of all defense attorneys in gaining charge reductions for defendants pleading guilty is evident in the data shown

Table 6.6 Given the indictment charge, are publicly appointed attorneys more or less likely to gain a dismissal?

	Public defenders		*Assigned and contract attorneys*		*Privately retained attorneys*		*Totals*	
	Dismissed	*Not dismissed*	*Dismissed*	*Not dismissed*	*Dismissed*	*Not dismissed*	*Dismissed*	*Not dismissed*
Crimes against the person (%)	11	89	10	90	12	88	11	89
(No.)	(65)	(550)	(17)	(160)	(35)	(259)	(117)	(969)
Burglary/theft (%)	9	91	13	87	11	89	10	90
(No.)	(91)	(970)	(25)	(174)	(30)	(243)	(146)	(1387)
Drug sale/possession (%)	7	93	7	93	12	88	8	92
(No.)	(65)	(927)	(16)	(201)	(39)	(294)	(120)	(1422)
Other types of felonies (%)	12	88	6	94	20	80	13	87
(No.)	(42)	(311)	(4)	(61)	(27)	(107)	(73)	(479)

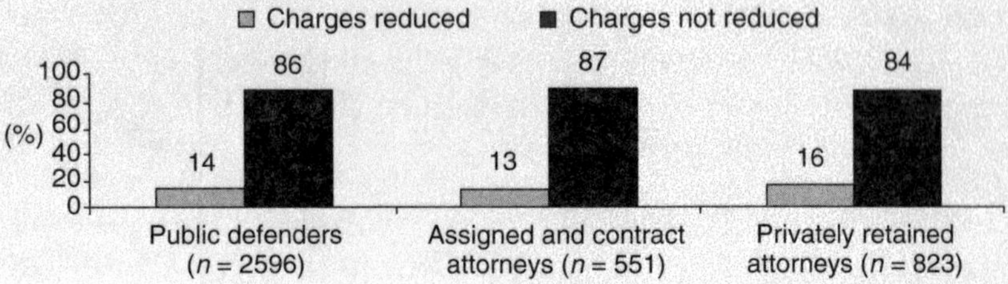

Chi-square = 3.24 Significance level = 0.198

Figure 6.4 Do privately retained attorneys gain charge reductions more frequently than appointed attorneys in cases resolved by guilty pleas?

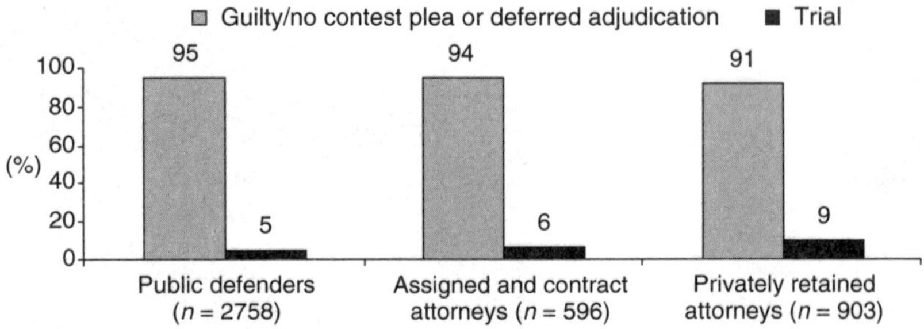

Chi-square = 18.03 Significance level = 0.001

Figure 6.5 How do different types of criminal defense attorneys resolve cases?

in Figure 6.4. While relatively few indictment charges were reduced, privately retained attorneys were slightly more successful in gaining charge reductions (16 percent) than were assigned/contract attorneys (13 percent) and public defenders (14 percent).

Concerning the manner of case resolution, public defenders, assigned counsel, and contract attorneys are more likely than private counsel to have clients who plead guilty, but the actual differences are small (Figure 6.5). The trial rates are about the same, ranging between 5 and 9 percent for all three groups of attorneys. One preliminary conclusion is that publicly appointed and privately retained attorneys have caseloads that are more similar than different from each other and that they do not resolve their caseloads in radically different ways. Hence, it seems fair to compare the conviction rates at trial among the different types of defense attorneys.

Conviction rates at trial

One basic goal of the defense attorney is to minimize the possibility of criminal sanctions. The lower the conviction rate at trial for a given set of defense attorneys, the more successful they are in gaining favorable outcomes for their clients.

As shown in Figure 6.6, the conviction rates of defendants represented at trial by public defenders, assigned and contract attorneys, and privately retained attorneys are strikingly similar. Public defenders and privately retained attorneys have an overall conviction rate of 88 percent, while assigned and contract attorneys have a rate of 83 percent. No statistically significant difference in conviction rates implies that defendants are equally well off with either group of attorneys. In other words, defendants with privately retained attorneys do no better or worse, on average, than defendants with publicly appointed attorneys. Moreover, the lack of substantial difference in conviction rates exists in all four of the felony case types under study. For example, in the area of crimes against the person, the conviction rates for public defenders, assigned and contract attorneys, and privately retained attorneys are 90, 95, and 88 per cent, respectively (see Table 6.7). Privately retained attorneys achieve a higher level of performance among other types of felonies (for example, driving under the influence): 75 percent of their clients are convicted, while 81 percent of the clients of public defenders are convicted.

Incarceration rates

The data indicate that privately retained attorneys have the largest advantage over publicly appointed attorneys in the area of sanctions.

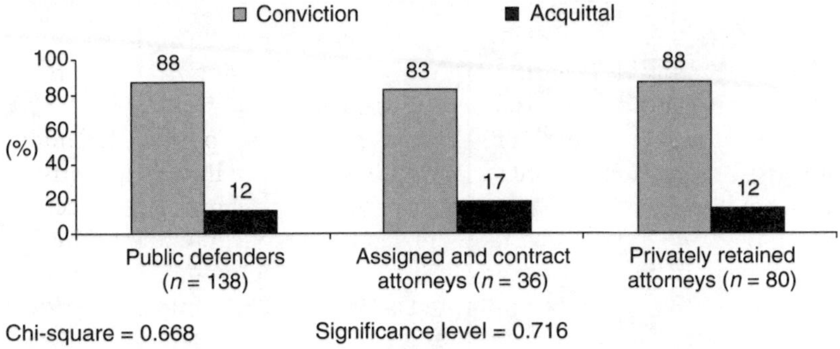

Figure 6.6 Are defendants represented by publicly appointed attorneys more likely to be convicted at trial than defendants represented by privately retained attorneys?

Table 6.7 Are defendants represented by publicly appointed attorneys more likely to be convicted at trial than defendants represented by privately retained attorneys?

	Public defenders		*Assigned and contract attorneys*		*Privately retained attorneys*		*Totals*	
	Convicted	*Acquittal*	*Convicted*	*Acquittal*	*Convicted*	*Acquittal*	*Convicted*	*Acquittal*
Crimes against the person (%)	90	10	95	5	88	12	90	10
(No.)	(52)	(6)	(19)	(1)	(43)	(6)	(114)	(13)
Burglary/theft (%)	83	17	43	57	100	0	80	20
(No.)	(24)	(5)	(3)	(4)	(10)	(0)	(37)	(9)
Drug sale/possession (%)	94	6	100	0	85	15	93	7
(No.)	(33)	(2)	(6)	(0)	(11)	(2)	(50)	(4)
Other types of felonies (%)	81	19	67	33	75	25	78	22
(No.)	(13)	(3)	(2)	(1)	(6)	(2)	(21)	(6)

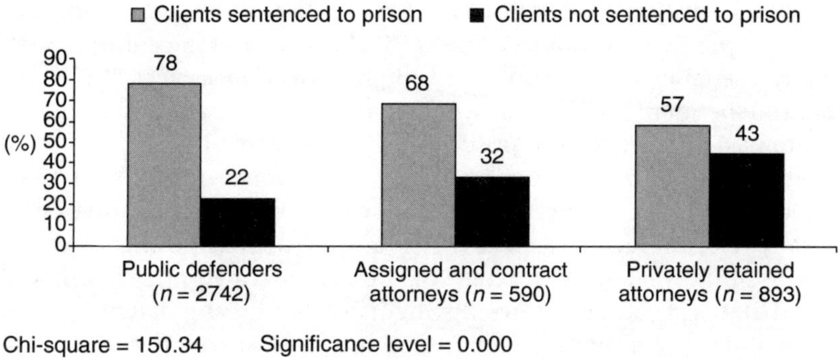

Figure 6.7 Are privately retained attorneys more successful in keeping their clients out of jail or prison?

The incarceration rates are lower for clients represented by privately retained attorneys (57 percent). Public defenders (78 percent) and other types of appointed attorneys (68 percent) are less successful in keeping their clients out of penal institutions (Figure 6.7).

On the one hand, Figure 6.7 shows that defendants represented by privately retained attorneys are less likely to be sentenced to prison. On the other hand, we also know (Figures 6.1 and 6.2; Table 6.4) that publicly appointed attorneys are more likely to represent defendants who have a prior record or who have been held in pretrial detention – factors which the criminal justice literature suggest are strongly correlated with the decision to incarcerate. These observations lead us to question which factors actually determine the likelihood that a convicted offender will receive prison time. Does it have more to do with the potential liabilities of poor defendants (for example, prior record and bail status) or with the type of representation (public or private attorney) that the defendant received? This question is addressed through an alternative statistical technique.

Part VI Factors affecting the decision to incarcerate

Whether an offender will be sentenced to prison is difficult to predict with certainty, but it is possible to estimate reasonably the *probability* of incarceration. In this section we examine the relationship between different case and defendant characteristics and the probability that a particular defendant will receive a prison sentence. The method for identifying which factors do and do not shape the decision to incarcerate is logistic regression. This statistical technique allows us to control simultaneously for the influence of multiple factors (called independent or predictor variables) on the likelihood of incarceration. Such analysis enables us to discern the unique contribution of each individual independent variable on whether the offender will or will not be sentenced to serve time in prison (the dependent variable).

Four types of independent variables are examined in this analysis. First, the decision to incarcerate is known to be influenced directly by legally relevant factors such as the severity of the charge at conviction, the use of a weapon, the extent of the defendant's prior record, and bond status. In addition, we distinguish whether the defendant was represented by a public defender, an assigned attorney, or privately retained counsel. We also examine whether certain extralegal factors – the defendant's gender, race, and age – influence the in/out decision. Finally, we include a set of site variables that control for basic differences in local legal culture in the 11 jurisdictions.[8] Table 6.8 defines briefly all the variables used in the analysis and provides each variable's mean and standard deviation.

The results of the analysis and the variables that are statistically significant in explaining whether an individual receives a prison sentence are displayed in Table 6.9. The coefficients (and their measures of significance) indicate the relative influence of each independent variable on the probability that a convicted offender will be incarcerated.[9] The last row of the table shows the overall success of the model in correctly distinguishing whether an offender will be sent to prison (that is, the percentage of cases correctly predicted by the model).[10] The percentage is compared to the "null hypothesis," defined as the most common outcome.[11] Note that this model improves considerably our ability to predict the likelihood of incarceration over chance alone (83 percent to 70 percent).

Examining the significance of the individual variables in the model shows that the "legally relevant" factors were all significant. The type of charge for which the defendant was convicted was influential in predicting the in/out decision; individuals convicted of violent crime, drug crime, and other felony charges were more likely to receive a prison sentence than those convicted of burglary and theft. Likewise, the existence of a prior criminal record, the use of a weapon during the offense, and the failure to make bail each had an independent, positive, and significant impact on the likelihood of going to prison. Of concern is the finding that race has an independent effect on the probability of going to prison. Nonwhite offenders are more likely to be incarcerated relative to similarly situated white offenders.

Table 6.8 Descriptive information for variables in the logistic regression

Variable name	*Variable label*	*Mean*	*Std. Dev*
Dependent variable			
Incarceration	Sent to prison?	0.71	0.45
Independent variables			
Severity of charge at conviction:			
Violent	Convicted of a crime against person?	0.23	0.42
Drug	Convicted of drug sale or possession?	0.33	0.47
Other felony	Convicted of other felony?	0.12	0.32
Burglary/theft	Convicted of burglary or theft?	0.32	0.47
Procedural aspects:			
Bail	Defendant released on bail?	0.49	0.50
Weapons charge	Case involved a weapons charge?	0.16	0.37
Prior felony conviction	Defendant had at least one prior felony conviction?	0.40	0.49
Type of defense counsel:			
Public defender	Defendant had a public defender?	0.63	0.48
Assigned counsel	Defendant had assigned counsel?	0.14	0.34
Privately retained counsel	Defendant had a private attorney?	0.22	0.41
Extralegal characteristics:			
Age of defendant	Age of defendant	30.17	9.33
Race of defendant	Defendant was white?	0.48	0.50
Gender of defendant	Defendant was male?	0.84	0.37
Jurisdictions:			
Fort Worth	Case occurred in Fort Worth?	0.08	0.27
Omaha	Case occurred in Omaha?	0.10	0.30
Riverside	Case occurred in Riverside?	0.10	0.30
San Jose	Case occurred in San Jose?	0.10	0.30
Seattle	Case occurred in Seattle?	0.10	0.30
Tucson	Case occurred in Tucson?	0.09	0.29
Baltimore City	Case occurred in Baltimore City?	0.09	0.29
Baltimore County	Case occurred in Baltimore County?	0.06	0.24
Spokane	Case occurred in Spokane?	0.10	0.30
St Petersburg	Case occurred in St Petersburg?	0.10	0.30
Des Moines	Case occurred in Des Moines?	0.08	0.27

Note: All variables (except age of defendant) are dichotomous, coded 1 for yes and 0 for no.

Table 6.9 Results of the logistic regression

Variable name	*Estimated coefficient*	*Significance*	*Significant difference (0.05 level)*
Severity of charge at conviction			
Violent	0.466	0.001	*
Drug	0.294	0.016	*
Other felony	1.244	0.000	*
Procedural aspects			
Bail	–1.397	0.000	*
Weapons charge	0.398	0.013	*
Prior felony conviction	1.165	0.000	*
Type of defense counsel			
Assigned counsel	0.037	0.795	
Privately retained counsel	–0.175	0.198	
Extralegal characteristics			
Age of defendant	0.002	0.647	
Race of defendant	–0.342	0.001	*
Gender of defendant	0.578	0.000	*
Jurisdictions			
Fort Worth	0.147	0.455	
Omaha	0.680	0.536	
Riverside	2.459	0.000	*
San Jose	3.063	0.000	*
Seattle	2.817	0.000	*
Tucson	0.565	0.002	*
Baltimore City	1.986	0.000	*
Baltimore County	–0.346	0.215	
Spokane	3.145	0.000	*
St Petersburg	0.143	0.425	
Constant	–0.6139	0.018	*
Nagelkerke R2	0.51		
–2 × LLR	2641.6		
% Correct (Null)	83 (70)		

The probability of receiving a prison sentence varies by jurisdiction. The model suggests that in five sites (Des Moines, Fort Worth, Omaha, Baltimore County, and St Petersburg), the case- and defendant-related factors included in the model have a similar effect on the likelihood of incarceration. The large and positive coefficients for the remaining sites indicate that local sentencing practice in these jurisdictions is to make greater use of incarceration for otherwise similar offenders.

Of particular interest to this research is the finding that the type of criminal defense counsel does not have an independent effect on the probability of incarceration. Once other factors such as type of offense at conviction, prior record, and bail status were taken into account, knowing whether the defense counsel was a publicly appointed attorney or a privately retained attorney had no impact on our ability to predict the in/out decision. Factors related to the defendant – which are outside the control of the defense counsel – primarily determine whether a defendant will be sentenced to prison. This finding supports the notion that publicly appointed attorneys perform as well as privately retained attorneys in keeping their clients out of prison once we consider important differences in defendant backgrounds and behaviors.

Part VII Conclusions

The institution of publicly appointed attorneys for criminal defendants operates relatively effectively in the 11 courts under study. This observation conflicts with previous criticisms. How can we account for the positive performance we observed?

Explaining the relatively positive performance of publicly appointed criminal defense attorneys is more difficult than assembling data on case outcomes. However, clues concerning effectiveness can be found in a previous study of court-appointed attorneys in nine communities, including Denver and Detroit, conducted by the National Center for State Courts.

Publicly appointed attorneys, especially public defenders, perform well when they are adequately compensated for their services. A fair salary for advocates of poor defendants is a salary level equal to that of prosecutors. Where that degree of parity occurs, public defenders perform reasonably well (Hanson et al., 1992). When salaries become competitive among all types of public sector attorneys, public defenders can receive financial rewards in addition to the psychic benefit of protecting the constitutional rights of defendants (ibid.).

Publicly appointed attorneys also perform well because they receive on-the-job and external training. Because most publicly appointed attorneys work on a vertical system of representation (the attorney representing the defendant at the first appearance hearing takes the case to resolution), experienced attorneys become proficient at all stages of criminal case processing. As a result, more experienced attorneys are able to share their knowledge with less experienced attorneys during brown-bag sessions at the office. Some courts have been imaginative in financing very up-to-date legal training programs. Detroit, for example, deposits 0.5 percent of each assigned counsel fee into a training fund. As a result, Detroit offers very sophisticated courses on cutting-edge legal defense skills, despite the impoverished nature of Detroit's public treasury (ibid.).

The problem of case shedding can be and has been averted, at least in some courts. Obviously, liberal declaration of conflicts might lead to the assignment of cases to less qualified counsel. However, the Denver experience shows how this pitfall can be avoided. The Denver public defender's office also controls the budget for counsel in conflict cases. Hence, public defenders do not profit by declaring conflicts where they do not exist. In fact, there is an incentive for the public defender to keep conflicts to a minimum and to gain credit with the state legislature by returning part of the conflict budget each year. Proof that this arrangement works lies in the very small number of conflict cases in Denver (ibid.).

Thirdly, public defenders may be more experienced than is commonly believed. In Chicago and other cities, the tenure of public defenders is more extensive than it is for prosecutors (McIntyre, 1987; Hanson et al., 1992). After years of experience, the defense attorneys know how to negotiate and how to deploy strategies to gain the best possible outcome for their client.

Finally, all publicly appointed attorneys are not considered equivalent. Courts try to screen and to grade attorneys in assigned attorney systems to match attorney qualifications with the severity of the offense. In contract systems, not all attorneys who seek contracts gain them, and initial contracts seldom cover a full range of cases. Where public defender offices exist, each attorney must work his or her way up the ladder, beginning with juvenile and misdemeanor offenses before tackling felony murder trials.

For all these reasons, the system of advocacy for the poor works reasonably well, although more research is required to refine the explanation behind the success of publicly appointed criminal defense attorneys. The conditions for positive performance do not exist everywhere, and every system has room for improvement. However, there are a sufficient number of communities in which effective advocacy prevails.

Notes

1. The existence of three types of publicly appointed criminal defense attorneys in American state courts contrasts with Japan's almost exclusive reliance on an assigned attorney system. Historically, the American states relied exclusively on an assigned system. That situation has changed with the development of public defender offices and more recently with contract

systems. In our opinion, the American system has improved because of the organizational variety of appointment systems available to communities that vary in size, resources, culture, and tradition.

From our perspective, circumstances suggest the establishment and use of one type of a system over another. For example, in small communities, a public defender system is probably unworkable because a staff of only one, two, or three full-time attorneys would find itself in constant conflict in codefendant cases. Yet an assigned system may not be desirable in a small community because too few attorneys might agree to accept court appointments. Many attorneys might lack interest in criminal law, feel that they are not qualified, or regard the fees as too low. A contract system might work. There may be enough attorneys who together can handle virtually all of the appointments in criminal cases. Moreover, the contract attorneys might view their contracts as very desirable. A guaranteed amount of money might enable an attorney to cover his or her overhead while still leaving enough work time to handle retained criminal or civil cases.

2. For reports of other findings, see Hermann et al. (1977), Willison (1984), and Hanson et al. (1992).
3. For differing points of view concerning the relationships between defense attorneys and other court personnel, see Sudnow (1965, pp. 255–76), Blumberg (1967, pp. 15–40), Eckart and Stover (1974, pp. 665–85), Levine (1975, pp. 215–40), Balbus (1973), Mounts and Wilson (1986, pp. 193–201), Cole (1992).
4. See Rovner-Pieczenik et al. (1977), especially pp. 38–43 concerning measures of "attorney competence"; American Bar Association Project on Standards for Criminal Justice (1971), especially pp. 225–8 concerning the "duty to investigate"; Genego (1984, pp. 181–212); National Legal Aid and Defender Association, National Study Commission on Defense Services, (1976), especially pp. 428–47 on "insuring effectiveness".
5. In essence, defendants must prove their indigency by their inability to make bail.
6. The chi-square test of significance indicates whether there is a systematic connection as opposed to a coincidental connection between the different types of defense attorneys and performance. This technique generates a number and a corresponding level of significance. The smaller the significance level, the less likely the observed pattern could have happened by chance alone. In this report, the benchmark of 0.01 is used (that is, results could have happened by chance alone one time out of 100). In all of the tables, the chi-square value and the level at which it is significant are reported.
7. Interestingly, the burdens placed on publicly appointed attorneys in the US are similar to the burdens placed on publicly appointed attorneys in Japan. The court-appointed attorneys in Japan are much more likely than privately retained criminal defense attorneys to have clients with prior records and to be detained before trial. See Murayama, Chapter 4 of this volume.
8. All variables but the age of defendant are structured as dichotomous variables. These dichotomous variables are coded as 1 if the criterion applies in a particular case or 0 if the criterion does not apply. Researchers call these categorical variables "dummy variables."

9. A positive coefficient indicates that larger values of the independent variable are associated with an increased probability of incarceration, while a negative coefficient indicates a diminished probability of incarceration.
10. The primary measures of "goodness of fit" are displayed at the bottom of the table. The most frequently used indicators in logit are the "–2 log likelihood" and the Nagelkerke R2. On the basis of both measures, the model fits the data very well and is highly significant. The –2 log likelihood is a chi-square variate with 21 degrees of freedom (because there are 21 explanatory variables in this model). It is the analog of the *F*–statistic in linear regression and tests the hypothesis that all of the coefficients are equal to zero. The Nagelkerke R2 is a statistic that attempts to quantify the proportion of variation explained by the logistic regression. The purpose of this statistic is similar to the R2 used in linear regression.
11. That is, in about 30 percent of the cases in our sample, the offender was sentenced to prison, and in 70 percent of the cases, the offender was not sentenced to prison. Therefore, the null hypothesis or best guess is to predict that the offender does not receive a prison sentence and to be right 70 percent of the time.

References

American Bar Association Project on Standards for Criminal Justice (1971) *Standards Relating to the Prosecution Function and the Defense Function* (New York: Institute of Judicial Administration).

Argersinger v. Hamlin, 407 US 1972, 25.

Balbus, I. (1973) *The Dialectics of Legal Repression: Black Rebels before the American Criminal Courts* (New Brunswick, NJ: Transaction Books,).

Blumberg, A. (1967) "The Practice of Law as a Confidence Game: Organizational Co-optation of a Profession," *Law and Society Review*, Vol. 1, pp. 15–40.

Cole, G. (1992) *Criminal Justice: Law and Politics* (Belmont, Calif: Wadsworth, Inc.).

Eckart, D. and R. Stover (1974) "Public Defenders and Routinized Criminal Defense Processes," *Journal of Urban Law*, Vol. 51 (May), pp. 665–85.

Genego, E. 1984 "Future of Effective Assistance of Counsel: Performance Standards and Complete Representation," *American Criminal Law Review*, Vol. 22 (Fall), pp. 181–212.

Gideon v. Wainwright, 372 US, 1963, 335.

Hanson, R., B. Ostrom, W. Hewitt, and C. Lomvardias (1992) *Indigent Defenders: Get the Job Done and Done Well* (Williamsburg, Va.: National Center for State Courts).

Hermann, R., E. Single, and J. Boston (1977) *Counsel for the Poor: Criminal Defense in Urban America* (Lexington, Mass.: Lexington Books).

Klein, R. and R. Spangenberg. (1993) *The Indigent Defense Crisis: A report for the American Bar Association Section of Criminal Justice* (Washington, DC: American Bar Association).

Levine, J. (1975) "The Impact of 'Gideon': the Performance of Public and Private Criminal Defense Lawyers," *Polity*, Vol. 8, pp. 215–40.

McIntyre, L. (1987) *The Public Defender: the Practice of Law in the Shadows of Repute* (Chicago, Ill.: University of Chicago Press).

McConville, M. and C. Mirsky (1986–87) "Criminal Defense of the Poor in New York City," *New York University Review of Law and Social Change,* Vol. 15 pp. 581–694.

Mounts, S. and R. Wilson (1986) "Systems for Providing Indigent Defense: an Introduction," *New York University Review of Law and Social Change,* Vol. 14, pp. 193–201.

National Legal Aid and Defender Association, National Study Commission on Defense Services (1976) *Guidelines for Legal Defense System in the United States* (Chicago, Ill.: National Legal Aid and Defender Association).

Ostrom, B. and N. Kauder (eds) (1997) *Examining the Work of State Courts, 1996: a National Perspective from the Court Statistics Project* (Williamsburg, Va.: National Center for State Courts).

Rovner–Pieczenik, R., A. Rapoport, and M. Lane (1977) *How Does Your Defender Office Rate? Self–Evaluation Manual for Public Defender Offices* (Washington, DC: National Institute of Law Enforcement and Criminal Justice).

Scott v. Illinois, 440 US, 1979, 367.

Sudnow, D. (1965) "Normal Crimes: a Sociological Feature of the Penal Code in a Public Defender Office," *Social Problems*, Vol. 12, pp. 255–76.

Willison, D. (1984) "The Effects of Counsel on the Severity of Criminal Sentences: a Statistical Assessment," *Justice System Journal*, Vol. 9, pp. 87–101.

7

Adversarial Procedure without a Jury: Is Japan's System Adversarial, Inquisitorial, or Something Else?

*Satoru Shinomiya**

Part I The Simpson trial and adversarial procedure in the United States

The O.J. Simpson case greeted me on my first day as a visiting scholar at UC Berkeley. Although in the course of my stay I had the chance to attend many hearings in Berkeley municipal courtrooms, Oakland superior courtrooms, and federal courtrooms in San Francisco, the Simpson trial had a totally different atmosphere than the ordinary cases I observed. Quite unlike its less spectacular counterparts, O.J.'s trial took nine months and enjoyed heavy media coverage; it involved the latest electronic devices in the courtroom, eloquent and garrulous lawyers, and a bearded Japanese-American judge. While the trial did have many extraneous, gladiatorial features,[1] I realized that the fundamental structure of the trial was identical to that of the other American trials I had been observing: adversarialism with a jury.

The Simpson verdict was highly controversial. However, on the issue of whether Mr Simpson had a fair trial or not, there was far less controversy. If the trial had been held according to inquisitorial procedure, it certainly would have been less noisy. But would the American people have considered the procedure fair? Surely not. I wondered why. After I discussed this question with many people, I found that many Americans believe that a fair trial results from thorough adversarial procedure, especially in criminal matters, even if the lawyers might be extremely aggressive and zealous.

* I would like to thank David Johnson and Kay Levine for their advice and assistance with this chapter.

Part II Japan's dispute resolution process: "adversarial process" without a jury

We define an adversary system as a style of decision-making in which two contestants argue their cases before a neutral and largely passive judge (Feeley, 1987, p. 753). After World War II, Japan introduced an adversary system, closely modeled on the American system, as a method of criminal dispute resolution. But the Japanese system was also unique in practice, for it did not put the defendant in the adversary seat during the investigative phase, and it had no jury during the trial phase.

The first unique feature signifies that the defendant is not an actual adversary against the police or prosecution in Japanese criminal procedure, but rather more of an isolated "hostage." This hostage characterization stems from statistical facts related to arrestees' detention status throughout the course of criminal procedure in Japan, as presented in Tables 7.1–7.3.

The latter feature means that in Japan, only the judge finds the facts. That is, under our "adversarial" system of criminal justice, judges decide the guilt or innocence of defendants. You may wonder: Are Japanese judges still neutral and passive, as is expected in an adversarial system? Or do judges adopt a markedly different role under Japanese-style adversarial procedure? Let me paint a portrait of judges in Japan's adversarial system by describing some cases in which I was involved as a defense counsel. The picture I paint starkly contradicts the normative logic of a healthy adversarial system.

Table 7.1 Percentage of detention warrants granted (for ten days' detention)

	Granted (%)	*Denied*	*Withdrew*
1996	95 091 (99.7)	293	22
1995	90 664 (99.7)	287	26
1994	90 027 (99.6)	316	23
1993	87 285 (99.6)	360	24
1992	81 590 (99.5)	365	15
1991	78 327 (99.6)	336	18
1990	76 525 (99.5)	378	11
1989	81 641 (99.7)	261	14
1988	90 081 (99.7)	269	24
1987	97 071 (99.6)	301	85

Note: Approximately 118,000 arrest warrants are issued each year. More than 99% of requests for warrants are granted. About 25–30% of arrestees are not detained.
Source: Supreme Court, Annual Judicial Statistics 1985–96.

Table 7.2 Percentage of requests for extension of detention granted (usually for ten more days)

	Claims	*Granted (%)*	*Denied*
1996	42 489	42 445 (99.9)	44
1995	38 527	38 509 (99.9)	18
1994	37 608	37 551 (99.8)	57
1993	35 493	35 441 (99.9)	52
1992	32 011	31 911 (99.7)	100
1991	28 638	28 612 (99.9)	26
1990	27 430	27 405 (99.9)	25
1989	28 777	28 750 (99.9)	27
1988	30 263	30 250 (99.9)	13
1987	31 617	31 594 (99.9)	23

Source: Supreme Court, Annual Judicial Statistics 1985–96.

Table 7.3 Court orders to prohibit communication with suspects (except by lawyers)

	Claims	*Granted (%)*
1996	26 596	25 435 (95.6)
1995	23 503	22 359 (95.1)
1994	20 032	18 541 (92.6)
1993	19 696	18 596 (94.4)
1992	18 395	17 415 (94.7)
1991	18 305	17 248 (94.2)
1990	17 146	16 355 (95.4)
1989	18 267	17 564 (96.2)
1988	21 921	21 189 (96.7)
1987	24 114	23 232 (96.3)

Source: Supreme Court, Annual Judicial Statistics 1985–96.

Reluctance to maintain party symmetry

(1) Reluctance to grant bail

Japanese judges are exceedingly reluctant to grant bail to defendants, especially to those who do not confess (see Table 7.4). In return for bail, some judges give defense counsel suggestions such as "Plead guilty" or "Do not make any objections to the admissibility of the prosecution's evidence." Since we do not have a so-called bail hearing in open courtrooms, these suggestions are usually given in chambers.

Table 7.4 Pretrial status of defendants at the trial phase (bailed only after indictment)

	No. of detention orders after indictment	*Bail granted (%)*
1996	53 881	8 778 (16.3)
1995	50 859	9 017 (17.7)
1994	49 961	9 387 (18.8)
1993	48 051	10 249 (21.3)
1992	45 615	10 477 (23.0)
1991	44 670	11 034 (24.7)
1990	43 960	11 100 (25.3)
1989	47 588	11 289 (23.7)
1988	53 047	11 797 (22.2)
1987	57 602	13 331 (23.1)

Source: Supreme Court, Annual Judicial Statistics 1985–96.

The judge's reluctance to allow bail often encourages defendants to give up and to plead guilty. Since there is no jury, trial sessions take place approximately once a month; it takes a long time for the judge to reach a verdict if the defendant does not confess.

(2) Reluctance to compel disclosure of prosecution evidence

Under the prewar Code of Criminal Procedure (CCP, Section 44.1), the prosecution had to send all documents and evidence to the trial court, whereupon defense counsel could review and copy the evidence. But the postwar CCP has no such provision for prosecutorial discovery obligations. The prosecutor has to disclose only the evidence which he or she is going to submit to the court (CCP Section 299.1). The Supreme Court has instructed that, during the phase of testimony, defense counsel may ask the court to order the prosecution to disclose particular evidence upon a showing of concrete necessity. If the discovery of the evidence will materially contribute to the defense and if there is no possibility that disclosure will lead to destruction of evidence or to intimidation of witnesses, and if the court deems disclosure appropriate, the court may order the prosecution to disclose evidence to the defense (*Onuki v. Japan*, Judgment of April 25, 1969, Saikousai [Supreme Court]). Otherwise, the prosecution has no duty to disclose any evidence before or during the trial.

Judges are reluctant to order disclosure. In Japan, investigations and interviews are conducted not only by the police but also by the prosecutor. Usually, for the defendant and for crucial witnesses, the police prepare many written statements based on these interviews. The prosecutor later reinterviews the interviewees and prepares final summary statements. At trial, especially in contested cases, the prosecutor submits only the final summary written statement as evidence, and not those made by the police, even though the latter were made just after the incident.

Easy rules of evidence

The postwar CCP includes rules of evidence similar to those of the United States. While the CCP restricts the admissibility of evidence in many ways, many trial judges interpret the exception clauses broadly. Hence, they admit a wide range of evidence, much of which would not be acceptable in most American courtrooms.

(1) The voluntariness standard

I will demonstrate the way in which Japanese trial judges handle the voluntariness of a confession by describing an incident from the Sasaki double murder case. The following is a partial transcript of a police officer's testimony at a hearing concerning the admissibility of audio tapes on which the police officer secretly recorded the defendant's statement. Note that the questioner is neither the prosecutor nor the defense attorney; the judge is asking these questions to the officer. In the end, of course, the tape was admitted into evidence by the judge himself.

> *Q* To the defendant's question "You threatened and coaxed me, didn't you," you answered "Yes I did," didn't you?
> *A* Yes, I did.
> *Q* What do you mean "threatened"?
> *A* I mean, for example, at that time the defendant got close to Ms M., and I admonished him. Then he argued over extravagant issues, and I said to him "I would never be close to that kind of woman." I threatened him in such a way.
> *Q* You again stated the word "threaten." What did you actually do?
> *A* As I answered before.
> *Q* Do you mean that you admonished him in a rather loud voice?
> *A* Well, admonished or ... I said, "I would never do like you did." I made a loud voice.
> *Q* Did you roar him down?
> *A* Yes, I think so on this issue.

Q On this issue?
A Yes, on this issue.
Q Did you threaten him regarding the content of the incident?
A No, I didn't.
Q You did not?
A No, I didn't. I told him about my background, and I interviewed him frankly. He knew everything, even about the polygraph. He talked to me, and asked me many difficult questions.
Q Were they irrelevant to the incident?
A Yes, they were. He read a novel titled *Jashumon* [Heretic] in his cell, and I also bought it and read it. We discussed issues other than the incident.
Q Did you discuss or argue with him?
A That's right. The interview went on in that way. He is not one who succumbs to threats.
Q Then you never threatened him when he confessed to killing his mother, did you?
A No I didn't.
Q Then can you say that you did not threaten him when he confessed to killing his parents?
A Yes I can. He is not one who succumbs to threats.[2]

(2) The exclusionary rule

The Japanese CCP does not have a clause on exclusionary rules. Nonetheless, the Supreme Court has authorized the exclusion of evidence when the procedures used to search and to seize the evidence demonstrate such grave illegality as to jeopardize the spirit of the warrant requirement embodied in Article 35 of the Constitution and Article 218.1 of the Code, and when it is deemed inappropriate to admit the evidence from the standpoint of deterring future illegal investigations (*Hashimoto v. Japan*, Judgment of September 7, 1978, Saikousai [Supreme Court]).

I can best describe the way in which Japanese judges handle this rule by referring to a typical instance: the *Kan* illegal drug use case. In *Kan*, the police had been watching an apartment which was the residence of a suspect in a fraud case. The defendant, who was a friend of the suspect, drove up to the apartment and went into the room. Police then rushed into the room and forced the defendant out of the building. He was surrounded by seven police officers and questioned. Since he did not answer, the police took him by the arms and put him into a police car. Although he resisted, he was forced to get in; he was then taken to the police station located six kilometers from the apartment. After they arrived at the station, he was taken to an interview room, where a police officer opened his bag without consent. They found his ID and learned his name. They asked him many questions, but he did not answer.

Since they recalled that he was driving, they phoned the driving license center and learned that he had no driver's license. They arrested him for driving without a license. He was detained in a police cell overnight. The next morning they asked him to give a urine sample, contending that if he refused, they would take him to the doctor. He succumbed to the police pressure and gave a sample. An examination of his urine revealed that he had used an illegal drug. In the police report, the officers wrote that they had arrested the defendant in the front of the apartment for driving without a license. He was indicted only for one count of illegal drug use.

The defense counsel argued that the urine sample was obtained illegally and hence should be excluded. The court disagreed, finding that the procedure of taking him to the police station was illegal. However, because he did drive the vehicle without a license, he could have been arrested legitimately. Thus, under the circumstances, the court held that it could not blame the police and the evidence should not be excluded (*Japan v. Kan*, Judgment of January 21, 1988).

In this case, the court found that the police illegality was not grave enough to justify excluding the evidence. In Japan, "illegal but not grave enough to exclude" is the cavernous space through which much illegally obtained evidence is admitted.

Judicial activism in finding guilt

Japanese trial judges actively find defendants guilty. The easy rules of evidence provide one outlet for judicial activism, but there are others. Consider, for example, the *Nemoto* attempted extortion case. Note the number of questions asked by the presiding judge.

Examination of a witness (Mr T.)

Number of questions asked by:

- prosecution: 29
- defense counsel: 48
- presiding judge: 42

Examination of the defendant

Number of questions asked by:

- prosecution: 177
- defense counsel: 105
- presiding judge: 174

In both cases, all of the judge's questions served to establish the guilt of the defendant, including queries such as the following:

> *Q (Court)* Can you recall telling Mr T. to "Train her to buy the goods?"
> *A (Defendant)* No I cannot.
> *Q* No?
> *A* No.
> *Q* But can you say you might have told him?
> *A* I cannot say for sure.
> *Q* I am sorry for asking you this question even though you are telling me you cannot recall for sure, but if you said to Mr T. to train her, what was your intention?
> *Defence Counsel* I have an objection, your honor. I think your assumption is incorrect.
> *Court* He admitted it might be, so I asked this question.[3]

Part III The causes and consequences of Japan's unique adversary system

Are there consequences of Japan's adversary system, as described above? Most definitely. First, Japan has a very low percentage of not-guilty verdicts. Statistics show that the average rate of not-guilty verdicts is only 1.8 percent (excluding election offenses). Tables 7.5–7.8 summarize the data for recent years. In addition, Japanese lawyers, especially young ones, have become very reluctant to represent criminal defendants, because their efforts always seem to be in vain, and because they feel that they are not and will not be treated fairly.

While the consequences may be obvious, the causes of Japan's style of the adversary system are more obscure. Many commentators contend that Japanese criminal procedure has been taken over by a foreign adversarial system. If so, what changed the system to make it so unlike its Anglo-American parents?

Table 7.5 Acquittal rates in Japan, 1985–96 (district and municipal courts)

No. of accused	*Pled not guilty (%)*	*Acquitted (%)*
1996 64 421 (63 586)	4 142 (6.4)	54 (1.3)
1995 61 475 (60 429)	3 966 (6.5)	56 (1.4)
1994 60 286 (59 537)	4 098 (6.8)	60 (1.4)
1993 58 871 (58 098)	4 043 (6.9)	135 (3.3)*
1992 56 604 (55 879)	3 957 (7.0)	75 (1.8)
1991 56 922 (56 153)	4 000 (7.1)	200 (5.0)*
1990 60 195 (59 413)	4 289 (7.2)	101 (2.3)
1989 64 183 (63 385)	4 681 (7.3)	134 (2.8)
1988 70 441 (69 586)	5 203 (7.4)	81 (1.5)
1987 76 483 (75 528)	5 626 (7.4)	99 (1.7)
1986 78 602 (77 333)	6 126 (7.9)	113 (1.8)
1985 81 093 (79 903)	6 368 (7.9)	113 (1.7)

Average acquittal rate: 2.16%
Average acquittal rate excluding election offenses: 1.8%
* The figures for 1991 and 1993 include acquittals in election offense cases. Excluding such cases, the acquittal rates for those years is 1.9 and 2.0%, respectively.
Source: Supreme Court, Annual Judicial Statistics 1985–96.

Table 7.6 Acquittal rates in Japan, 1928–43 (%)

Jury trial acquittal rate: 17.6
Bench trial acquittal rate: 3.0

Source: Okahara (1943).

Table 7.7 Acquittal rates in the state of California, 1992–94 (%)

	Jury trials (88.2%)	*Bench trials (11.8%)*
July 1, 1993–June 30, 1994	15.6	15.3
July 1, 1992–June 30, 1993	18.2	15.3

Source: Judicial Council of California, Annual Data Reference (1993–94).

Japanese courts resemble the Diplock courts of Northern Ireland

In Northern Ireland, a commission chaired by Lord Diplock decided that jury trials were not practicable for handling terrorist crimes, for two reasons: the threat of intimidation of jurors, and the risk that Loyalist defendants would be perversely acquitted by what were then predomi-

Table 7.8 Acquittal rates in England and Wales (cases in which the defendant pled not guilty to all charges)

	Total jury verdicts	*Not guilty (%)*
1993	16 807	6 127 (36.4)
1992	19 068	6 794 (35.6)
1991	20 114	7 341 (36.4)
1990	20 015	7 263 (36.3)

Average acquittal rate: 36.1%
Source: Hoyano (1997).

nantly Protestant juries. The Northern Ireland Emergency Provisions Act, including suspension of jury trials and recommendations for jury-less "Diplock courts," was enacted in 1973 (Greer and White, 1988, pp. 173–5).

There are at least five noteworthy consequences of the Diplock Courts, all of which can be found in Japanese criminal courts:

(a) Diplock courts produced conviction rates approximately 20 percent higher than those produced by jury trial courts.
(b) Judges become more inquisitorial in Diplock settings. According to one study comparing a Diplock court and a jury court presided over by the same judge, the number of witnesses questioned by the judge and the amount of time used by the judge for questioning were far greater in Diplock trials than in jury trials. Moreover, cross-examination by the judge occurred only in the Diplock court.
(c) Admissibility and reliability of evidence become empty standards. Once the judge has admitted the prosecution's evidence, the defense can hardly convince the same judge of its dubious reliability. Even when the judge does not admit the prosecution's evidence, his or her decision to do so comes after a lengthy hearing or discussion. Consequently, such evidence usually makes a lasting impression on the judge which the defense cannot erase.
(d) Warnings by the judge to the jury about, for example, the credibility of eyewitness testimony or of accomplice testimony, become meaningless.
(e) The functions of summation and instruction by the judge to the jury also become meaningless (Greer, 1997, pp. 128–35).

What has changed the judge's role?

Even though logic does not require the jury to be an element in the adversary system, the jury appears to have been an important catalyst in the development of the culture of that system (Feeley, 1987, p. 755). As suggested above, from the "experiments" in Japan and in Northern Ireland, a jury system may actually be an indispensable pillar of the adversary system. Indeed, the Japanese and Northern Ireland courts help illuminate why these two elements – a neutral, passive jury and a disinterested judge who presides over party-controlled proceedings – evolved as crucial elements of the adversary system in England (ibid., pp. 755–6).

The adversary system divides power into many pieces. The lawyers, not the judge, present the evidence at trial. The jury, not the judge, decides who wins. And the judge sits primarily as an umpire, making sure that the lawyers obey the rules. The adversary system assumes that justice emerges when each player carries out his or her limited role.

If we deprive the adversary system of the jury, the judge is given, in addition to the powers mentioned above, the most important power at the trial: the power to decide the defendant's guilt or innocence. If we give the judge that power, the judge has three roles: to preside over the proceedings; to collect evidence, especially by asking questions of witnesses and of the defendant; and to decide the accused's guilt. With such power, the judge is sure to become more than just a neutral and disinterested participant. In fact, this system undermines the neutrality and disinterestedness of the judge (ibid., p. 759). In the absence of neutrality and disinterestedness, the judge naturally tends to undermine other salient features of the adversarial system of criminal justice (ibid., p. 756), such as:

- the presumption of innocence (for the judge may presume the defendant guilty);
- the standard of proof (for the judge may construct or interpret "beyond a reasonable doubt" to be a very low hurdle);
- the right to have compulsory process for obtaining witnesses (for the judge may think the defendant is guilty and therefore not allow the defense to submit more evidence);
- the right to silence (for the judge may examine the defendant until the desired answer is forthcoming);
- exclusionary rules (for the judge may want to see all evidence and therefore not exclude even that which is illegally obtained).

In these manifold ways, the absence of a jury in Japanese criminal justice deprives adversarialism of several of its most crucial ingredients.

Part IV The jury-for-Japan movement

Recently a remarkable movement has emerged to restore the jury system in Japan.[4] Both the public and legal scholars have become involved. After 50 years of postwar Japanese administration, the people are realizing that there is little room for their participation in judicial proceedings. In the criminal field, people can only participate as members of a Committee on Inquest of Prosecution, which only examines the prosecutor's determination not to indict a suspect. No room is available for citizens to participate in any criminal trials, except as witnesses and defendants. As Japan's democracy develops, people are starting to insist on increased public participation in legal matters.

Scholars and lawyers are arguing for the restoration of the jury system in order to ensure that several crucial principles of due process are respected, such as the presumption of innocence, the protection of human rights, the symmetry of the parties, and the fairness of the courts. Greater participation of the people would also inject more of the community's common sense into the court and thereby bolster the legitimacy of verdicts.

The Japan Federation of Bar Associations has formed an ad hoc committee to research and to act on restoring the jury system to Japan. Local bar associations are doing likewise. Remarkably, a former Chief Justice of the Supreme Court, Koichi Yaguchi, strongly supports jury restoration for two reasons: to develop Japanese democracy, and to lend legitimacy to verdicts (Iimuro, 1997, p. 2). Currently Japan has five civilian groups working to restore the jury system, in Niigata, Saitama, Tokyo, Kyoto, and Osaka. They are performing mock jury trials, publishing books, and so on. Some political parties are also interested in jury restoration.

Part V Conclusion

It is a truism that the structure of the legal process reflects the larger society of which it is a part (Feeley, 1987, p. 765). Japan's "adversary system" in criminal procedure reflects Japanese society. Japanese society has been dominated by bureaucrats and lacks the free flow of information. As a result, there has been very little room for the people to participate, and the relationship between the people and the state has been badly asymmetrical. While the democracy of Western societies has been modified in Japan, so too has the adversary system. I think the absence of a jury in Japan has produced several troubling results: it has given bureaucrats – judges and prosecutors – predominance;[5] it has undermined the neutrality and disinterestedness of judges; and it has fostered easy detention, no discovery, the nonexclusion of illegal evidence, and an unbelievably high conviction rate.

The integrity of an adversarial system depends not only on effective fact-finding but also on a sense of fairness. Of course, either an adversarial or an inquisitorial system can accomplish "justice." However, a sense of "fairness" might be better implemented by a truly adversarial system, because the parity and symmetry of the parties, the presumption of innocence, and the protection of human rights thrive better in an adversarial system than in an inquisitorial one. And a sense of fairness will cause the public to be satisfied and to accept the legitimacy of the judicial system. In short, I believe that the JURY imbues adversarialism with life. It is the wick of the candle named FAIRNESS.

Notes

1. For a discussion of the gladiatorial nature of the justice system, see Feeley (1987, p. 760).
2. For a complete transcript, see *Japan v. Sasaki*, transcript of witness Nomura, September 13, 1983.
3. For a complete transcript, see *Japan v. Nemoto*, transcript of May 29, 1997.
4. Japan had a criminal jury system from 1928 through 1943. The Jury Act was suspended in 1943 because of World War II, but it has never been abolished.
5. Besides the absence of juries, we should also pay attention to the training and recruitment of judges in Japan.

References

Feeley, M. (1987) "The Adversary System," in Robert Janosik (ed.), *Encyclopedia of the American Judicial System II* (New York: Charles Scribner's Sons).

Greer, Steven (1997). "The Suspension of Jury Trial for Terrorist Offenses in Northern Ireland," in Itsuhiro Namazugoshi (ed.), *Baishinseido Wo Meguru Shomondai* [The Substantial Issues Related to the Jury System] (Tokyo: Gendaijinbunsha).

Greer, Steven and Anthony White (1988) "Restoring Jury Trial to Terrorist Offenses in Northern Ireland," in Mark Findlay and Peter Duff (eds), *The Jury under Attack* (London: Butterworths).

Hashimoto v. Japan, Judgment of September 7, 1978, Saikousai [Supreme Court], 32 Keishu 1672.

Hoyano, Laura (1997) "The Legitimacy of Modern Jury Trials," in Itsuhiro Namazugoshi (ed.), *Baishinseido Wo Meguru Shomondai* [The Substantial Issues Related to the Jury System] (Tokyo: Gendaijinbunsha).

Iimuro, Katsuhiko (1997) "Report of the Former Chief Justice's Address at the 1997 Summer Meeting," *Baishin-Saiban* [Jury Trials], Vol. 13.

Japan v. Kan (1988), Chiba District Court, Criminal Division 1. Judgement of January 21, 1998 (unpublished opinion).

Japan v. Nemoto (1997) Chiba District Court, Criminal Division 3. Transcript of hearing, May 21, 1997 (unpublished hearing).

Japan v. Sasaki (1983) Chiba District Court, Criminal Division 2. Transcript of hearing, witness Nomura, September 13, 1993 (unpublished hearing).

Judicial Council of California, Annual Data Reference (1993–94) Caseload data by individual courts.

Okahara, Masao (1943) "On the Jury Suspension Act of 1943," *Hosokai Zassi,* Vol. 21, No. 4, pp. 20–1.

Onuki v. Japan, Judgment of April 25, 1969, Saikousai [Supreme Court], 23 Keishu 248.

Supreme Court [Japan], Annual Judicial Statistics 1985–96.

8
The Miranda Experience in Japan

Takashi Takano

Part I Introduction

In early 1946, an American military lawyer[1] concluded that:

> The most serious abuses of individual rights in Japan have been through the uncontrolled actions of the various police agencies, particularly the Higher Secret Police and the Kempei-Tai[2] and the conduct of the procurators (Kenji). All manner of abuses have been practiced by the police and procurators in the enforcement of general law, but primarily in the enforcement of the thought control law. It is not unusual for people to be incarcerated for months and years without charges being filed, during all of which time attempts are made to force confessions from the accused.[3]

The first version of the Draft Japanese Constitution (the so-called "GHQ Draft") included two safeguards, proposed by the American quoted above, Colonel Rowell: No person shall be compelled to testify against himself; and no confession shall be valid unless made in the presence of counsel for the accused (Inumaru et al., 1983, p. 144).

The first clause, which is identical to a clause of the Fifth Amendment to the United States Constitution, became Article 38, Section 1 of the Japanese Constitution. The second clause, in contrast, was revolutionary; it was 20 years before the US Supreme Court's decision in *Miranda v. Arizona*. According to Colonel Rowell, "this provision [is] valid as a hedge against special Japanese abuses. Traditionally, the procurator is unwilling to go into court unless he has a confession, so he will go to extreme lengths, using third-degree, torture, and threats, to secure a confession before bringing the case to trial" (Tanaka, 1979). However, the second clause was later omitted from the Japanese Constitution following a suggestion made by General Courtney Whitney: "This [clause] outlaws the use of spontaneous confession made immediately after the commission of a crime. Confession without counsel should be accepted in evidence if it is made without duress" (Tanaka, 1979).

In response to the concerns voiced by Colonel Rowell, Section 2 of Article 38 of the Japanese Constitution provides that: A confession made under compulsion, torture or threat, or after prolonged arrest or detention shall not be admitted in evidence (Takayanagi et al., 1972, pp. 212–13).[4]

When I started legal practice, 35 years had passed since Colonel Rowell first argued for protections against interrogation abuses. From time to time in the course of my work, I have reached almost the same conclusion as Rowell. For various reasons, Whitney's version of safeguards does not work well in Japan.

First of all, it is impossible for ordinary individuals in Japan to exercise their right to remain silent. Police officers and public prosecutors insist that suspects under arrest or in detention remain in the interrogation room and be questioned, even though, legally, they have a "right" to remain silent.[5] Suspects in detention usually are kept in a police station jail, for as long as 23 days, during which time they are questioned by the police and prosecutor. Shortly before the expiration of the first ten days, lower court judges routinely grant extension requests from prosecutors, reasoning that "the interrogation of suspect(s) or other concerned person(s) has not been completed."[6] Even for suspects who are not under arrest and therefore have a statutory right to refuse interrogation,[7] the situation is not easy. If a suspect exercises this "right" and refuses interrogation, the police can request an arrest warrant in order to bring him or her to their interrogation room. A judge rarely denies this request.[8] Of course, a judge will not agree that the police can arrest someone simply because they need him to answer questions. Instead, the judge will insist that the person's refusal to appear for interrogation is a reasonable ground for believing that he or she may destroy evidence or flee from justice.[9]

Second, persons other than the interrogating officers and the suspect are, as a rule, kept away from the interrogation room. Attorneys or relatives of the suspect are not allowed inside the room. The interrogation itself is neither tape-recorded nor videotaped. The only material that may reflect what the accused has said is a written statement composed by the officer and signed by the suspect. In Japanese courts, this written statement gives the police officer victory in a swearing contest about the validity of the defendant's confession. Countless times I have heard judges state that the "defendant's allegation is incredible, since officer so-and-so testifies that he has never done that sort of outrageous behavior and since the accused has voluntarily stated, as his written statement shows . . ."

Third, and apart from the invisibility of interrogation and the difficulty the defendant faces proving what happened in the interrogation room, Japanese judges are extremely reluctant to exclude written confessions from evidence. Although I have no precise statistics, I believe I have defended more than 50 defendants in a variety of contested trial cases where the admissibility of written confessions was one of the issues. Of all these cases, in only five did the trial judge finally exclude the defendant's written confession. And the same judge presided over four of these five cases!

Japanese judges seem to harbor no suspicions about confessions obtained after several hours of continuous questioning. For example, in a 1989 robbery-murder case, the Supreme Court upheld the admissibility of a confession obtained after continuous interrogation from midnight until the following afternoon. The justices had no doubt that this confession was voluntarily made, for the defendant had voluntarily reported to the police station, asking officers to interrogate him, and he had never asked to stop the interrogation.[10]

What should we Japanese lawyers do if we believe that our professional norms require us to defend our client's best interests, as well as to realize the rule of law instead of the rule of power? In answer to this question, I have created – along with a group of like-minded lawyers – an innovative method of defense. We seek to initiate a trend powerful enough to change the system itself. As a representative of *Miranda No Kai* (Miranda Association), I would like to introduce our Association, to recount some recent events involving this group, and to describe two specific cases on which I worked.

Part II The Miranda Association

In February of 1995, 18 Japanese private attorneys (including me) organized a group called *Miranda No Kai* (Miranda Association). We announced that we would exercise the following defense strategies as a first step to secure the right against self-incrimination:

1. In contested-charge cases, the accused should not be interrogated without counsel; we will advise our clients to refuse interrogation without counsel present.

2. In all cases, including those in which the accused admits the charge, we will advise our clients not to sign the draft written statements composed by the police or prosecutor until defense counsel reviews the contents.
3. At the trial stage, we will contest the admissibility of written statements that have been obtained without compliance with the above-mentioned requests.

The first strategy – triggered by a suspect's request to have a lawyer present in the interrogation room – is almost always ignored by the officers, especially when the accused is under arrest or in detention. However, occasionally in nonarrest cases police have allowed defense counsel inside the interrogation room.

Obviously, the main strategic point is located in the second strategy. Police officers or public prosecutors never allow attorneys to look at their clients' unsigned written statements. Following our advice, our clients will refuse to sign, which is itself a very easy practice.[11] According to the Article 322 of the Code of Criminal Procedure, a defendant's unsigned written statement cannot be admitted in evidence. Thus, at the trial stage, public prosecutors can no longer expect to rely on written confessions. Sometimes they will abandon the written statements of the accused altogether, while on other occasions they will introduce the written statements in court subject to objections made by defense counsel. In either event, by eliminating the signed confession, we can eliminate the arguments about voluntariness and the swearing contests.[12]

Many lawyers who participated in the creation of these strategies feared that our clients would be treated unfavorably by police officers, public prosecutors, or even judges. When I first considered these strategies, I argued that if a judge issued a detention order because our client had refused to sign a paper, the order would be illegal: if an accused had a legal right to refuse to sign, it would be a violation of the law to detain the accused because he or she exercised that right. But now I realize how naive those initial arguments were. In the following pages, I will discuss the reactions to our activities from both leading prosecutors and judges, all of which add context and complications to my original naive approach.

How we have been treated

In 1995, a member of the Miranda Association defended one of the accused who allegedly put sarin gas in a Tokyo subway train in Tokyo, an action which killed 18 people and injured more than 1000. He advised the suspect to refuse any interrogation. This provoked a strong response from some leading figures of the Public Prosecutors' Offices and commentators for the mass media. On May 24, 1995, Mr Tatsuo Kainaka, Deputy Chief of the Tokyo District Public Prosecutor's Office, commented at a press conference, "if this was advised by a Toban-Bengoshi (duty-attorney),[13] it would be beyond the limits. Suspects under arrest or detention, having a right to remain silent, may not refuse interrogation under the Code of Criminal Procedure."[14] One of the major newspapers published an editorial entitled "Defending Suspects or National Security?" It read, "We could not accept those lawyers' activities, ignoring the security of the people" (Shucho (Opinion), *Sankei Shimbun*, May 26, 1995). Right after this editorial, my office ceased operations for several days due to the receipt of numerous anonymous phone calls. I even received a blackmail threat.

On May 31, 1995, a representative of the Ministry of Justice, at a session of the "Joint Conference on the Duty-Attorney Scheme" (sponsored by both the Ministry of Justice and the Japan Federation of Bar Associations), criticized our activities and warned that "people may not support the JFBA's position if it seeks taxpayers' money for the scheme"(*Asahi Shimbun*, June 1, 1995, evening edition). On June 7, while serving as a representative at a conference of the Legal Committee of the House of Representatives, the Chief of the Criminal Affairs Bureau of the Ministry of Justice expressed the same opinion (*Horitsu Shimbun*, June 16, 1995).

In December of 1995, Mr Nobuyoshi Tanabe, the Chief of the Okayama District Public Prosecutor's Office, published an article entitled "The Miranda Association and Public Prosecutors," in which he criticized our defense strategies and declared that any suspect who refuses interrogation without reasonable ground or who refuses to sign the written statement shall be indicted as long as his or her guilt may be proved. This should not be deemed retaliation since those suspects can be said to lack remorse (Tanabe, 1995).

On April 4, 1996, Mr Kanji Mizukami, the Chief of the Urawa District Public Prosecutor's Office, criticized us by asserting that

> defense counsel in criminal procedure shall protect the interests of the suspect while also contributing to finding the truth. Counsel has a duty not to obstruct the investigation. It should be illegal under Article 1 of the Lawyer Act and the Code of Criminal Procedure for defense counsel to advise suspects under arrest or in detention not to go out of their cell or not to be interrogated.[15]

This criticism echoed that made exactly one year earlier, by Mr Isao Shimizu, the Chief of the Urawa District Public Prosecutor's Office. He openly criticized us at a press conference: "it is intolerable that there are some young lawyers who stress the rights of the suspect, advising not to sign any written statements or not to say anything. These lawyers have forgotten their professional obligation to preserve social justice."[16]

This is the criticism voiced by the prosecutors; their comments are predominantly theoretical and hypothetical in nature. The next examples are real cases in which individuals were victimized, not just by prosecutors but also by judges.

Amphetamine abuse by a battered woman

On September 30, 1995, Mrs O., a 43-year-old housewife, was arrested for abusing stimulant drugs. She stated that her husband, Mr O., a chronic amphetamine addict who had recently battered her, had forcibly injected the stimulant into her arm. The local police did not accept her story. They believed Mr O. instead: he said that Mrs O. was an addict and that she injected the drug into both of their arms. During the preindictment investigation, which lasted more than two weeks, she was kept in a police jail and intermittently interrogated by police officers and prosecutors. Mrs O., following my advice, refused to sign any written statements, except one which contained the following passage:

> Today, I met with an attorney named Takano Takashi. He advised me to request his presence at an interrogation and to refuse to sign any written statements unless he reviewed the contents. Although I think I admitted the facts and told you the truth, I would like to follow my attorney's advice and refuse to sign any written statement until he reviews it.

Based on the story told by Mr O., she was indicted by the Koshigaya branch of the Urawa District Public Prosecutor's Office. As in ordinary contested-charge cases, Mrs O. was denied bail. At trial, Mr O.'s story lost credibility. My cross-examination established that (a) he was a chronic amphetamine addict who groundlessly suspected that Mrs O. had affairs with several men, and (b) he had told several different stories other than the one to which he testified during the case-in-chief. At the final stage of the trial, the prosecution suddenly requested the court to modify the charge as follows:

> "The defendant, Mrs O., during the period between the latter half of September 1995 and the first day of October 1995, within the border

of Saitama prefecture or somewhere around it, used stimulant drug by having it inside her body."

This new count did not specify the time, place or manner of the crime; it nullified most, if not all, of the previous defense strategy. I objected to the modification. The trial judge overruled my objection and granted this request for modification. He then found Mrs O. guilty of the new charge and sentenced her to imprisonment for one and a half years. The judge accused me of conducting "improper defense activities" and harshly rebuked me for advising my client not to sign the statements, for asking questions which he called "improperly leading" (although nobody, including the judge himself, ever objected to them at trial), for raising objections to the questions asked of some witnesses by the prosecutor and by the judge, and for making a "groundless" objection to the request for modification. Then he concluded, "Considering these improper activities on the part of the defense counsel, we could not obtain the truthful statements from the defendant or from witnesses for the defense."[17]

The defendant appealed to the Tokyo High Court. As one ground for reversal, we alleged that the trial judge's statements about my defense activities violated the defendant's right to effective assistance of counsel secured by the Constitution and by the United Nations Convention on Civil and Political Rights. A three-judge panel of the Tokyo High Court reversed the judgment on other grounds and sentenced Mrs O. to a suspended term of imprisonment. As for the right to counsel issue, the appellate judges held that the trial judge's comments about my activities were "unnecessary and improper," but they did not constitute a violation of the Constitution, of the United Nations Convention, or of procedural law material to the judgment.[18]

Assault by an estranged husband

Mr K., a 46-year-old bookstore clerk, had been married to Mrs K. for more than 13 years and had five children with her. In the summer of 1994, Mrs K. left their home alone. Mr K. suspected that his wife was having an affair with Mr S., her art school classmate. One day in October, Mrs K. appeared home and spoke to her husband. They argued, and Mr K. slapped her in the face. In November, Mrs K. filed for divorce. In December, Mr K. filed a damage suit against Mr S., alleging adultery.

In March of 1995, Mrs K. filed a criminal complaint with the Urawa police station concerning Mr K.'s violence in October of 1994. Shortly thereafter, Mr K. accepted the police's request and reported to the police station to answer some questions. He admitted that he slapped his wife several times, but the officer was not satisfied. The officer told him that the victim had said he punched her more than 20 times, and the officer suggested to him that it would be reasonable for him to admit to approximately ten slaps. Mr K. agreed; he signed a written statement affirming this story. Mr K. later became angry with the officer's attitude; he came to my office for advice.

Late in May of 1995, Mr K. received a request to report to the police. I called the police and notified them that Mr K. would like to be interrogated in my presence. The police replied, "We would not like to interrogate the suspect in Mr Takano's presence." In August, Mr K. received another request to report for interrogation, this time from a prosecutor in the Urawa District Public Prosecutor's Office. I asked the prosecutor to let me stay with my client in the interrogation room. He denied my request, saying, "I have never done that before."

When nothing happened for six months, I thought the police and the prosecutors had abandoned their plan to interrogate Mr K. But I was wrong. In the early morning of January 30, 1996, Mr K. was arrested by a prosecutor's assistant. A district court judge issued a detention order, finding reasonable grounds to believe that Mr K. would destroy evidence or escape. I appealed this order to a three-judge panel of the Urawa District Court, asking the court to disclose the evidence that supported the detention order. I also asked the judge who issued the detention order to state in open court the reason for detention, as required by Article 82 of the Japanese Code of Criminal Procedure. The three-judge panel denied my request, stating that the documents submitted by the prosecutor for the detention order were *not* evidence; they were simply "the prosecutor's case file the judge borrowed for his convenience." The judge who ordered Mr K.'s detention also refused my request for disclosure. He even refused to state the detailed reasons for detention, claiming the secrecy of the investigation prevented him from commenting.

Mr K. was indicted and denied bail. After 102 days of detention, he was allowed bail on the following conditions, which included a 1,500,000 yen deposit:

1. He must live in an apartment I had rented near the courthouse.
2. He must work as my law office employee under my supervision from 9:00 a.m. to 6:00 p.m. on weekdays.
3. If he goes out after 6:00 p.m. on weekdays and during weekends and holidays, he must be accompanied by at least one of his defense attorneys.

During trial, I applied many times for a discovery order to compel disclosure of the prosecutor's file, which served as the basis for Mr K.'s detention. The three-judge panel of the Urawa District Court, however, ignored my requests. They did not even issue a discovery order for the concrete materials which, according to the prosecutor's testimony, supported his allegation that Mr K. should be detained. On August 19, 1997, the panel of judges declared Mr K. guilty of the battery charge and fined him 200,000 yen.[19] While the judges denied that the detention and the indictment of Mr K. were in retaliation against the Miranda Association, they implied in their judgment that he was a victim of my defense strategy:

> Such consequences [detention and formal indictment] were a result of the defendant's continual refusal to report to the station for interrogation as well as of Takano's advice to him, that is, that the defendant request the officers to allow his counsel present in the interrogation room with him. . . . *We have difficulty understanding why in this case where the accused had already admitted the assault itself Takano should have stuck himself to the idea of his presence at the interrogation.* He testified that he did not feel any danger in this case that his client would be arrested while refusing interrogation, but rather that he expected he would be allowed inside the interrogation room at sometime during the investigation of this case. However, as Takano admitted at trial, his forecast and judgment were clearly too optimistic.[20]

Mr K. appealed to the Tokyo High Court. As one of the grounds for appeal, we contended that the judges' refusal to compel discovery of the documents which were the basis for Mr K.'s detention violated several constitutional provisions, including Article 34 of the Constitution and Article 14, Section 3, Subsection (b) of the UN Convention of Civil and Political Rights. The Tokyo High Court, however, affirmed the trial court's judgment of conviction on April 8, 1998. As for the discovery issue, the court withheld comment on the merits, stating that even if it were a violation of law, there was no evidence that this violation materially affected the final judgment.[21]

Part III Final comment

As of April 1998, the Miranda Association consisted of 40 private attorneys and 3 scholars. Generally speaking, our defense strategies work well for our clients. Cases like Mrs O. and Mr K. are, I would like to believe, rare exceptions. These cases, however, clearly show that the adversary system has a long way to go in Japan. There is no doubt that defending the accused is one of the hardest jobs in Japan. Our Constitution contains the same language as the Fifth Amendment to the US Constitution, so there can be no doubt that Japanese suspects have a constitutional right against self-incrimination. This "constitutional right," however, is both chimerical and terribly hard to exercise. Even lawyers are extremely hesitant to advise their clients to use it. The Japanese criminal justice system could not work if the accused routinely exercised this constitutional right.

Is this a natural consequence of Japanese culture or is it somehow deeply rooted in traditional ways of Japanese life? Neither explanation is satisfactory. I see no willingness or pride on the part of suspects who are pressured to give up their rights. Once a person is in this system, whether or not he or she is Japanese, he or she cannot escape the severe pressure to "voluntarily" forget, or to pretend to forget, his or her rights, both constitutional and statutory. This system is wrong, regardless of the culture or nation in which it appears. As Justice Goldberg stated for the United States Supreme Court in *Escobedo v. Illinois* (1964, p. 490):

> We have also learned the companion lesson of history that no system of criminal justice can, or should, survive if it comes to depend for its continued effectiveness on the citizens' abdication through unawareness of their constitutional rights. No system worth preserving should have to fear that if an accused is permitted to consult with a lawyer, he will become aware of, and exercise, these rights. If the exercise of constitutional rights will thwart the effectiveness of a system of law enforcement, then there is something very wrong with that system.

Notes

1. Mr Milo E. Rowell practiced at a private law firm in Fresno and served as an Assistant US Attorney in Los Angeles before he started serving in the military (Tanaka, 1979, pp. 72–3).
2. "Kempei-Tai" is the Japanese military police.
3. This quote can be found in "Memorandum for Chief of Staff" (January 11, 1946), cited in Takayanagi et al. (1972, p. 28).
4. Second Meeting of the Steering Committee with the Committee on Civil Rights (original draft) (February 9, 1946).

5. Article 198, Section 1 of the Code of Criminal Procedure provides that

   > A public prosecutor, public prosecutor's assistant officer and judicial police official may ask any suspect to appear in their offices and question him, if it is necessary for pursuing criminal investigation. However, the suspect may, *except in the case where he is under arrest or under detention,* refuse to appear or after he has appeared, withdraw at any time" (emphasis added).

   Public prosecutors, police officers and some scholars say that, from a natural reading of the second sentence of this section, one must conclude that suspects under arrest or in detention may not refuse to appear or withdraw from the interrogation room. Recently, 15 Justices of the Japanese Supreme Court *unanimously* held this reading of the provision constitutionally valid, since "there is no doubt that to obligate a suspect under custody to report and stay for the interrogation does not necessarily mean to deprive the suspect of the freedom not to testify against his or her will." Sup. Ct. Grand Bench, Order, March 24, 1999, *Minshu* 53–3–514, 518.
6. A judge may grant the request of extension when "unavoidable circumstances exist." Art. 208, Section 1, Code of Criminal Procedure. On these extension orders, the judge typically uses a rubber-stamp imprinted with the phrases cited in the text.
7. This right is contained in Art. 198, Section 1, Code of Criminal Procedure.
8. Each year, out of 110,000 requests for arrest warrants from officers, only 50 are turned down by judges throughout Japan. For statistics, see the Supreme Court of Japan (1997, pp. 16–17).
9. Statutory grounds for detention are: (1) lack of a fixed residence, (2) reasonable grounds to suspect that the accused may destroy evidence, and (3) previous escape attempts by the accused or reasonable grounds to suspect that he or she may escape (Art. 60, Code of Criminal Procedure).
10. Sup. Ct. 3rd Petty Bench, Order, July 4, 1989, *Keishu* 43–7–581.
11. The right to refuse to sign a written statement is another example of a statutory right which is secured in the language of the law but is almost always waived in the interrogation room. See Art. 198, Section 5, Code of Criminal Procedure.
12. It seems that the police and prosecutors have developed a countermeasure. In one Tokyo case, the prosecution, after introducing unsigned written confessions, called a police officer to testify about the contents of the defendant's confession. The officer, however, obviously had memorized the contents of the unsigned written statements and simply recited them in the courtroom. The presiding judge overruled the defense counsel's objection and let the officer testify (Morino, 1997, pp. 148–49).
13. The Toban-Bengoshi system, planned by the Japan Federation of Bar Associations following the English model of the duty solicitor scheme, was put into practice in every local bar association in 1992. Lawyers on duty respond without charge to a call from detainees, advise them of their basic rights, and explain the procedure.In 1997, private attorneys volunteering for this scheme responded to 22,910 calls from detainees throughout Japan (JFBA Criminal Defense Center, 1998, pp. 124–5).
14. See quotes in these newspapers: *Sankei Shimbun*, May 25 and 26, 1995; *Yomiuri Shimbun*, May 30, 1995.

15. See quotes in these newspapers: *Mainichi Shimbun*, April 5, 1996 (Saitama edition); *Saitama Shimbun*, April 5, 1996.
16. See quote in *Mainichi Shimbun*, April 8, 1996 (Saitama edition).
17. This case was reported as the Koshigaya Branch of Urawa Dist. Ct. Judgment, January 21, 1997, 1599 *Hanji* 155. The trial judge's ruling concerning improper defense activities can be found on p. 157.
18 The appellate court decision can be found at Tokyo High Ct. Judgment, September 17, 1997, 1623 *Hanji* 155, at pp. 156–7.
19. This case was reported as Urawa Dist. Ct. Judgment, August 19, 1997, 1624 *Hanji* 152.
20. This quote can be found on pp. 161–2 of the Urawa District Court's judgment, cited in n. 19.
21. Tokyo High Ct. Judgment, April 8, 1998, 1640 *Hanji* 160, 167.

References

Asahi Shimbun, June 1, 1995 (evening edition).

Escobedo v. Illinois, 378 US 478 (1964).

Horitsu Shimbun, June 16, 1995.

Inumaru, H., H. Yasuda, O. Nishi and Y. Ogoshi (eds) (1983) *Nihonkoku-Kempo Seitei No Keii* [Details of the Drafting of the Japanese Constitution] (Tokyo: Daiichihoki).

JFBA Criminal Defense Center (ed.) (1998) "Toban-Bengoshi Seido Unyo Jokyo Shukei-hyo" [Statistical Tables on the Administration of the Duty-Attorney System], *Kikan-Keijibengo*, Vol. 15, p. 124.

Mainichi Shimbun, April 5, 1996 (Saitama edition); April 8, 1996 (Saitama edition).

Morino, Y. (1997) "Dare no Kenri wo Mamoru no ka?: Watashi no Miranda Nikki" [Who Do We Defend?: My Miranda Diary], *Kikan Keijibengo*, Vol. 11, p. 144.

Saitama Shimbun, April 5, 1996.

Sankei Shimbun, May 26, 1995.

Supreme Court of Japan (ed.) (1997) *ShihoTokei Nempo Keijihen Heisei 8 Nen* [Annual Statistical Report on Judiciary-Criminal Justice in 1996] (Tokyo: Hosokai).

Takayanagi, K., I. Otomo and H. Tanaka (eds) (1972) *Nihonkoku-Kempo Seitei No Katei* [The Development of the Japanese Constitution] (Tokyo: Yuhikaku).

Tanabe, N. (1995) "Miranda No Kai to Kensatsu" [Miranda Association and Public Prosecutors], 13 *Okayama Bengoshi Kai Keijibengo News*, Vol 13, p. 1.

Tanaka, Hideo (1979) *Kenpo Seiteikatei Obegaki* [A Memorandum on the Development of the Japanese Constitution] (Tokyo: Yuhikaku).

Yomiuri Shimbun, May 30, 1995.

9

Plea Bargaining in Japan

David T. Johnson

> The Japanese prosecutor does not consult with the defendant or defense attorney and then institute a lesser charge in exchange for a confession.
>
> Fumio Aoyagi (1986, p. 201)

> The somewhat lower frequency of contested prosecutions in Japan probably reflects the greater predictability of trials there.
>
> J. Mark Ramseyer and Eric B. Rasmusen (2001, p. 51)

Is plea bargaining absent in Japan, as former prosecutor Aoyagi argues, or is plea bargaining even more common in Japan than in the United States, as the American scholars Ramseyer and Rasmusen assert? This chapter rejects both polar positions in favor of an intermediate answer which possesses one singular advantage: it fits the facts. After establishing that Japan has plea bargaining, though in lesser amounts and in different forms than the US, this chapter explores two related questions. First, compared to the United States, why does Japan have *so little* plea bargaining? And second, given that Japan's system of criminal justice is decidedly nonadversarial, why does it have *any* plea bargaining at all?

Part I Does Japan have plea bargaining?

Consider the first quote: plea bargaining does not exist in Japan. This claim is often repeated but seldom scrutinized to see how closely it accords with reality (Aoyagi, 1986, pp. 201ff; Sato, 1974; Sanders, 1996, pp. 338, 344; Inagawa, 1994; Sasaki, 1994; Kitada, 1995). Indeed, it sometimes seems that the truth of this claim derives, illegitimately, from the force with which a related normative claim is made: Japanese criminal justice officials must not plea-bargain because doing so is inconsistent with the principle that is supposed to animate the entire criminal process, namely, the pursuit of truth (*jittai teki shinjitsu shugi*; Code of Criminal Procedure, Article 1). Though there is little doubt that most Japanese – legal professionals and lay people alike – oppose the practice of plea bargaining, I am less interested in their normative views than in what happens, as a matter of fact, in Japan's criminal process. Plea bargaining is illegal in Japan (Ukawa, 1997; Bayley, 1991, p. 147; Westermann and Burfeind, 1991, pp. 111, 165), and many knowledgeable Japanese are "appalled by the American judicial system, which seems to them more a matter of plea bargaining than [of] justice" (Reischauer, 1977, p. 265). However, these are different assertions than the empirical claim that plea bargaining does not occur in Japan.[1]

In this section I use two approaches to evaluate the veracity of the claim that Japan is a land without plea bargaining. First, I attempt to delineate, in broad terms, the various kinds and meanings of plea bargaining. The Japanese have an almost visceral aversion to the words "plea bargain" (usually translated as *shiho torihiki* or *toben torihiki*) which interferes with their ability to assess dispassionately whether what they do rightly falls under that rubric (Sato, 1974, pp. 168ff; Ukawa, 1997). Thus, my first job is to clear the air of conceptual and empirical misunderstandings about the practice of plea bargaining in the US and elsewhere so that we can recognize if it appears in Japan. After that, I do what one ought to do with any empirical claim – weigh the evidence. Taking these two steps leads to the conclusion that plea bargaining occurs in Japan, notwithstanding the long-standing fiction to the contrary.

What is plea bargaining?

Definitions of plea bargaining vary widely. The modal American view is that "plea bargaining occurs when the prosecutor induces a criminal accused to confess guilt and to waive his right to trial in exchange for a more lenient criminal sanction than would be imposed if the accused were adjudicated guilty following a trial" (Langbein, 1978, p. 8). Because defendants in Japan can neither plead guilty nor give up their right to trial, by this definition plea bargaining cannot and therefore does not occur in Japan.[2] This narrow definition is widely employed, and reliance on it (rather than on some broader definition) allows many people to conclude that Japan does not have plea bargaining.

However, if instead of this narrow nomenclature one adopts a broader definition of plea bargaining, whether or not Japan "has it" is a question which must be answered empirically, not formally. In an analysis of criminal procedure in the United States, France, and West Germany, the German comparativist Thomas Weigend (1980, pp. 404–5) advances a more expansive definition:

> The basic structure of plea bargaining can be described in terms of two models of case processing. The first, which I shall call the complicated model, is designed for defendants who claim to be innocent.... [It] is costly in terms of time, labor, and money. The second, "simple" model can be used only if the defendant does not seriously contest the charges against him.... [It is] swift, convenient and inexpensive.

This definition is designed to make cross-national comparison possible. It posits two crucial elements in plea bargaining: defendants must have a choice between complicated and simple models of case processing, and the criminal justice system must exert pressure on defendants to be "cooperative" and choose the simple model. On this understanding, Japan can rightly be called a "land without plea bargaining" only if at least one of the two crucial elements in the definition is absent: either Japan does not have two different models of criminal procedure, or else suspects and defendants are not pressured to choose the simple one. Conversely, if both elements are present in Japan, then Japan has plea bargaining.[3]

Two Japanese shortcuts

Like France, Germany, Great Britain, Italy, Singapore, South Korea, and the United States, Japan has more than one system for handling criminal cases (Weigend, 1980, p. 407; Frase, 1990, p. 626; Miller, 1990, p. 221; Langbein, 1978; Spencer, 1995, p. 315; Horiuchi, 1995; Feeley, 1985). In fact, since Japan has developed "two shortcuts to criminal trial . . . in order to deal efficiently with uncontested cases," it actually has three models of case processing: summary procedure, the more or less uncontested trial, and the contested trial (D. Johnson, 2002, p. 245; Westermann and Burfeind, 1991, p. 111; Araki, 1985).

First, prosecutors can request summary procedure for minor offenses in which the fine upon conviction is no more than 500,000 yen (about $3850, at $1=130 yen). Guilt is determined *in camera* by the judge, without the defendant, prosecutor, or complainant ever appearing in court. Almost all traffic offenses are handled in this way, as are many other minor offenses.

The second shortcut for case processing is the more or less uncontested trial. As in France so too in Japan: the great majority of defendants fully confess to the charges against them and consent to the admission of all evidence the prosecution wants to introduce at trial (Frase, 1990). For example, between 1987 and 1992, about 92 percent of all Japanese defendants appearing in district court confessed to the charges against them.[4] In these uncontested cases the public trial is greatly streamlined. Most of the evidence introduced in court is in the form of dossier (*chosho*) which police and prosecutors have prepared during the investigation, and few (if any) witnesses besides the defendant are questioned in court (Westermann and Burfeind, 1991, p. 111; Araki, 1985, p. 619; Hirano, 1989, p. 138).

The third and final model of case processing results in a contested trial in which the defendant disputes all or part of the prosecution's case. However, because the Japanese system relies so heavily on the two shortcuts – summary procedure and uncontested trials – only a small handful of cases are seriously contested (Araki, 1985; Feeley, 1985). Indeed, just after retiring from Japan's Supreme Court, Masataka Tanaguchi noted that criminal trials in Japan "tend to begin and end with the non-procedural steps of confirming the subjectivity of the prosecutors in their investigation and deliberating on the sentence" (quoted in Ishimatsu, 1989, p. 143). The preponderance of uncontested trials helps explain why one sees so many judges, prosecutors, and defense lawyers dozing during trial.

The evidence: pressure to choose the shortcuts

Since Japanese criminal justice has both simple and complicated methods for disposing of cases, it does possess the first of the two crucial elements of plea bargaining. The critical question is thus whether officials pressure suspects and defendants to choose one of the two simple procedures instead of opting for the complex procedure and the full range of rights, privileges, and costs that accompany it. Evidence from my survey of Japanese prosecutors, my fieldwork inside Japan's procuracy, and the reports of police, exoffenders, lawyers, judges, and journalists show that Japan is hardly a stranger to plea bargaining.

(1) The survey

From January of 1994 to May of 1995, I administered a survey to 231 Japanese prosecutors (D. Johnson, 2002). In it I asked four questions relevant to plea bargaining. In response to the most direct question about plea bargaining, the vast majority of Japanese prosecutors said they do not practice it. In fact, only 10 out of 231 prosecutors (4.3 percent) said they "sometimes engage in plea bargaining," while 209 (90.5 percent) said they do not (survey part 4, question 57). The wording of this question, however, undoubtedly elicited a large proportion of *tatemae* answers, that is, "principles describing how something should be ideally" rather than the *honne* or "real truth" (Ames, 1981, p. 230; van Wolferen, 1989, p. 8). As any resident of the country eventually learns, Japanese officials regularly employ this institutionalized dichotomy for distinguishing between "what the truth is and how that truth is described for public consumption" (Fingleton, 1995, p. 114). The rhetoric often misleads.

Japanese prosecutors are reluctant to use the direct translation of the English term "plea bargaining"[5] to describe their own practices because plea bargaining is officially outlawed in Japan and because it is widely believed that plea bargaining is fundamentally incompatible with "the principle of substantive truth" (*jittai teki shinjitsu shugi*) which is supposed to stand at the heart of the Japanese criminal process (Code of Criminal Procedure, Article 1). I constructed question 57 expecting that responses would reveal far more *tatemae* than *honne*. The question not only uses the disdained term but also describes the practice as an explicit promise of lenient treatment in exchange for a confession. Given this blunt phrasing, it is surprising that even ten prosecutors admitted that they plea-bargain.[6]

Responses to other, more nuanced survey questions can be used to begin sketching a more accurate portrait of prosecutor practices. Most strikingly, nearly four in five prosecutor respondents agreed or strongly agreed that "in a case which will result in conviction, if a suspect denies the facts and does not express remorse, this influences the sentence we seek" (survey part 4, question 88). Thus, a suspect's defiant, noncompliant, or uncooperative attitude influences most prosecutors to pursue additional punishment. This "denial tariff" (or *hininryo*, as prosecutors call it), is a Japanese counterpart to the so-called "asshole enhancements" which American prosecutors use to punish defiant or uncooperative suspects and defendants. In both systems, a primary prosecutor aim is to pressure suspects into confessing and thereby to avoid the costs and risks of a fully contested trial.

Two other survey questions suggest that prosecutors and suspects believe it often pays for the latter to confess. The first item, borrowed from a survey administered to American prosecutors and judges (Nardulli et al. 1988, p. 68), strongly asserts that prosecutors should reward compliant offenders: "cooperative defendants who confess and thus save the state investigative and trial resources should be given as lenient a disposition as possible" (part 4, question 10). In response to this question, nearly half of all prosecutors said that "it depends," thus indicating the contextual nature of many prosecutor decisions. More than half of the remainder, however, agreed that cooperative defendants should be rewarded. The second survey question shows that prosecutors believe that many defendants expect to be rewarded for confessing: "suspects think prosecutors will treat them more leniently if they confess and display remorse" (part 4, question 58). Here, only 35 of 235 (15 percent) prosecutors disagreed, while nearly three and one-half times that number agreed.[7]

In sum, the survey reveals three important truths about plea bargaining in Japan. First, most prosecutors are reluctant to label their practices plea bargaining, though a small but significant handful are not. Second, prosecutors believe that it pays for suspects to confess and that suspects believe likewise. Third, prosecutors seek extra punishment for suspects who do not confess, in order to compel them to choose one of the alternatives to the fully contested trial. In short, and despite the survey's inherent limitations, the data show that suspects are pressured to choose shortcuts.

(2) Field observations and interviews

In field observations and interviews, I found substantial corroborating evidence for the last and most important survey finding and thus for the second crucial element of plea bargaining in Japan. To start with, even people who argue that "confessions are obtained without plea bargaining in Japan" acknowledge the existence of certain highly publicized "exceptions" (DeSombre, 1995, p. 36). In the Lockheed scandal, for example, which ultimately ended in the indictment and conviction of former Prime Minister Kakuei Tanaka, the Prosecutor General gave (and the Supreme Court approved) a promise of immunity from prosecution to an American employee of the Lockheed company from whom prosecutors needed testimony.[8] Nearly two decades after this immunity was granted, the Supreme Court reversed itself when it ruled that such grants are illegal because the Code of Criminal Procedure does not confer explicit authority on prosecutors to give immunity in exchange for testimony (Tsuchiya, 1995).

I was working at a branch of the Ministry of Justice (UNAFEI: The United Nations Asia and Far East Institute for the Prevention of Crime and the Treatment of Offenders) in Tokyo on the day this decision was announced and thus had the opportunity to ask several prosecutors about their reaction to it. Their responses reveal that plea bargaining in Japan is far from "exceptional." One prosecutor was so upset by the decision that when he arrived at work he immediately rushed into my office and began berating the Supreme Court for its "ridiculous" ruling. With scarcely a prompt or probe from me, this prosecutor described how he and his colleagues commonly plea-bargain, give immunity, and make promises to suspects and witnesses during investigations.

Sometimes, as in the Lockheed case, prosecutors offer complete immunity from prosecution to a small fish in order to build a stronger case against a bigger one.[9] Sometimes, in lieu of formal prosecution, prosecutors promise summary prosecution and the concomitant fine in exchange for cooperation. Sometimes prosecutors assure suspects – especially gangsters – that they will leave the suspects' wives or bosses alone only if they provide the desired information. And sometimes prosecutors flatly state that confessions will be rewarded with suspended prosecution or a reduced sentence recommendation. In short, in the emotional wake of the Supreme Court's decision reaffirming the illegality of plea bargaining, I listened for over 20 minutes as a prosecutor described plea bargains of all kinds – explicit and implicit, charge and sentence, immunity – in which he and his colleagues "often" engage. Two other prosecutors, albeit in more qualified tones, had similar responses.

I also observed prosecutors make subtle suggestions to suspects that a confession would be in their own interest, and impose not so subtle "denial tariffs" on suspects deemed unreasonably uncooperative. In one such case, the prosecutor wanted to suspend prosecution of a man arrested for possession of hashish because the amount of the drug was relatively small, the suspect had no prior record, and the suspect could be deported and thus punished sufficiently without being formally tried and convicted. The suspect, however, was British, and did not believe the prosecutor's claim that confessing would be in his own interest, so in the end the prosecutor had no choice but to charge. A year later the suspect (now defendant) was still protesting his innocence at trial. He spent most of the intervening months in detention, having been deemed a bad bail risk because, alas, he had not confessed. By invoking his legal rights instead of heeding the prosecutor's suggestion, this foreign suspect incurred severe "process costs" (Feeley, 1992) and potentially, at least, a far more serious sanction than deportation.

Another case, involving a Japanese man arrested for possession of amphetamines (*kakuseizai*), suggests that unlike the British suspect, few Japanese suspects are willing to so steadfastly ignore a prosecutor's suggestions or to incur such heavy "process costs" in order to contest their innocence. Like much Japanese speech, prosecutor "offers" are usually implied and indirect rather than explicit and direct (Maynard, 1984). Since the success of such communications "depends as much on the sensitivity of [the] recipient as on the quality of the message sent" (Smith, 1983, p. 57), Japanese suspects are far more likely to understand what prosecutors mean than are foreigners unskilled at the language.

In this case, however, the offer was neither implied nor indirect. The police found about 10 g of amphetamine in the Japanese man's apartment. Early in the investigation the suspect told authorities he did not know how the drug got there or to whom it belonged. The prosecutor, unconvinced by this story, presented the suspect with a stark choice: if he confessed, the prosecutor would recommend that the suspect receive two years' imprisonment (likely to be suspended) and that he be released on bail pending trial; if he did not confess, the prosecutor would seek three years and continued detention throughout the trial. The judge who would ultimately decide the bail and sentence issues was almost certain to follow the prosecutor's bail request and very likely to impose about 80 percent of the sentence which the prosecutor requested. In effect, the prosecutor gave the suspect this choice: would you like more punishment, or less? Predictably, the suspect chose to be punished less, the prosecutor did as he promised, and the court eventually imposed a suspended sentence. The point is not that the suspect was unjustly convicted, for there was little doubt as to his substantive guilt. Likewise, the suspect could have refused to confess, as this was a real, albeit unwise, option. Rather, the point is that the suspect was pressured to "choose" one of the criminal process "shortcuts" described above – an uncontested and therefore expedited trial instead of a fully contested one. Much like suspects in American systems of criminal justice, this suspect was threatened with a materially increased sanction if he availed himself of his rights and was subsequently convicted. And, as in America, it was the "sentencing differential" which made this encounter a plea bargain and made this plea bargain coercive (Langbein, 1978, p. 12). In principle, the suspect could have refused to confess (as the British suspect did). In practice, however, this was an "offer which cannot be refused" (Zeisel, 1980, p. 558).

(3) But do they calculate?

Critics of my argument will contend that what I observed in Japan may look like plea bargaining from the outside but is in reality something quite different, because the actors do not calculate self-interest before making their choices. When neither prosecutors nor defendants regard the confession as part of a bargain, the argument goes, neither should we. A more appropriate image depicts the defendant as "throwing himself on the mercy of the prosecutors, confessing to his transgressions, and imploring their forgiveness" (Foote, 1986, p. 100).

There is an important element of truth in this argument, for there is little doubt that more Japanese suspects confess "spontaneously" than do American suspects. The difference, while difficult to measure, is unmistakable to anyone who has observed the criminal process in both countries.[10] As a result, in order to obtain confessions and cooperation, police and prosecutors in Japan do not have to pose the "stark choice" for suspects – more punishment or less – as often as their American counterparts.

But there are two problems with this argument. First, the same kind of noncalculating exchange often occurs in American criminal justice. When it does, it is routinely called a plea bargain (Heumann, 1978, p. 156; Feeley, 1992, p. 185; Nardulli et al., 1988).[11] Does it not make sense to denote the same behavior with the same name, in the US *and* in Japan?

Notwithstanding this semantic point, however, an empirical problem also exists: Japanese suspects *do* calculate self-interest in response to cues, suggestions, and offers from police, prosecutors, and judges. In a work which otherwise stresses that Japanese suspects are characteristically submissive, remorseful, cooperative, and compliant in the face of authority, even David Bayley acknowledges that guilt is sometimes admitted in Japan because it is "a quid pro quo for leniency"(Bayley, 1991, pp. 136, 141). I observed several clear examples of such calculated, self-interested behavior (and heard ex-offenders describe many more), but here present only one of the most striking cases.[12] Though it is not about plea bargaining per se, it vividly illustrates that one wellspring of defendants' behavior is self-interest – in Japan too.

In January of 1994, I dropped in at a private lawyer's office to thank him for introducing me to an ex-offender for an interview. We had just begun to sip our green tea when a young couple entered the office. Both bowed repeatedly as they entered the waiting room, and the woman carried a wrapped package which we soon discovered to be Japanese rice crackers. In the moments that followed, my tea time with the attorney was transformed into a criminal defense strategy session that was comically calculating in intent. The man, aged 41, had recently been arrested in a sting operation for possessing 4.7 g of marijuana (*taima*), or slightly less than one-sixth of an ounce, and had retained as private counsel the attorney on whom I had called. Caught with the goods, the man confessed to both police and prosecutors and was released after ten days' detention on bail of 4,000,000 yen (about $30,000). Two and one-half years earlier, the man had been convicted of a similar offense for which he was sentenced to eight months in prison, suspended for three years. Since the suspended sentence had not yet expired, the man and his girlfriend were deeply worried that this time he would have to do "real time" in prison. Japanese judges rarely impose a second suspended sentence on top of a first, though such "double suspended sentences" are slightly more common in the Kansai region (where this offense occurred) than in the Kanto area around Tokyo. The question which consumed the defendant was natural: what could he do to increase his chances of getting a second suspended sentence?

The defendant, his girlfriend, and the lawyer shrewdly drew up a plan for stage-managing a performance in court that would maximize the defendant's chances of getting the second suspended sentence. First of all, the man would have to marry his girlfriend before the trial began. Being married would help more than simply "going together," as the couple were doing at the time. The couple did marry, a mere eight days after our meeting in what, for Japan at least, must have been an extraordinarily simple ceremony. The defendant's girlfriend, who was somewhere in her early to mid-thirties, also asked the attorney if it would be helpful to be pregnant during the trial. She was told it would. While the defense did not introduce at trial any evidence that the couple would soon become a trio, I have no way of knowing if they tried to conceive in the period preceding the trial. At the very least they appeared to take seriously the attorney's counsel on the matter. Next the girlfriend wondered aloud if she should cry during the trial. In this she was greatly encouraged. The judge might not be much moved, the attorney explained, for judges get hardened after hearing so many cases, but it is certainly better to cry than not to. She did cry at the trial. It was also agreed that the defendant should apologize to the judge when given a chance, as all defendants are, to make a final statement before the court adjourns to decide the verdict and sentence. The defendant asked if it would help to get down on his hands and knees (*dogeza suru*) and beg for mercy, but when the attorney predicted that the judge would simply tell him to stand up, this idea was abandoned in favor of a more dignified apology. While the defendant was in jail during the investigation, his apartment building had burned to the ground in a suspected arson. The attorney instructed the couple to bring to trial at least three photographs of the charred ruins in addition to the fire department's records of the losses they had sustained. Finally, and as happens in most Japanese trials, the attorney queried the defendant about who could appear at trial on his behalf as a "circumstantial witness" (*jojo shonin*), to vouch for his good character and to promise to "supervise" (*kantoku suru*) him if he was released on a second suspended sentence. The defendant's parents had both died some years earlier, and since the defendant owned and managed his own restaurant he had no employer-like figure who could fill in. After considerable discussion the threesome agreed that the defendant should get one of his employees at the restaurant – a subordinate – to play the supporting role of "supervisor" (*kantokusha*) at the trial.

At trial, the defense put on the performance much as they had rehearsed it, and the defendant received the second suspended sentence he so badly wanted (ten months' imprisonment suspended for three years, with probation). It is impossible to tell what effect the various elements of the performance had. After trial, the defense attorney told me that the acts described above probably had some influence, but that more important still was the effect of a "double suspension of sentence" precedent he had found and submitted to the court. The point of the story, however, is not that Japanese offenders can be as cynically manipulative as Americans,[13] nor that Japanese judges can be duped, but rather that Japanese suspects and defendants do calculate self-interest in response to the cues and incentives provided by repeat players in the criminal process and in anticipation of the likely effects various actions will have on police, prosecutors, and (as in this case) judges. In short, they do calculate.

(4) Evidence from other sources

If plea bargaining occurs in Japan as clearly and as commonly as I claim, why have so few people written about it? One reason, of course, is that prosecutors, publicly at least, deny that they do it.[14] However, if one pays careful attention to what prosecutors say and write, even for public consumption, it is possible to discern indirect admissions of plea bargaining (Ugawa, 1997). For example, in July of 1989, the "First Joint Canada–Japan Symposium on Crime and Criminal Justice" was held at Simon Fraser University in British Columbia. Shu Sugita, then a prosecutor in the Tokyo District Office, participated in a panel on "The

Handling and Disposition of Criminal Cases." When the moderator asked Sugita if plea bargaining occurs in Japan, Sugita first replied with the orthodox formula: "System plea negotiations or plea bargaining do not exist in Japan." Later, however, Sugita acknowledged that defendants do make requests and prosecutors do consider them:

> However, before the indictment, at the investigation stage, the defense makes a few requests to the public prosecutor. Take an injury case for example. Suppose I am investigating an assault injury case and I could indict for a fine or for a trial. But suppose the suspect is very remorseful, decides to make restitution, and wants to be convicted for a fine. If I think that the defense counsel's request is reasonable, I would consider it, but, as a legal procedure, the process of plea bargaining and negotiations does not exist in Japan (Boyd and Layton, 1991, p. 57).[15]

Even without direct access to prosecutors, there is ample evidence that Japan has plea bargaining. Consider data from the following six sources: police, ex-offenders, journalists, judges, lawyers, and "old-boy" prosecutors.

(a) Police. I asked many experienced police officials in Japan whether or not prosecutors plea-bargain. A few had to have the term (*shiho torihiki*) explained to them, but once they understood what I was asking about, most agreed that prosecutors do it. For example, shortly after he retired from the Tokyo Metropolitan Police Department, a former high-ranking police executive told me that prosecutors frequently plea-bargain with defense attorneys. Prosecutors, he observed, do not want to admit that it occurs, but it "often" does, sometimes very explicitly. He added that most police think plea bargaining is a good thing, since in their view it reduces the risk of charging cases with weak evidence, avoids long trials and their associated costs, enables the authorities to get information they otherwise could not obtain, and rewards lawyer friends and cooperative suspects. Prosecutors acknowledge that all of these are "benefits" of plea bargaining, even the ability to reward lawyer friends, but they rarely admit that such considerations influence their decisions – especially "rewarding one's friends."

Interestingly, several lawyers told me that police, too, engage in a practice closely analogous to plea bargaining, and at least as routinely as prosecutors. One attorney, a veteran "cause lawyer" well-known for her vigorous criminal defense work, said that during interrogation police frequently promise to "close their eyes" (*me o tsuburu*) to some cases if suspects confess to others. She told me that when prosecutors honor the officer's pledges, she has no objection to the practice, but that problems arise when prosecutors ignore police promises or renege on their own oaths. Similarly, in his seminal study of Japanese police detectives, Setsuo Miyazawa observes that during police interrogation, "sometimes a lighter sentence is held out as an instrument of persuasion" and that "at least the possibility of such an exchange is one of the instruments Japanese detectives use in dealing with suspects." Miyazawa contends that the Japanese detectives he studied, like the prosecutors I observed, "are far more manipulative" than previous scholarship on the subject has supposed (Miyazawa, 1992, p. 160).

(b) Ex-offenders. Ex-offenders report that plea bargaining commonly occurs in Japanese criminal justice. A man who had previously broken ties with Japan's largest organized crime group (the Yamaguchi *gumi*), said that during the interrogations which followed his 13 arrests, police and prosecutors often pressured him to confess by threatening more severe punishment or a negative bail recommendation if he did not cooperate. This former gangster further stated that he obeyed prosecutors' orders to make restitution to victims, not because he was remorseful or wanted to repair a damaged relationship, as some commentators have argued, but because he knew that doing as he was told was "in my own best interest" (*yuri ni naru kara*).

(c) Journalists. I interviewed seven journalists who cover or used to cover the procuracy for major newspapers in Japan's ubiquitous "press clubs" (*kisha kurabu*). Since press clubs function as "information cartels" to restrict access to and the dissemination of information about the organizations around which they form, mainstream journalists seldom write controversial articles about prosecutors (Freeman, 1996; van Wolferen, 1989, p. 93). Nevertheless, after gaining proper introductions and guaranteeing their anonymity, the journalists I interviewed were exceptionally candid. All had spent years cultivating relationships with prosecutors in the major offices in Tokyo and Osaka, and most said that plea bargaining, especially in political and other "big" cases, may be "hidden" (*ankoku*) from public view but is "common knowledge" (*joshiki*) among insiders. One journalist, familiar with the workings of American criminal justice, ventured a comparison that is consistent with my own observations:

> Plea bargaining in Japan is usually tacit (*anmoku*) and indirect (*kansetsu teki*). In the US it is explicit (*meihaku*). This is the main difference. We

> don't make written records of it. Our prosecutors communicate with suspects by "belly art" (*haragei*). They are, after all, Japanese (see also Fingleton, 1995, p. 114; Nomura, 1988, p. 24; Hasegawa, 1978, p. 145).

(d) Judges. Unlike their prewar predecessors, contemporary Japanese judges do not participate in pretrial investigations or procedures. Thus, concerning plea bargaining, they are the least informed members of the criminal court community. Nevertheless, some judges believe it happens regularly. Once when I was eating lunch in a courthouse cafeteria, a Japanese judge who had often observed me taking notes in his courtroom sat down across from me and introduced himself. As it turns out, the night before we both had watched *The Accused*, a movie starring Jodie Foster which gives plea bargaining a prominent place in the plot. I took the opportunity to ask the judge if anything like plea bargaining occurs in Japan. Here is his reply, as best as I could reconstruct it in my field notes:

> Of course plea bargaining happens. It is hidden (*kakureta*) but it happens rather often, doesn't it (*kanari ooi ja nai*)? However, if the practice were openly revealed the evidentiary value of the confession would suffer a lot, so prosecutors and police do their best to keep it concealed.

(e) Lawyers. If Japanese judges know comparatively little about what really happens in the pretrial process, lawyers know a lot. They, too, acknowledge that Japan is hardly a land without plea bargaining (Wakamatsu, 1992). On April 10, 1995, I gave a talk on "Plea Bargaining in America" to a group of 15 Japanese people – about half of whom were lawyers – gathered at the Tokyo First Bar Association. During the two-hour lecture I defined plea bargaining, described several of its forms, and attempted to explain why it occurs and how various groups of Americans feel about it. Immediately after the lecture but just before beginning the one-hour discussion session, I posed two questions to my audience about their own system of criminal justice: Do you have plea bargaining? If so, what kinds?

A Japanese scholar spoke first, arguing that since plea bargaining is illegal in Japan, it does not occur. Since one cannot get to an "is" from an "ought," I pressed the audience to discuss what actually happens. All said that they hear about or participate in conversations which resemble most of the forms of plea bargaining I had just described – explicit and implicit deals, sentence and charge bargains, and horizontal and vertical charge bargains. At the same time, some of the lawyers recognized that there remain real differences between the two countries' approaches to plea bargaining. Japan has no arraignment system, for example, so prosecutors cannot guarantee a sentencing outcome with the same authority that an American prosecutor can. Similarly, the system of case consultation and approval (*kessai*) in Japan's procuracy prevents some of the rougher forms of bargaining common in the US. It also is clear that Japanese legal professionals are far more reluctant to talk about plea bargaining than Americans are, largely because plea bargaining practices are considered illegitimate by both the Japanese public and Japanese law.

But in addition to these important differences, the lawyers noticed clear parallels: some acknowledged telephoning prosecutors to ask what could be done to gain the desired disposition; others said that while prosecutors often tell suspects the punishment will be more severe if they do not confess, they seldom promise lenient treatment in exchange for a confession. One even described a form of "bargaining" over the way the dossier (*chosho*) gets worded, wherein suspects allow prosecutors or police to write what they like in the hope they will thereby gain more favorable treatment. In short, while the lawyers spoke in different voices about the precise forms and occasions of plea bargaining, all agreed that it occurs.

(f) "Old-boy prosecutors". Finally, "old-boy prosecutors" (*OB kenji*) who have quit or retired from the procuracy acknowledge that plea bargaining is an ordinary prosecutor practice. I interviewed four "old boys," two of whom had extensive experience working in the "Special Investigation Divisions" (SID) (*tokusobu*) that handle Japan's highest-profile cases. One told me flatly that plea bargaining "happens a lot" and that negotiations are often explicit. Two important factors, he stressed, were "how much influence the defense lawyer possessed" and whether or not the lawyer was able to make a "connection" with the prosecutor before the charge decision was made. It is widely believed that old-boy prosecutors who become defense attorneys ("old-boy lawyers") have an especially big influence on their former colleagues, something two "old-boys" confirmed, as did a former chief of the Tokyo SID. Since prosecutors are more likely to trust "old-boy lawyers" to keep their promises, they are more likely to enter into agreements with them than with outsiders. This may help to explain why politicians often hire old-boy lawyers when they are being investigated or tried for a crime. In the various Lockheed trials that have rocked Japan for the last 20 years, for example, 15 of the 50 defense lawyers were "old-boy lawyers," and six of those 15 came

from the procuracy's executive ranks. An additional six were "old-boy judges" (*Zaikai Tenbo*, 1979). Similarly, when Shin Kanemaru, the former "godfather" of Japanese politics, was investigated for accepting bribes in 1992, his lead attorney was an "old-boy lawyer" who had worked as a prosecutor in the SID.[16]

Part II Is Japan different?

Japan is not a land without plea bargaining. Its criminal procedure has both simple and complicated methods for processing cases, and its criminal justice officials sometimes pressure suspects and defendants to choose the simple methods instead of the complicated one. In short, Japan has the two crucial elements of plea bargaining. Summary procedures and (more or less) uncontested trials are far more swift, convenient, and inexpensive than Japan's notoriously slow contested trials. Similarly, an abundance of evidence – from field observations, the survey, and interviews with defendants, ex-cons, police, lawyers, journalists, judges, and prosecutors themselves – shows that suspects and defendants are pressured to avoid a full-scale trial war. The conclusion is unequivocal: Japan has plea bargaining.[17]

This conclusion, however, does not mean that plea bargaining in Japan is just like plea bargaining in the United States.[18] Given the many historical, cultural, and structural differences between the two countries and their respective criminal justice systems, that implication would be implausible on its face and inconsistent with several crucial distinctions, including the fact that the US Supreme Court has officially approved plea bargaining (*Brady v. U.S.*, 1970) while Japan's Supreme Court has forbidden it (*Enomoto v. Japan*, 1995). In short, there are similarities and parallels, but there are notable differences as well.

Quantity of plea bargaining

Most strikingly, while plea bargaining is the modus operandi for disposing of criminal cases in most American jurisdictions, it is far less central in Japan. In the US, upwards of 90 percent of cases are concluded through plea agreements; in Japan, while the corresponding figure cannot be known precisely (since plea bargaining is illegitimate, it cannot be openly acknowledged) it is surely far lower. I estimate that perhaps 10–20 percent of criminal cases are disposed of through plea bargains as defined in this chapter. Even if the true figure is two or three times higher, plea bargaining in Japan would still not be the routine dispositive procedure it is in the United States.

Style of plea bargaining

There are qualitative differences as well. Most importantly, plea bargaining in Japan is more "consensual" and less "concessional" than plea bargaining in the US, and it is more tacit and implicit.

Two main models are used to describe the American plea bargaining process (Nardulli et al., 1988, p. 205). The "concessions model" depicts plea bargaining as a process involving routine charging manipulations and sentencing concessions. This model "forms the basis for most popular conceptions of the guilty plea process," but actually fits the facts of American plea bargaining less well than the "consensus model." The consensus model states that plea bargaining resembles a modern supermarket more than a Middle Eastern bazaar (Feeley, 1992, p. 187). Thus, rather than the "higgling and haggling" over dispositions that characterizes the concessions model, "strong, well-established going rates" are the rule, and "most cases are disposed of in cooperative agreements reaching a consensus on facts and, therefore, on appropriate punishment" (Rosett and Cressey, 1976, p. 15). In short, in American criminal justice, the role of "shared perceptions and accepted norms" is greater than the most visible and therefore controversial results seem to suggest,[19] for the plea bargaining process "is not overly dependent upon explicit, concrete exchanges or manipulations" (Nardulli et al.,1988, p. 245).

If the "consensus model" of plea bargaining fits the United States better than the "concessions model," it also fits Japan better – indeed, far better – than the United States. This is true for several reasons. First, most Japanese police and prosecutors have lighter caseloads than their American counterparts (Miyazawa, 1992, p. 13; D. Johnson, 2002, p. 23). As a result, the press of heavy caseloads less often compels them to make concessions (Alschuler, 1968, p. 50; Weigend, 1980, p. 419; Langbein, 1978, p. 10).[20] Second, Japanese police and prosecutors benefit from a highly "enabling" legal environment which gives them almost complete control over the construction of case information and the "making" of crime. Since confessions can be obtained by manipulating voluntary compliance, concessions (and coercion) are seldom necessary (Miyazawa, 1992). Like the American prosecutor who told me he prefers the "Joe Stalin approach to plea bargaining," Japanese prosecutors usually get what they want because they have all the "weapons" on their side.[21] Third, the criminal process is far less adversarial in Japan than in America (D. Johnson, 2002, p. 71). In particular, since Japanese defense attorneys are accustomed to "going along" in order to "get along" with the other actors in the criminal court, they solicit and elicit fewer concessions from police and prosecutors than do defense attorneys in the US. Indeed, Japanese law confers so many powers on police and prosecutors and so few on the defense that in most cases the defense has little choice but to comply with official "suggestions." Finally, while Japan is not the Shangri-La of harmony that it often is reputed to be, it *is* a more consensual society than the United States (Upham, 1987; Pharr, 1990). That general "culture of consensus" channels plea bargaining in a distinctly consensual direction, albeit in ways and by mechanisms that are difficult to measure.

Plea bargaining is also more often tacit and implicit in Japan than in the US. A deal is not recorded in writing, of course, because doing so would document an illegal act. Moreover, most offers are made and most deals are struck indirectly, through innuendo and inference more than through clearly articulated negotiations. In this regard, communication in the criminal process reflects communication norms more generally (Yamada, 1997).

Legality and the enforcement of plea bargains

Plea bargaining is legal in the US but illegal in Japan. As a result, defendants in Japan do not enjoy the same right to challenge the outcome of a "deal" if the prosecutor fails to act in the manner anticipated (Foote, 1986). Broken promises are of more than merely theoretical concern. Three Japanese defense lawyers told me about cases in which they reached agreements with the prosecution only to have them violated when the prosecution sought substantially heavier punishment at trial than had been promised during the investigation. In neither case did the defense have any legal recourse. *Caveat confessor.*

Deliberation and the factual basis of the plea

Since the American style of plea bargaining allows for "condemnation without adjudication," the trial function is systematically circumvented: no court ever decides whether the facts implied in the plea support an inference of guilt beyond a reasonable doubt (Langbein, 1978, p. 14). To be sure, American law imposes a requirement that there be "adequate factual basis for the plea," but the procedures used to establish that foundation belie their chimerical character. In the extreme, the US Supreme Court has even found that there is adequate factual basis for a murder defendant's plea that "I ain't shot no man.... I just pleaded guilty because they said if I didn't they would gas me for it.... I'm not guilty but I plead guilty" (*North Carolina v. Alford*, 1970).

Two features of criminal justice in Japan help ensure that confessions induced through plea bargains rest on an adequate factual basis. First, except for cases disposed of through summary procedure, there is no condemnation without adjudication. All serious cases get tried in a court of law by one or three judges. Second, before indicting a suspect, front-line prosecutors must obtain the approval of one or more of their superiors. This system of hierarchical review (*kessai*) requires the charging prosecutor to justify his or her findings of fact and selection of charges. Like judicial review at trial, *kessai* helps guarantee that the case has been thoroughly investigated, analyzed, and discussed. Since thorough deliberation is the hallmark of good plea bargaining, this is no small virtue (McCoy, 1993, p. xvi).

Remorse and rehabilitation

Finally, the defendant's subjective experience of plea bargaining in Japan and the US differs considerably. Some students of American plea bargaining argue that since a guilty plea evidences a defendant's remorse, plea bargains have a legitimate jurisprudential rationale: repentant defendants are less likely to reoffend. But real repentance is rare in the American guilty plea process (Alschuler, 1968, p. 57; Heilbroner, 1990). Subjectively, most American defendants seem to view plea bargaining as a market transaction in which rights are traded for leniency. For many American offenders, the explicit trade-off confirms that they are little more than pawns in a game between defense counsel and prosecutors.

Though the evidence presented above suggests that some Japanese suspects view confessing in a similarly transactional way, pleas of guilty in Japan are less likely to be motivated purely by self-interest and more likely to be accompanied by remorse (Haley, 1991, p. 129; Bayley, 1991, p. 126). Insofar as remorse facilitates rehabilitation and reform, this type of plea bargaining probably produces more "special prevention" than does bazaar-like bargaining. And insofar as the remorseful defendant regards leniency as benevolently "bestowed" rather than grudgingly granted, his perception of the prosecutor's motivations may further encourage rehabilitation (Foote, 1992). Of course, "genuine" remorse is difficult to measure, as is the hypothesized causal connection between remorse and gratitude, on the one hand, and lower rates of recidivism on the other. Even so, the apparent differences in modal motivations suggest that something like this may be occurring. If so, then more crime control benefits accrue to plea bargaining in Japan than to plea bargaining in the US (D. Johnson, 2002, p. 185).

Part III Why is Japan different? Explaining variation in plea bargaining

Although Japan has plea bargaining, it occurs less often and more discreetly than in the United States. Why? And compared to Germany, where plea bargaining is all but absent in serious cases, plea bargaining in Japan seems prominent (Langbein, 1979; Felstiner, 1979; Weigend, 1980; Blankenburg, 1996). Why? How can we explain the variations in plea bargaining between Japan and the two countries from which it has most self-consciously adopted and adapted its institutions and procedures of criminal justice? This section briefly explores the causes of these comparative differences.

First, why is plea bargaining less central in Japan than in the US? Whether lauded or lamented, the Japanese criminal justice system's heavy reliance on confessions (*jihaku no hencho*) is universally regarded as one of the defining features of the Japanese way of justice (D. Johnson, 2002, p. 243; Hamada, 1992; Foote, 1991; Ishimatsu, 1989; Igarashi, 1994). Writing over a quarter century ago, the Japanologist Chalmers Johnson (1972, pp. 149, 402) noted that

> in dealing with criminal cases Japanese police, procurators, and judges think of the confession as the "king of evidence" (*shoko no o*). It is the decisive element of proof sought by every procurator . . . and the single most important item determining the reception his efforts are likely to receive from most Japanese judges.

Little has changed since. "The attitude that confessions *must* be extracted" still rules the psyches and governs the behavior of Japanese police and prosecutors (Miyazawa, 1992, p. 165; emphasis in original; D. Johnson, 2002, p. 264).[22] On this view, given the centrality of confessions throughout the criminal process, it is natural that officials sometimes induce them through plea bargains.

This explanation, however, rings tautological: prosecutors seek confessions and suspects provide them because confessions are important, yet we know confessions are important mainly because they are earnestly sought and frequently provided. By failing to account for the primacy of confessions in the first place, this explanation begs a fundamental question. Hence, one must search for other causes of Japan's lower level of plea bargaining. There are plenty:

1. *Lighter caseloads*: In general, caseloads are lighter in Japan than in comparable American jurisdictions. Hence, Japanese prosecutors

are less compelled to deal out of expediency (D. Johnson, 2002, p. 23).

2. *Smaller "gap"*: In Japan, the "gap" between the simple and complex models of case processing is narrower than in the US, largely because Japan has no jury trials. As a result, prosecutors can be less preoccupied with how the choice of models affects workloads, schedules, and resources (Langbein, 1978, 1979).[23]
3. *Enabling law*: Japan's highly "enabling" Code of Criminal Procedure makes it possible for prosecutors and police to obtain confessions without making concessions, especially in ordinary street crime cases. Like Joe Stalin, Japanese prosecutors possess almost all the "weapons" in their encounters with suspects. Compared to American prosecutors, they seldom *need* to negotiate (Miyazawa, 1992; Steinhoff, 1993; D. Johnson, 1999).
4. *Bureaucracy*: The *kessai* system of hierarchical review in Japan's procuracy requires front-line prosecutors to gain the approval of one or more supervisors before instituting a charge. This restricts "higgling and haggling" by multiplying the number of participants and thereby complicating the negotiation process. It also requires front-line prosecutors to provide principled reasons for their charge decisions (D. Johnson, 1998).
5. *The form of indictment*: Japan's system of single-charge indictments makes it difficult to "overcharge." Since prosecutors cannot indict in a scattershot way, threats to overcharge are not credible. This reduces the room for charge bargaining (Peters, 1992, p. 283; Alschuler, 1968, 1975).
6. *No condemnation without adjudication*: Japan has no arraignment system, so all cases – even uncontested ones – must be tried. Since it is judges who impose sentence after trial, Japanese prosecutors cannot guarantee sentences as confidently as their American counterparts can (Itoh, 1993; Langbein, 1978).
7. *Fewer harsh laws*: American criminal law is harsh. When statutory penalties exceed the prosecutor's conception of a substantively just outcome, the prosecutor will use plea bargaining to reacher a fairer disposition. Since Japan has fewer harsh laws, judges impose less severe sentences, and prosecutors are less often motivated to plea-bargain out of the substantive concern to reach a just outcome (Lynch, 1995; Feeley, 1992; Weigend, 1980; Alschuler, 1968).
8. *Norms*: Confession is more of a moral imperative in Japan than in the US. Since many confessions are obtained spontaneously, Japanese investigators less often need to apply pressure on suspects

to get them (Wagatsuma and Rosett, 1986; Haley, 1991; Foote, 1991; Bayley, 1991; Inagawa, 1994).

9. *Cultural resistance*: The idea of commercialized criminal justice is abhorrent to Japanese legal tradition. It frustrates legislative intent and the legitimate expectations of victims, generates uncertainty and inconsistency, and compromises the rule of law. In this regard, Japanese legal culture resembles legal culture in the civil law tradition (Ukawa, 1997; Merryman, 1985, p. 130).

Clearly a variety of causes – structural, legal, organizational, political, cultural, and historical – account for the American–Japanese difference in propensity to plea-bargain. In this sense, plea bargaining, like other penal events and institutions, is overdetermined (Garland, 1990, p. 280). What, then, of the second comparative question? Why is plea bargaining more conspicuous in Japan than in Germany? There appear to be at least three reasons:

1. *Discretion*: Germany's Code of Criminal Procedure prescribes the "rule of compulsory prosecution" (*Legalitatsprinzip*), requiring prosecutors to charge "all prosecutable offenses, to the extent that there is a sufficient factual basis," and provided that the crime is sufficiently serious (as defined by law). The German rule is meant to achieve ends that are immensely important in the German tradition: treating like cases alike, obeying the legislative determination to characterize something as a crime, preventing political interference with prosecution, and so on. It has largely succeeded (Langbein, 1978, p. 211; Davis, 1969, p. 191). In contrast, Japanese prosecutors have discretion not to charge, regardless of the severity of the crime and even if there is sufficient evidence to support a conviction. The Japanese rule makes it possible for prosecutors to give charge reductions in exchange for confessions. In this way, the principle of discretionary prosecution enables plea bargaining while the principle of compulsory prosecution discourages it.
2. *The meaning of acquittals*: Acquittals in Japan convey a markedly different meaning than do acquittals in Germany (or, for that matter, in the US). With few exceptions, acquittals in the latter two countries are "meaningless" in the sense that they do not declare innocence in the same clear way that convictions declare guilt (Givelber, 1997). By comparison, acquittals in Japan carry a much clearer meaning: if a prosecutor fails to gain a conviction, he or she should never have instituted charges in the first place. Politically, this means that the Japanese public holds prosecutors responsible for

acquittals, and rebukes them accordingly. Organizationally, Japan's procuracy has designed a rigorous set of controls to minimize acquittals, if not to eliminate them altogether (D. Johnson, 1996, p. 492). Procedurally, Japanese prosecutors have a strong incentive to plea-bargain in order to avoid the risk of acquittal (Ukawa, 1997).

3. *The size of the "gap"*: Finally, it appears that the "gap" between the simple and complex models of case processing is wider in Japan than in Germany. Vigorously contested trials can drag on for years, or even decades, in Japan. At the grotesque extreme, consider the Matsukawa and Kabutoyama murder cases, each of which lasted more than 20 years (C. Johnson, 1972; Kibe, 1993). The wider the gap, the greater the incentive to use the simple model, and the harder the system will try to ensure that defendants choose that form of case processing.

Part IV Conclusion

I have tried to show that Japan has plea bargaining: less than the US, more than Germany, and for a variety of reasons. I also have argued that the Japanese style of plea bargaining differs from the American in several important respects. To construct a more adequate causal account of cross-cultural differences – a comparative theory of plea bargaining – it would be instructive to compare Japan with other countries, especially France and South Korea. Like Germany, France was a source of many important features in Japan's system of criminal justice. Unlike Germany, however, France does not subscribe to the rule of compulsory prosecution. Thus, we may expect to find significant similarities in the incidence and significance of plea bargaining between France and Japan (Frase, 1990; Weigend, 1980; Provine, 1996). Comparisons with South Korea may also be illuminating. When Japan colonized South Korea (1905–45), it imposed many of its own institutions and procedures of criminal justice. As a result, the two systems of criminal justice closely resemble each other (Horiuchi, 1995). If the Japanese models of case processing produce the plea bargaining practices described in this chapter, then we should expect to find more similarities in quantity and style of plea bargaining in South Korea than in France. Researchers tend to compare Japan only to the US. The result often obscures as much as it illuminates (Reed, 1993, p. 6). Casting the comparative net more broadly may well reveal new insights about what is distinctive and ordinary in Japanese criminal justice.

I have said little about the conspicuous gap between the Japanese law on the books – "thou shalt not plea-bargain" – and the law in action which generates the plea bargaining practices described above. Of course, Japan is hardly the only country where one finds dissonance between legal norms and actual practice. Moreover, the Japanese way of plea bargaining – to condemn it in principle but to permit it in practice – may curb some of the excesses found in countries like the US, where courts not only tolerate plea bargains but legitimate and even encourage them (Schulhofer, 1984, p. 1107). Yet that restraint comes at a cost, incurred in abstract values like fidelity to law, and suffered by real defendants who cannot challenge prosecutors for reneging on deals.

The gap between the law on the books and the law in action could stimulate reforms aimed at creating greater consistency between legal principle and actual practice. This could happen in two ways: by trying harder to identify and to eliminate plea bargaining that does occur, or by legalizing plea bargains. While the latter course seems more likely, if it occurs, the motive is less likely to be a desire to close the "gap" than a desire to give prosecutors more tools to "make crimes" out of cases that are presently difficult to solve.

The most articulate spokesperson for legalization is prosecutor Haruhiko Ukawa (1997). His point of departure is the observation, widely shared by practitioners and scholars alike, that prosecutors and judges are "too precise" in their demands for evidence to indict and to convict. Ugawa believes it has become more difficult for investigators to obtain the confessions on which they have so long and so heavily depended. The rise of more adversarial defense lawyering (as by attorneys in the Miranda Association), the spread of "rights consciousness" in Japanese society, and the diffusion of knowledge that sometimes "denial works" all inhibit prosecutors' pursuit of confessions. In Ukawa's view, since the standards of proof have not been relaxed, and since the king of proof is increasingly difficult to obtain, many criminals are escaping justice. The solution, he maintains, is to make plea bargaining legally legitimate. By granting prosecutors the explicit authority to bargain, especially with suspects who cooperate by providing information about bigger offenses and offenders, prosecutors will be more able to bring to justice precisely those wrongdoers who are most difficult to charge and to convict. Among these are corrupt officials and other white-collar offenders (D. Johnson, 2002, p. 269).

If Ukawa is correct, if forbidding a technique like plea bargaining is tantamount to sanctioning high levels of corruption and certain other crimes, then legalizing plea bargains may facilitate a duty that has long vexed prosecutors – corruption control. Yet this, too, would come at a cost, for by adding another arrow to the prosecutors' quiver, legalization would exacerbate the already extreme imbalance of advantage in Japan's ostensibly adversarial system.[24] It is unclear whether the change would be worth the price.

Notes

1. It seems many Americans share the Japanese distaste for plea bargaining.

   > Among all the discretionary decisions in the [American] criminal justice system, plea bargaining is most often the focal point of general public dissatisfaction with the criminal justice system. The idea that most cases are settled by "deals" is a convenient symbol of everything that people believe is wrong with the justice system (Walker, 1993, p. 81).

2. Unlike the United States, Japan has no arraignment system. Thus, defendants cannot be found guilty or sentenced without first being tried in court. Similarly, even if a defendant confesses and contests no part of the prosecution's case, the state is still constitutionally required to present additional evidence corroborating the confession (Constitution of Japan, Article 38; Code of Criminal Procedure, Article 319). In this sense, what I describe below as plea bargaining may also be characterized as "confession bargaining."
3. There is nothing unorthodox about this definition of plea bargaining. For instance, Professor Stephen Schulhofer of the University of Chicago Law School also defines plea bargaining broadly. To Schulhofer, plea bargaining is "any process in which inducements are offered in exchange for a defendant's cooperation in not fully contesting the charges against him." Thus, plea bargaining includes "not only formal, officially sanctioned plea bargaining, but also the wide variety of informal *sub rosa* behavior patterns in which indirect inducements, unspoken commitments, and covert cooperation create the functional equivalent of explicit bargaining" (Schulhofer, 1984, p. 1037; see also Standen, 1993, p. 1474; Maynard, 1984, pp. 25, 202; Littrell, 1979, p. 193; Blumberg, 1979; Heumann, 1978).
4. Confession rates differ by type of trial. All summary court cases and most district court cases are heard by a single judge. Confession rates in these cases range from 91 to 94 percent. A collegiate court made up of a panel of three judges hears all district court cases for which the offense is punishable by at least one year's imprisonment, as well as some other cases deemed particularly important or serious. Confession rates in these cases range from 68 to 71 percent in "obligatory" three-judge cases and from 50 to 66 percent in "discretionary" three-judge cases (Itoh, 1993).
5. As mentioned earlier, "plea bargaining" is usually translated into Japanese as *shiho torihiki* (lit. "administration of justice transaction" or "justice deal") and as *toben torihiki* (lit. "reply transaction"). Occasionally the word *dango* ("bid-rigging") is borrowed from the world of construction contracting to refer to that species of plea bargaining which Americans call "immunity"

(Hasegawa, 1978, p. 148; Woodall, 1996, p. 14). Question 57 of my survey used both *toben torihiki* and *shiho torihiki*, the second in parentheses after the first. I wanted to ask the question without employing the alarm-word but was not permitted to do so. The entire question thus reads as follows: "Sometimes I engage in plea-bargaining-like practices, that is, I tell a suspect that if he confesses he will be treated more leniently (via suspended sentence, suspended prosecution, fine, or the like)." There are at least two ways in which the question is defective. First, it uses the alarm-word "plea bargaining." Second, the question asks if prosecutors explicitly tell suspects about the potential exchange of leniency for a confession. As I explain later, plea bargaining in Japan, like Japanese communication more generally, is typically subtle, tacit, and indirect (Hasegawa, 1978).

6. I also distributed the survey to several senior and retired prosecutors, asking them to mark questions that seemed most likely to elicit *tatemae* responses. All prosecutors marked this question as highly likely to produce *tatemae* answers.
7. I was not permitted to ask another, more direct, question about prosecutor behavior: "Prosecutors treat suspects more leniently if they confess and display remorse." I also wanted to survey former suspects and defendants about their experiences in the criminal process, as Jonathan Casper has done in the US (Casper, 1972, p. 77). Unfortunately, this proved impossible. Below, however, I do report from interviews with some ex-offenders.
8. Another widely cited "exception" to the purported rule that Japanese prosecutors do not plea-bargain is the summary prosecution of Shin Kanemaru, once Japan's most powerful politician, in September of 1992 (DeSombre, 1995, p. 40; Woodall, 1996, pp. 12, 39, 95, 109). Kanemaru confessed to accepting nearly five million dollars in illegal political contributions. Chalmers Johnson argues that "prosecutors fined Kanemaru a mere $1820 without even having him come to their office for an interview," thus proving that "the fix was in at the Ministry of Justice" (C. Johnson, 1995, pp. 219, 222; *Shukan Bunshu*, October 1, 1992, pp. 36–9, and October 22, 1992, pp. 34–40). I talked to several prosecutors who worked on the *Kanemaru* case. All deny Johnson's allegation. However, Michio Sato an elite prosecutor in Sapporo, harshly criticized his colleagues for the Kanemaru disposition in a front-page editorial in the *Asahi* newspaper shortly after the Kanemaru case was decided (Mukaidani, 1993, p. 195).
9. Grants of immunity in exchange for cooperation are one species of the genus plea bargaining which even critics of plea bargaining – some Japanese prosecutors included – consider unproblematic (Ukawa, 1997). It is wrong, these critics say, to give concessions out of convenience in order to expedite the flow of cases and to avoid the complications that might arise in a contested trial. But it is perfectly acceptable, they continue, to use concessions as an investigative tool. Those who endorse this distinction may thus have a "so what?" reaction to evidence that Japanese prosecutors grant immunity. I have three responses. First, my primary aim is to demonstrate that Japan has plea bargaining, not to persuade readers that plea bargaining is good (or bad). Even critics of plea bargaining acknowledge that immunity is a form of plea bargaining. Second, the normative claims that plea bargaining for convenience is bad but plea bargaining for investigative

reasons is good are usually couched in similar utilitarian terms: the end does not justify the means in one case (convenience), but does in the other (investigative need). Using the same utilitarian framework, it is easy to see that immunity may sometimes be objectionable: what if the big fish is not big enough? Third, granting immunity is officially illegal in Japan (*Enomoto v. Japan*, 1995).

10. The difference, however, is easy to exaggerate. In 1993–94, Richard Leo (1996) observed 122 American police interrogations in person and another 60 on video tape. He found that 78 percent of his sample ultimately waived their *Miranda* rights and talked to the police. Furthermore, 64 percent of the suspects gave police information that hurt their case: 23 percent made incriminating statements; 18 percent partially confessed; and 24 percent fully confessed. By comparison, in Japan, over 90 percent of criminal defendants confess at trial. Of course, one must remember that Japanese investigators have far longer to obtain confessions than American investigators do. In Leo's study, only 8 percent of the interrogations lasted more than two hours (the longest was four and one-half hours), and each suspect was only interrogated once. In Japan, interrogations in even minor cases last far longer, and often are repeated over several days during the preindictment period (Hamada, 1992; Tokyo Sanbengoshikai, 1984).
11. In fact, the most exhaustive empirical study of American-style plea bargaining in recent years concludes that "the plea process is not overly dependent upon explicit, concrete exchanges or manipulations.... Most pleas probably result from the fact that, given the circumstances surrounding most cases, they appear to be the best way to proceed, simply because there was so little to contest" (Nardulli et al., 1988, p. 245).
12. Daniel Foote (1986, p. 99) describes another Japanese case where the defendant clearly regarded his confession as something to be traded for more lenient treatment. The defendant was "the picture of contrition at trial," but in the elevator a few minutes later, after having received a suspended sentence for driving while intoxicated, he "was triumphantly telling a friend that his demeanor was exactly what judges wanted to see and that was how one had to act to get off lightly." The kind of calculating behavior Foote and I observed is more common than many commentators suppose.
13. There is no doubt the defendant's behavior *was* manipulative. During the strategy session at the lawyer's office, I asked him how he felt about the offense for which he was arrested and charged. The defendant argued passionately that possessing marijuana for personal use should not be considered such a big deal. "The only thing I regret," he complained, "is getting caught."
14. Of course, this answer suggests another question: why do prosecutors deny doing it? John Langbein (1979, p. 213) maintains that there are only two possibilities: either prosecutors know not what they do (the delusion thesis), or else they knowingly engage in plea bargaining, despite its illegality, thus lying and lawbreaking (the deception thesis). Both answers apply to Japanese prosecutors.
15. In his memoirs, Kiyoshi Hasegawa, who worked as a prosecutor from 1921 until his retirement in 1952, describes several functional equivalents to plea bargaining, though he is careful to insist that what he describes does not constitute plea bargaining as such. In a section entitled "Bid-Rigging Which

Should Be Admonished" (*Imashimu Beki Dango*), Hasegawa uses the term *dango*, or "bid-rigging," that is normally associated with the awarding of construction contracts, to refer to a plea-bargaining-like exchange between a prosecutor and a suspect. The prosecutor tells the suspect that "if you inform me of another big case, I will not prosecute you for the present one," and the prosecutor is then informed of the other case (Hasegawa, 1978, p. 148).

For Hasegawa, *dango* is a grant of immunity in exchange for information. After positing this definition, Hasegawa first declares that such a "base means" of obtaining notice of other cases is "absolutely unthinkable" (*zettai ni arienai*) for Japanese prosecutors, and he reasserts that orthodoxy in subsequent passages as well. However, in the bulk of this section of his book, Hasegawa analyzes seven methods for telling a criminal suspect that his case will be dropped if he tells the prosecutor about another case, and for doing so without violating the norm against *dango*. The passage is hopelessly muddled and internally contradictory, as a Japanese professor of law to whom I showed it agreed. Some of the methods Hasegawa describes (such as prosecutors' "hints" and suspects' desires to please the prosecutor) narrowly escape Hasegawa's definition of *dango* but they do not pass the American "duck test": if it looks like a duck and sounds like a duck, bet that it is a duck.

16. One former prosecutor told me that, as an "old boy," he once defended a company executive who was being investigated for having evaded 300,000,000 yen (then about 3 million dollars) in taxes. The suspect could afford to pay only one-third that amount, otherwise he would need to declare bankruptcy. During the investigation, the OB persuaded prosecutors and tax officials to let the suspect pay the reduced amount. The suspect was thus able to keep his Mercedes car and several other luxury possessions that, in retrospect, the lawyer thinks he should have had to give up. "It was a good deal for my client," the lawyer explained, "but sometimes the outcome bothers me a little. I still have a sense of justice you know."
17. This conclusion is not the artifact of an unreasonably broad definition of plea bargaining. Indeed, Weigend (1980) employs the same definition and concludes that the French and (former West) Germans do not practice plea bargaining. Langbein (1979) and Felstiner (1979) agree that the former West Germany was a land without plea bargaining, while Blankenburg (1996) suggests that for serious crimes it still is. Likewise, Provine (1996) and Frase (1990) argue, respectively, that France has no plea bargaining and that it has only weak analogues to plea bargaining.
18. Many Asian governments with an Anglo-American legal heritage acknowledge that their countries have plea bargaining. They include Australia, India, Malaysia, Pakistan, the Philippines, Singapore, and Sri Lanka. In contrast, South Korean prosecutors state that they do not plea-bargain (Horiuchi, 1995).
19. In some highly controversial but unrepresentative American cases, rich drug dealers use the proceeds of their crimes to bargain for lighter sentences.
20. Note that while some analysts argue "the press of heavy caseloads" does not explain the variance in plea bargaining across jurisdictions, even they

admit that "case-pressure variables should be taken into account" when doing comparative studies (Heumann, 1978, p. 168; Feeley, 1992, p. 224).

21. Significantly, the same American prosecutor said he seldom could employ the "Joe Stalin approach" because (mixing his metaphors) "prosecutors always have to sell at a discount." Another way of describing the comparative difference is to say that Japanese prosecutors are less often pressured – by heavy caseloads, by unpredictable juries, or by adversarial lawyers – to sell at a discount.
22. The attitude that confessions *must* be extracted concerns some Japanese prosecutors, for at least two reasons. First, prosecutors' reluctance to charge cases in the absence of confessions means that many offenders who should be charged and punished are not (interviews with prosecutor executives in the Ministry of Justice Criminal Affairs Bureau, spring 1995). Second, some prosecutors feel that "rights consciousness" is spreading in Japan, making more and more suspects reluctant to confess and thereby exacerbating the first problem (Ukawa, 1997). However, most senior prosecutors seem to share the view of the veteran who told me that "the right to silence is a cancer (*gan*) in the criminal justice system. We must obtain confessions." Further evidence that the "cancer view" is widespread can be seen in the harsh criticism prosecutors level at defense lawyers who advise their clients to remain silent during investigations (Miranda no kai, 1997, p. 59).
23. The absence of juries produces unclear effects on the frequency of plea bargaining in Japan. Some argue that the absence of juries actually produces more plea bargaining. This view starts from the premise that without juries, Japanese prosecutors and lawyers can investigate the history of judges to determine the way they approach a case, and therefore can agree on the expected litigated outcome before trial. On this view, the prosecution and defense are likely to settle many cases in the shadow of the law (Ramseyer and Rasmusen, 2001).

    While this theory is plausible, an equally plausible one predicts the opposite effect. This view starts from the observation that, at least for prosecutors, the jury is a perversely unpredictable institution. It is unpredictable because, unlike a judge, it has no track record; it is perversely unpredictable because juries are far more likely to acquit than judges (Kalven and Zeisel, 1966; D. Johnson, 2002, p. 42). Facing the heightened risk of acquittal by jury, American prosecutors are likely to make concessions in order to get a sure something (a plea to a lesser charge) instead of a possible nothing (acquittal). In contrast, Japanese prosecutors face a lower risk of acquittal at trial. They are thus less likely to feel the need to make concessions.

    It is unclear which of these two effects of Japanese bench trials – greater predictability or reduced risk – is bigger. However, since the absence of juries in Japan helps keep the "gap" between the simple and complex methods of case processing narrower than in the US, it seems clear that the overall effect of the absence of juries on plea bargaining is negative.
24. See, for example, the chapters in this volume by Miyazawa, Shinomiya, and Takano.

References

Alschuler, Albert W. (1968) "The Prosecutor's Role in Plea Bargaining," *University of Chicago Law Review*, Vol. 36, pp. 50–112.

—— (1975) "The Defense Attorney's Role in Plea Bargaining," *Yale Law Journal* (May), pp. 1179–314.

Ames, Walter L. (1981) *Police and Community in Japan* (Berkeley: University of California Press).

Aoyagi, Fumio (1986) *Nihonjin no Hanzai Ishiki* (Tokyo: Chuo Koronsha).

Araki, Nobuyoshi (1985) "The Flow of Criminal Cases in the Japanese Criminal Justice System," *Crime and Delinquency*, Vol. 31 (October), pp. 601–29.

Bayley, David H. (1991) *Forces of Order: Policing Modern Japan*, 2nd edn (Berkeley: University of California Press).

Blankenburg, Erhard (1996) "Changes in Political Regimes and Continuity of the Rule of Law in Germany," in Herbert Jacob et al., *Courts, Law, and Politics in Comparative Perspective* (New Haven:Yale University Press).

Blumberg, Abraham (1979) *Criminal Justice: Issues and Ironies*, 2nd edn (New York: New Viewpoints Press).

Boyd, Neil, and Monique Layton (1991) *Crime and Criminal Justice in Canada and Japan: Understanding Our Differences* (Vancouver: Simon Fraser University School of Criminology).

Brady v. US, 397 US, 1970, 742.

Casper, Jonathan (1972) *American Criminal Justice* (Englewood Cliffs, NJ: Prentice-Hall).

Davis, Kenneth Culp (1969) *Discretionary Justice: a Preliminary Inquiry* (Urbana and Chicago: University of Illinois Press).

DeSombre, Jean Choi (1995) "A Comparison of Japanese and U.S. Criminal Justice: Reforming the U.S. Criminal Justice System through Greater Emphasis on Substantive Justice." Unpublished manuscript, Harvard Law School.

Enomoto v. Japan, 40 Keishu, 1995, 1.

Feeley, Malcolm M. (1985) "Introduction," *Crime and Delinquency*, Vol. 31 (October), pp. 601–4.

—— (1992) *The Process Is the Punishment* (New York: Russell Sage Foundation).

Feeley, Malcolm, M. and Charles Lester (1994) "Legal Complexity and the Transformation of the Criminal Process," *Subjektivierung des Justiziellen Beweisverfahrnes* (Frankfurt am Main: Vittorio Klostermann), pp. 337–75.

Felstiner, William (1979) "Plea Contracts in West Germany," *Law and Society Review*, Vol. 13, pp. 309–25.

Fingleton, Eamonn (1995) *Blindside: Why Japan Is Still on Track to Overtake the US by the Year 2000* (Boston: Houghton Mifflin Company).

Foote, Daniel H. (1986) "Prosecutorial Discretion: a Response." *Pacific Basin Law Journal*, Vol. 5, pp. 96–106.

—— (1991) "Confessions and the Right to Silence in Japan," *Georgia Journal of International and Comparative Law*, Vol. 21, pp. 415–88.

—— (1992) "The Benevolent Paternalism of Japanese Criminal Justice," *California Law Review*, Vol. 80, No. 2 (March), pp. 317–90.

Frase, Richard S. (1990) "Comparative Criminal Justice as a Guide to American Law Reform: How Do the French Do It, How Can We Find Out, and Why Should We Care?" *California Law Review*, Vol. 78, No. 3 (May), pp. 539–683.

Freeman, Laurie A. (1996) "Japan's Press Clubs as Information Cartels," Japan Policy Research Institute Working Paper Number 18 (Cardiff, Calif.: JPRI, April).

Garland, David (1990) *Punishment and Modern Society: a Study in Social Theory* (Chicago: The University of Chicago Press).

Givelber, Daniel (1997) "Meaningless Acquittals, Meaningful Convictions: Do We Reliably Acquit the Innocent?" *Rutgers Law Review*, Vol. 49, pp. 1317–96.

Haley, John O. (1986) "Comment: the Implications of Apology," *Law and Society Review*, Vol. 20, No. 4, pp. 499–507.

—— (1991) *Authority without Power: Law and the Japanese Paradox* (Oxford: Oxford University Press).

Hamada, Sumio (1992) *Jihaku no Kenkyu* (Tokyo: 31 Shobo).

Hasegawa, Kiyoshi (1978) *Watakushi to Kenji* (Tokyo: Hyoronsha).

Heilbroner, David (1990) *Rough Justice: Days and Nights of a Young D.A.* (New York: Dell).

Heumann, Milton (1978) *Plea Bargaining: the Experiences of Prosecutors, Judges, and Defense Attorneys* (Chicago: University of Chicago Press).

Hirano, Ryuichi (1989) "Diagnosis of the Current Code of Criminal Procedure," translated by Daniel H. Foote. *Law in Japan*, Vol. 22, pp. 129–42.

Horiuchi, Kunihiro (1995) *Criminal Justice Profiles of Asia: Investigation, Prosecution, and Trial* (Tokyo: UNAFEI).

Igarashi, Futaba (1994) "Nihongo o Bokugo to Shinai Mono no Kyojutsu Chosho no Shoko Noryoku ni tsuite," *Jiyu to Seigi*, March, pp. 226–7.

Inagawa, Tatsuya (1994) "The Criminal Justice System in Japan: Investigation and Prosecution." Unpublished paper (Tokyo: UNAFEI).

Ishimatsu, Takeo (1989) "Are Criminal Defendants in Japan Truly Receiving Trials by Judges?" translated by Daniel H. Foote. *Law in Japan*, Vol. 22, pp. 143–53.

Itoh, Osamu (1993) "The Criminal Justice System in Japan: the Court." Unpublished paper. (Tokyo: UNAFEI).

Johnson, Chalmers (1972) *Conspiracy at Matsukawa* (Berkeley: University of California Press).

—— (1995) *Japan: Who Governs? The Rise of the Developmental State* (New York: W.W. Norton & Company).

Johnson, David T. (1996) "The Japanese Way of Justice: Prosecuting Crime in Japan." PhD dissertation, University of California at Berkeley Boalt Hall School of Law, June.

—— (1998) "The Organization of Prosecution and the Possibility of Order," *Law and Society Review*, Vol. 32, pp. 247–308.

—— (1999) "Kumo no Su ni Shocho Sareru Nihonho no Tokushoku," *Jurisuto*, Vol. 1148, pp. 185–9.

—— (2002) *The Japanese Way of Justice: Prosecuting Crime in Japan* (New York: Oxford University Press).

Kalven, Harry and Hans Zeisel (1966) *The American Jury* (Boston: Little Brown).

Kibe, Katsumi (1993) *Kabutoyama Hodo ni Miru Hanninshi to iu Kyoki* (Gunma Ken: Asaosha).

Kitada, Mikinao (1995) "The Role of Public Prosecutors in Japan." Unpublished paper (Tokyo: UNAFEI).

Langbein, John H. (1978) "Torture and Plea Bargaining," *University of Chicago Law Review*, Vol. 46, pp. 3–22.

—— "Land without Plea Bargaining: How the Germans Do It," *Michigan Law Review*, Vol. 78, pp. 204–25.

Leo, Richard Angelo (1996) "Inside the Interrogation Room," *The Journal of Criminal Law and Criminology*, Vol. 86 (Winter) pp. 266–303.

Littrell, W. Boyd (1979) *Bureaucratic Justice: Police, Prosecutors, and Plea Bargaining* (Beverly Hills: Sage Publications).

Lynch, James (1995) "Crime in International Perspective," in James Q. Wilson and Joan Peterselia (eds), *Crime* (San Francisco: Institute for Contemporary Studies).

McCoy, Candace (1993) *Politics and Plea Bargaining: Victims' Rights in California* (Philadelphia: University of Pennsylvania Press).

Maynard, Douglas W. (1984) *Inside Plea Bargaining: the Language of Negotiation* (New York: Plenum Press).

Merryman, John Henry (1985) *The Civil Law Tradition: an Introduction to the Legal Systems of Western Europe and Latin America*, 2nd edn (Stanford, Calif: Stanford University Press).

Miller, Jeffrey J. (1990) "Plea Bargaining and its Analogues under the New Italian Criminal Procedure Code and in the United States: Towards a New Understanding of Comparative Criminal Procedure," *New York Journal of International Law and Politics*, Vol. 12, pp. 215–51.

Miranda no kai (Miranda Association) (1997) *"Miranda no Kai" to Bengoshi Katsudo* (Tokyo: Daiku Tosho).

Miyazawa, Setsuo (1992) *Policing in Japan: a Study on Making Crime*, translated by Frank G. Bennett, Jr. with John O. Haley (Albany: SUNY Press).

Mukaidani, Susumu (1993) *Chiken Tokusobu* (Tokyo: Kodansha).

Nardulli, Peter F., James Eisenstein and Roy B. Flemming (1988) *The Tenor of Justice: Criminal Courts and the Guilty Plea Process* (Urbana and Chicago: University of Illinois Press).

Nomura, Jiro (1988) *Nihon no Kensatsu: Saiko no Kenryoku no Uchigawa* (Tokyo: Kodansha).

North Carolina v. Alford, 400 US, 1970, 25.

Peters, Antonie (1992) "Some Comparative Observations on the Criminal Process in Holland and Japan," *Journal of the Japan–Netherlands Institute*, Vol. IV, pp. 247–94.

Pharr, Susan (1990) *Losing Face: Status Politics in Japan* (Berkeley: University of California Press).

Provine, Doris Marie (1996) "Courts in the Political Process in France," in Herbert Jacob et al., *Courts, Law, and Politics in Comparative Perspective* (New Haven: Yale University Press).

Ramseyer, J. Mark and Eric B. Rasmusen (2001) "Why is the Japanese Conviction Rate So High?" *Journal of Legal Studies*, Vol. 30, pp. 53–88.

Reed, Steven R. (1993) *Making Common Sense of Japan* (Pittsburgh: University of Pittsburgh Press).

Reischauer, Edwin O. (1977) *The Japanese* (Tokyo: Charles E. Tuttle Company).

Rosett, Arthur and Donald R. Cressey (1976) *Justice by Consent: Plea Bargains in the American Courthouse* (Philadephia: J.B. Lippincott Company).

Sanders, Joseph (1996) "Courts and Law in Japan," in Herbert Jacob et al., *Courts, Law, and Politics in Comparative Perspective* (New Haven: Yale University Press).

Sasaki, Tomoko (1994) "The Criminal Justice System in Japan: Investigation and Prosecution. Unpublished paper (Tokyo: UNAFEI).

Sato, Kinko (1974) *Torihiki no Shakai: Amerika no Keiji Shiho* (Tokyo: Chuo Koronsha).

Schulhofer, Stephen (1984) "Is Plea Bargaining Inevitable?" *Harvard Law Review*, Vol. 97, pp. 1037–107.

Smith, Robert J. (1983) *Japanese Society: Tradition, Self, and the Social Order* (Cambridge: Cambridge University Press).

Spencer, J.R. (1995) "Justice English Style," *The World & I*, August pp. 314–23.

Standen, Jeffrey (1993) "Plea Bargaining in the Shadow of the Guidelines," *California Law Review*, Vol. 81, pp. 1471–538.

Steinhoff, Patricia G. (1993) "Pursuing the Japanese Police," *Law and Society Review*, Vol. 27, pp. 827–50.

Tokyo Sanbengoshikai (1984) *Nureginu: Koshite Watakushi wa Jihaku o Sasereta* (Tokyo: Seihosha).

Tsuchiya, Shinichi (1995) "Experiences and Practical Measures Aimed at Combatting Corruption Involving Public Officials." Unpublished paper (Tokyo: Asia Crime Prevention Foundation).

Ukawa, Haruhiko (1997) "Shiho Torihiki o Kangaeru, 1-17," *Hanrei Jiho*, Nos 1583–84, 1586–7, 1590, 1592–3, 1596, 1598–9, 1601–2, 1604, 1613–14, 1616, 1627.

Upham, Frank K.(1987) *Law and Social Change in Postwar Japan* (Cambridge, Mass: Harvard University Press).

Van Wolferen, Karel (1989) *The Enigma of Japanese Power: People and Politics in a Stateless Nation* (New York: Alfred Knopf).

Wagatsuma, Hiroshi and Arthur Rosett (1986) "The Implications of Apology: Law and Culture in Japan and the United States," *Law and Society Review*, Vol. 20, No. 4, pp. 461–96.

Wakamatsu, Yoshiya (1992) *Hanzai Sosa no Subete wa Wakaru Hon* (Tokyo: Sogo Horei).

Walker, Samuel (1993) *Taming the System: the Control of Discretion in Criminal Justice, 1950–1990* (New York: Oxford University Press).

Weigend, Thomas (1980) "Continental Cures for American Ailments: European Criminal Procedure as a Model for Law Reform," in Norval Morris and Michael Tonry (eds), *Crime and Justice: an Annual Review of Research* (Chicago: University of Chicago Press).

Westermann, Ted D. and James W. Burfeind (1991) *Crime and Justice in Two Societies: Japan and the United States* (Pacific Grove, Calif.: Brooks/Cole).

Woodall, Brian (1996) *Japan under Construction: Corruption, Politics, and Public Works* (Berkeley: University of California Press).

Yamada, Haruo (1997) *Different Games, Different Rules: Why Americans and Japanese Misunderstand Each Other* (New York: Oxford University Press).

Zaikai Tenbo (1979) Tokushu (Special Report): "Homu – Kensatsu Kanryo no Jinji Kenkyu." May, pp. 58–90.

Zeisel, Hans (1980) "The Offer Which Cannot Be Refused," in Franklin Zimring and Richard Frase (eds), *The Criminal Justice System: Materials on the Administration and Reform of the Criminal Law* (Boston: Little, Brown and Company).

10
Witness Immunity and Bargain Justice: a Look at the Japanese Concept of the Adversary System

*Masahito Inouye**

Part I Introduction

On February 22, 1995, the Supreme Court of Japan handed down a final decision in the series of Lockheed bribery cases (*Enomoto v. Japan*, 1995), ending nearly two decades of legal actions over the biggest corruption scandal in postwar Japan. The decision upheld the lower courts' convictions of the last two defendants in the "Marubeni-route" trial, named for one of the four different routes of payoff involved in the Lockheed Aircraft Corporation's sale of TriStar airplanes to All Nippon Airways (*Zen-nikku*). The legal controversy surrounding these convictions centered on the prosecutors' pledge of immunity given to certain witnesses, who were former Lockheed officials. However, the Supreme Court affirmed the convictions by relying on other evidence found in the court records; it did not base its decision on the testimony of former Lockheed officials which had been given in exchange for immunity.

The granting of immunity, in itself an unprecedented practice in Japan, had generated a big sensation from the beginning, and eventually had become a major issue in the legal contests throughout the four route cases. The lower courts, despite their general doubt about the aspect of "bargain justice" associated with the measure, had managed to find a way to admit the depositions into evidence. In contrast, the Supreme Court flatly excluded them on the seemingly rather technical grounds that there was no statutory authorization for the granting of immunity.

---

* Professor of Law, University of Tokyo. The author is grateful to Professor Joseph L. Hoffmann of Indiana University School of Law for his helpful comment on an earlier draft of this chapter.

The decision left open whether a witness immunity procedure could be consistent with other substantive principles and with the public policies of the Japanese criminal justice system.

While in recent times law enforcement practitioners have contended that immunity would meaningfully assist in the prosecution of both large-scale bribery or corporate offenses and organized crime (see e.g. Fujinaga, 1991, p. 673; Hotta, 1995, p. 4), not a few Japanese resist the use of immunity. Among those who oppose immunity are contemporary lawyers and scholars who generally stress the principle of the adversary system (*Tojisha-shugi*) as the leading principle of Japanese criminal procedure. This resistance may reflect basic Japanese notions of justice and fairness that strongly affect the Japanese concept of the adversary system.

In this chapter, I will discuss whether and how this Japanese concept of justice differs from its American counterpart, using as a reference point the witness immunity issues involved in the Lockheed bribery cases.

Part II Lockheed bribery cases

The facts

In 1975, a Lockheed Aircraft Corporation accountant disclosed to a US Senate subcommittee that Lockheed had paid large illegal sums of money to win contracts in several countries, including Japan. Following this disclosure and several months of investigation, the Tokyo District Public Prosecutor's Office applied to a judge of the Tokyo District Court to conduct preindictment witness examinations of three former Lockheed officials, including its former vice president A.C. Kotchian.[1] The prosecutor's office sought to question these officials concerning the charge that President Hiyama and other officials of Marubeni Trading Corporation, then the official sales agent for Lockheed, bribed several unnamed persons for the sale of Lockheed airplanes in Japan. Anticipating that the US witnesses might claim their constitutional privilege against self-incrimination, the Prosecutor General, the highest office of the Japanese prosecutor, officially instructed the Chief Public Prosecutor of Tokyo to suspend prosecution against Kotchian and the other Lockheed officials for the matters on which they would testify. Such suspension of prosecution was to hold, pursuant to statutory prosecutorial discretion,[2] even if the questioners detected, from the testimony or evidence derived therefrom, that the officials had violated Japanese law. Shortly thereafter, Tokyo's Chief Public Prosecutor in turn made an official statement announcing the same.

Because the witnesses resided in California, the Tokyo District Court judge requested, with specific reference to the above declaration and official statement by the prosecution, that a specially assigned commissioner in the United States District Court for the Central District of California conduct the questioning. None of the witnesses was inclined to testify because each recognized the potential for prosecution in Japan.

On July 6, 1976, a presiding judge of the US District Court ordered the examinations of the witnesses to begin in camera. However, he also ruled that their testimony would not be transferred to the Japanese authorities unless and until the Japanese Supreme Court submitted to the US District Court an explicit order or ruling that the witnesses would not be indicted in Japan.

On July 21, the Japanese Prosecutor General submitted to the Supreme Court of Japan another declaration, reconfirming his first declaration. Three days later, the Supreme Court, by way of the decision of its judicial conference,[3] issued a declaration assuring US legal authorities that the Japanese prosecutors had promised not to indict the three witnesses. Upon receiving these declarations, the US District Court proceeded to examine the witnesses; it then supplied the Japanese authorities with more than ten volumes of testimony.

Based upon these depositions, as well as on other evidence collected during the investigation, the public prosecutors indicted four separate groups of defendants on various charges. The prosecution alleged the following: (1) Hiyama, in conspiracy with the other two Marubeni officials, asked then Prime Minister Tanaka to tell ANA to purchase Lockheed TriStar passenger planes, and Tanaka accepted the request in exchange for a 500 million yen bribe which was later paid by way of one of Tanaka's secretaries, Enomoto (the "Marubeni-route"); (2) President Wakasa and other officials of ANA, using a secret fund provided by Lockheed, gave 50 million yen to then Transport Minister Hashimoto and 2 million yen to then Parliamentary Vice-Minister of Transport Sato for their measures to delay a rival company's introduction of large-size passenger planes into the domestic lines (the "Zen-nikku-route"); (3) Kodama, a right-wing figure rumored to be an underground "fixer" in various matters involving politicians and big business, received a fee for his activities as a secret agent for Lockheed without abiding by the Foreign Exchange and Foreign Trade Control Act (the "Kodama-route"); and (4) Osano, an old companion of Prime Minister Tanaka who owned the transport company which was the single largest shareholder of ANA, committed perjury when he testified before a Diet committee regarding his suspected involvement in the Lockheed sale (the "Osano-route").

Lower courts' decisions

In the trial of the "Marubeni-route" defendants, which began in January of 1977, the defense objected to the admission into evidence of the US witnesses' testimony. The defense counsel asserted that such admission would violate the witnesses' privilege against self-incrimination, guaranteed by Article 38(1) of the Japanese Constitution,[4] because the Japanese authorities' declarations to suspend prosecution against them did not have the legal effect to eliminate their constitutional privilege. Additionally, such admission would violate due process of law guaranteed by Article 31 of the Constitution;[5] they argued that to obtain testimony in exchange for immunity contradicts "our traditionally held basic idea of criminal justice which has sought for the 100 per cent realization of justice and totally rejected any such bargain-like measures of convenience as are found in the Anglo-American legal systems."[6]

The trial court overruled the objection. It held that, for two reasons, there was no practical possibility of indicting the US witnesses: (1) the Japanese authorities had declared a suspension of prosecution, and (2) it was logistically impossible to initiate prosecution against persons who stayed out of the Japanese jurisdiction (*Japan v. Tanaka*, December 20, 1978). The court further held that the defendants had no standing to move to exclude the depositions based on the violation of the witnesses' constitutional privilege; their standing would only exist in exceptional cases involving serious intrusion into fundamental human rights, a high risk of inducing false statements, or such unfairness as deprivation of the privilege by coercion, torture, threat, or deception. In noting these exceptions to the standing rule, the court held that to force testimony with a grant of immunity might violate Japanese law for three reasons: (1) it "does not seem to be in conformity [with] the basic values of the legal system or [with] the people's traditional sense of justice in Japan," (2) it accompanies an appearance of unfairness, and (3) it fosters the production of false statements. However, the granting of immunity in the instant case was not impermissible because it did not implicate any of the above concerns. It did not substantially involve bargaining to exchange the testimony because the possibility of punishing the Americans was virtually nonexistent in any event. Granting immunity here would not cause any sense of unfairness when applied to American citizens, because they were accustomed to the witness immunity procedure in the legal environments of the United States. Finally, there was no danger of inducing false statements because the witnesses were not required to make any specifically indicated statement and were examined in accordance with ordinary procedure before a US court of law (ibid. pp. 1526–33, 1536).[7]

On appeal, the Tokyo High Court upheld the trial court's judgment of conviction against the defendants (*Tanaka v. Japan*, July 29, 1987). Affirming the trial court's denial of the defendant's standing to challenge the admissibility of the testimony in question, the High Court added that the statement of Tokyo's Chief Public Prosecutor to suspend prosecution itself could not eliminate, as a matter of law, the possibility of prosecution against the witnesses. However, the witnesses were, in effect, legally secured against prosecution because any indictment, if filed in breach of the repeatedly confirmed official promise, ought to be dismissed due to the violations of the prosecutors' loyalty obligation and of the international faith. The court opined that, from the nature of the matter, the legislature should decide whether to adopt "a measure of obtaining testimony at the price of granting immunity to some of those suspected of being involved in a crime." Hence, in the absence of statutory authorization, it would be illegal to force testimony from a witness who would otherwise assert his privilege against self-incrimination. Nonetheless, the court held that, in the matter of international judicial assistance – where we should assume differences in the legal systems of the relevant countries – evidence obtained as the result of a foreign procedure which is not recognized in the current law of Japan should be admitted in Japanese courts "unless the procedure is impermissibly unlawful in the light of our Constitution as well as the essential principles of our criminal procedure law" (ibid., pp. 120–8). In the opinion of the court, the American witness immunity procedure was not sufficiently impermissible even by Japanese standards to invoke the exception; consequently, the Lockheed witnesses' testimony was properly admitted (ibid., pp. 129–35).

In the trials of the defendants involved in the other three routes, the testimony of the Lockheed witnesses was admitted into evidence. The convictions of those defendants were upheld by the appellate courts for reasons more or less similar to those given in the above-referenced opinion of the High Court.[8]

The Supreme Court decision

The Supreme Court, in an en banc decision, overruled the Tokyo High Court's decision concerning the admissibility of the depositions. However, it found the error harmless because the convictions of defendants Enomoto and Hiyama could have been affirmed on the basis of the other evidence listed in the trial court judgment (*Enomoto v. Japan*, 1995, pp. 6–10).[9]

The court declared that the evidence submitted for fact-finding in a criminal case must be not only admissible according to the Code of Criminal Procedure (CCP), but also permissible in light of the whole spirit of criminal procedure law. In identifying this spirit, the court relied on the statement of purpose found in the CCP: "to clarify the true facts of cases and to apply and realize criminal laws and ordinances fairly and speedily, while thoroughly accomplishing the maintenance of public welfare and security of fundamental human rights of individuals" (CCP art. 1).

Although a witness immunity procedure would not be constitutionally prohibited, the court held that its adoption requires specific legislation. Such legislation should be supported by careful consideration of various factors – including the necessity for the measure, its appropriateness from the viewpoint of fair criminal process, and its conformity with the people's sense of justice and fairness. Moreover, legislation regarding immunity must specify its scope, procedural requirements and legal effects, because it would affect significantly the interests of those involved as well as the substance of criminal justice. The CCP, which evidently does not incorporate any witness immunity procedure, thus would not allow any statement made in return for immunity to be used as evidence in fact-finding. The court did not find that any different rule should apply when the evidence was obtained by way of international judicial assistance, because its admissibility in any case must be judged in accordance with the relevant Japanese laws (*Enomoto v. Japan*, 1995, pp. 9–10).

Part III Witness immunity and the privilege against self-incrimination

The witness immunity procedure, whose origin can be traced back to the early stage of the privilege against self-incrimination itself in Britain, was adopted as part of US federal court procedure in the late 1800s. Since then, it has been refined and used as an effective tool in the prosecution of cases involving organized crime or public corruption in the United States (see e.g. *Kastiger v. US*, 1972, p. 446 n.13; LaFave and Israel, 1992, section 8.11(a)). Nowadays, each state has a statute which authorizes the court to order a witness to testify in exchange for a grant of immunity, though the statutes differ in details (such as the offenses they cover and the scope of the immunity) (*Kastiger v. US*, 1972, p. 447, referring to Wigmore, 1961, section 2281, p. 495 n.11).

The concept of immunity stems from the American opinion that the Fifth Amendment privilege against self-incrimination does not apply in cases where there is no possibility that the witness will be criminally prosecuted or punished as a result of his testimony. He may be forced to give testimony which could otherwise incriminate him when such a possibility is eliminated by the granting of immunity (*Brown v. Walker*, 1896, p. 591; *Kastiger v. US*, 1972).

This type of witness immunity procedure would not be in conflict with the similar protection provided by Article 38(1) of the Japanese Constitution. Under the prevailing interpretation, the Japanese privilege against self-incrimination does not apply to a person who could not be prosecuted or punished due to the statute of limitations, double jeopardy, or a pardon (Hogaku, 1953, p. 662; Miyazawa, 1955, p. 308). The Japanese Supreme Court, in the Lockheed decision, probably suggested this interpretation was correct.

However, Japan has no existing statute that explicitly provides for such a procedure.[10] The issue, therefore, is whether we could somehow produce the same legal effect without specific statutory authorization.

In this regard, the Tokyo District Court in the "Osano- and Kodama-route" cases deemed the statement of Tokyo's Chief Public Prosecutor a total waiver of prosecution, which eliminated the prerequisite for the witnesses' privilege against self-incrimination (*Japan v. Osano*, 1978, pp. 1283–93, 1296–310).

As the state may waive a criminal punishment as a part of its sovereign power in the form of pardon, for instance, it also could waive prosecution, which is the means to realize the criminal punishment. The problem, however, is who is authorized to decide such a waiver. In Japanese law, only the Cabinet is empowered to decide a general pardon which shall extinguish the prosecution for the pardoned offense (Pardon Act art. 2(1)).

The "Osano- and Kodama-routes" trial court concluded that the public prosecutors, who under the current law are entrusted with vast prosecutorial discretion, could decide the total waiver of prosecution (*Japan v. Osano*, 1978, pp. 1297–8, 1300). In the United States, where prosecutors have similar discretion, federal as well as some state courts have held that prosecutors have an inherent power to make a promise of nonprosecution, which in itself could eliminate a witness's Fifth Amendment privilege.[11] In contrast, under German law, the principle of mandatory prosecution prevails, and immunity may be granted only with the consent of the Federal Supreme Court, and only to a *Kronzeuge* (Crown's witness) who makes a statement valuable to the detection or prevention of organized crime or terrorist offenses.[12]

The existence of prosecutorial discretion, however, does not automatically imply that the prosecutors can unilaterally waive prosecution. A majority of the American state courts[13] have refused to grant such extensive powers to prosecutors, in accordance with the advice of former Supreme Court Justice Benjamin Cardozo:

> Whether the good to be attained by procuring the testimony of criminals is greater or less than the evil to be wrought by exempting them forever from prosecution for their crimes is a question of high policy as to which the law-making department of the government is entitled to be heard. (*Doyle v. Hofstander*, 1931, p. 495; compare Note, 1974, p. 337)

Other courts have emphasized that the immunity power should not "inhere in the office of prosecutor;" rather, it should be obtained "only after legislative deliberation and the approval of carefully drawn legislation," because offering immunity is "a dangerous practice," "a clear invitation to (witnesses) to commit perjury," and "the kind of practice ... that is certain to be abused by law enforcement officials to the detriment of innocent people" (*State ex. rel. Munn v. McKelvey*, 1987, p. 769, citing *Commonwealth v. Brady*, 1974, p. 867).

A similar view was shared by many Japanese commentators, who criticized the Tokyo District Court's waiver decision in the Osano- and Kodama-routes cases (see e.g. Tamiya, 1978, p. 167; Mitsui, 1980, p. 107; Yamakawa, 1980, p. 107; Yokoyama, 1981, p. 185; Yamada, 1992, p. 136). The appellate court in the Osano-route case, like the trial and appellate courts in the other two routes cases, opined that Tokyo's Chief Public Prosecutor's declaration (to suspend prosecution) by itself cannot legally bar future initiation of prosecution.[14] Nonetheless, the trial courts in the two routes concluded that the prosecution against the witnesses had been impossible, by referring to the compiled effects of the repeated official declaration of non-prosecution, in addition to the impracticability of prosecuting non-residents. The courts arguably made a leap from factual impossibility to legal impossibility (Matsumoto, 1984, p. 191; Mitsui, 1980, p. 109).

Instead, the appellate courts in the three routes cases stressed that the prosecutors' estoppel-like loyalty obligation, as well as international good faith, should lead to the dismissal of any subsequent indictment (*Osano v. Japan*, 1984, pp. 190–1; *Japan v. Hashimoto*, 1986, pp. 51–2; *Tanaka v. Japan*, 1987, p. 127). Once the prosecutors have made an official commitment to a foreign government not to initiate prosecution against its witnesses, they have an obligation to keep this commitment. If they violate it, any subsequent prosecution derived from this testimony would be illegal. Such an effect, however, attaches as a corollary to the *fact* that the official promise of nonprosecution was made; it does not necessarily signify that the promise itself could *legally* have been made. Indeed, some American state courts have imposed a similar estoppel-type obligation upon prosecutors who, without any legitimate power to do so, gave their word not to prosecute a certain witness before that witness spoke.[15]

If, as described above, prosecutors are not empowered unilaterally to waive prosecution, we logically should not allow them to make any commitment that would have an effect tantamount to the waiver of prosecution. In other words, prosecutors should not be able to eliminate a witness's privilege against self-incrimination.

The Japanese Supreme Court in the Lockheed case did not directly decide whether the prosecutors' declarations and statements of nonprosecution could eliminate the witnesses' constitutional privileges. However, it would be correct if the court implicitly rejected this claim in holding that the granting of immunity is not permissible unless such procedure is specifically adopted in the existing law.

Part IV The admissibility of the depositions

It is well settled that any statement forced out of a witness who still held his privilege against self-incrimination is not admissible as evidence against him. It would be irrational to admit such a statement to punish him while guaranteeing him not to be forced to make such incriminating statements.

The protection does not, however, apply to any persons other than the one who made such a statement. The lower courts in the Lockheed cases correctly held that the defendants, as third parties, did not have standing to challenge the admissibility of the depositions on the grounds of the violation of the witnesses' constitutional privilege. If the depositions were to be excluded, the defendants needed another reason.

Rather than giving detailed reasons, the Japanese Supreme Court simply referred to the CCP, which does not adopt any witness immunity procedure. It is, however, doubtful that any evidence obtained through a measure which is not recognized by existing law must automatically or always be excluded, irrespective of whose rights or what interests were infringed, or how seriously. Indeed, the Supreme Court's precedent dictates that evidence seized from a search conducted outside of or contrary to statutory requirements should be declared inadmissible *only* when the search involved such serious illegality as to negate the spirit of the warrant requirements contained in Art. 35 of the Constitution[16] and in relevant provisions of the CCP, *and* if the admission of the evidence is deemed improper from the viewpoint of the deterrence of future illegal investigative activities (*Japan v. Hashimoto*, 1978, p. 1672).

Furthermore, international judicial assistance, which assumes differences in the legal systems of the countries concerned, would lose its meaning if the evidence collected through a procedure, legal in the requested country, could not be used in the requesting country because no similar procedure exists. American courts generally agree that evidence provided by a foreign government should not be suppressed only because the search or seizure would have been deemed illegal if it were conducted within the States (compare LaFave, 1996, section 1.8(h), p. 283).

There is not, however, a blanket rule which allows for admissibility no matter how illegal – by the domestic standards – the foreign collecting procedure was. The American courts have ordered the exclusion of the evidence when its collecting procedure (1) "shock[ed] the judicial conscience" (*Stowe v. Devoy*, 1978, p. 341), (2) "lacked fundamental fairness" (*US v. Salim*, 1988, p. 946), or (3) failed to satisfy the essential requirements of the US Constitution (see e.g. *Powell v. Zuckert*, 1966, p. 640).

The lower courts in the Lockheed cases also recognized, as a general rule, that the evidence should not be admitted if it was obtained by means impermissibly unlawful according to both the Japanese Constitution and the essential principles of criminal procedure law. In admitting the testimony, the courts found that immunity procedures had not been so unlawful.

The Japanese Supreme Court disagreed with this finding. Judging them in the light of "the whole spirit of the criminal procedure law," it held that the witnesses' statements were inadmissible despite their acquisition through international judicial assistance. According to the court, a decision concerning the adoption of a witness immunity procedure must evaluate the appropriateness of such a procedure in light of fair criminal process and conformity with the people's sense of justice and fairness. The court thus was dubious whether it is basically fair to obtain incriminating evidence by granting immunity to some of those involved in the suspected offense and then to use that evidence to convict and to punish the rest.

However, if granting immunity to obtain incriminating statements is so incongruent with "the whole spirit of the criminal procedure law" or with "the people's sense of justice and fairness," it would be natural to conclude that a similar procedure could not be adopted even by the legislature. Yet the court confirmed that legislative immunity would be constitutional. It might be more accurate to say that the court did provide decisive evaluation of the witness immunity procedure. The court, on suspicion, left it to the care of the legislature, whose members represent the opinions of the people of Japan.

Part V Witness immunity and the Japanese concept of the adversary system

Such basic doubt against witness immunity was shared by the lower courts throughout the four groups of Lockheed cases. They admitted that, by granting immunity, we would risk forfeiting the realization of justice against some of those involved in a crime, in order to gain a tactical advantage in the prosecution and punishment of the rest (*Japan v. Tanaka*, 1978, p. 1531). We also appear to unduly discriminate by granting immunity selectively (*Japan v. Hashimoto*, 1979, p. 1305), and import a kind of bargain into the administration of criminal justice, which ought to be rigid (*Japan v. Hashimoto*, 1986, p. 56; *Japan v. Tanaka*, 1978, p. 1531; *Japan v. Hashimoto*, 1979, p. 1305).

In Germany, there exists strong criticism against the *Kronzeuge* provisions from the standpoint that the integrity of the legal order must be secured by punishing the guilty (compare Kleinknecht and Meyer-Goßner, 1995, Rdnrs 5–8 vor Art 1. KronzG). It is, however, open to question whether the current Japanese law of criminal procedure aims exclusively to secure the complete punishment of the guilty. As indicated by art. 1 of the CCP, facts must be found and criminal laws realized according to fair procedure, tempered with the protection of the rights of individuals. In addition, Japanese public prosecutors are entrusted with discretion not to initiate prosecution, even against those whom they deem guilty.

The second point of doubt is not effective either. There is no violation of constitutional equal protection rights if other accomplices are unduly favored by the prosecutors (*Japan v. Fukumoto*, 1981).

It seems fair to say that the third point – hostility toward "bargain justice" – provides the core reason for the rejection of a witness immunity procedure. Such resistance against "bargain justice" presumably is rooted in the Japanese concept of the adversary system. The different feature of the Japanese concept from its American counterpart was already evident when the drafters of the present CCP rejected the adoption of an arraignment or guilty plea system.[17] Justice Dando, who played a leading role in its drafting, explains,

> (E)ffectuation of the right to punish is rightly enough a matter for the state. In this respect the concept of officially-controlled proceedings is inherently present in criminal adjudication. The adversary party principle is predominant in the new Code, but the concept of officially-controlled proceedings continues to lurk in the background, . . . in case . . . necessity comes to the fore. To conclude merely on a superficial examination that the adversary party principle has destroyed the concept of officially-controlled proceedings is to misjudge the essential nature of criminal adjudications. Accordingly, one may well say that criminal procedure comprises the adversary party system in form and the concept of officially-controlled proceedings in substance. (T)here are inherent limits on the so-called "change of criminal procedure into civil procedure" (*Zivilprozessualisierung*) or, the recognition that the parties are permitted to shape the action to achieve some desired result (*Dispositionsprinzip*). The arraignment system in Anglo-American law, at least in its pure form, is contrary to the essential nature of criminal judgments, and the failure of present law to incorporate it may be considered proper (see Dando, 1965, pp. 82–4; 1948a, p. 44; 1948b, p. 1011).[18]

As scholars and lawyers of the younger generation have emphasized the need to secure a fair trial and to protect the defendant's rights by allowing his active participation in the procedure, the adversary system has become a leading principle of current Japanese criminal procedure (Matsuo, 1972, p. 33; Tamiya, 1991, p. 457). However, while proposals for arraignment procedures have arisen sporadically, Japanese lawyers and scholars have not generally accepted that the adversary system goes so far as to justify the parties taking a more active role in disposing the case by themselves, as common in American criminal courts (Matsuo, 1972, p. 59).

It should be noted that the United States has harsh critics of plea bargaining arrangements, which typically accompany the guilty plea system (Alschuler, 1979, pp. 229ff). These critics warn that plea bargaining leads to possible abuses of the system, which harm innocent defendants who might be pressured or, on calculation, driven into pleading guilty (Finkelstein, 1975, p. 293; Rhodes, 1979, p. 370; Alschuler, 1968, p. 85). They also emphasize that injustice results when seriously guilty defendants receive inappropriately light sentences (Bradley and Hoffman, 1996, p. 1292; Heumann, 1975, p. 166). Opponents of plea bargaining also contend that this practice produces a "spoiling effect" upon guilty defendants: they wrongly conclude that the criminal justice system is no different from a business transaction, in which one who performs smarter gets a better deal (Casper, 1972, pp. 80–1, 92).

Plea bargaining has even been banned or restricted in some American jurisdictions (Rubenstein and White, 1979, p. 367; Bradley and Hoffman, 1996, p. 1292 n. 89; Kuh, 1975, p. 48; Heinz and Kerstetter, 1979, p. 349). However, no one in the States would dare suggest abolishing the guilty plea itself. While the heavy reliance on guilty pleas might diminish the significance of the adversary system by minimizing the opportunity for full adversary adjudication (LaFave and Israel, 1984, pp. 40–1), the guilty plea has become an essential tool of the adversary system. Guilty pleas help the system dispose of a large number of cases and allow an individual to express her dignity by allowing her to make a choice (ibid., p. 41; LaFave and Israel, 1992, p. 37). Despite its alleged philosophical illegitimacy, plea bargaining seems to be an inevitable practice vitally associated with guilty pleas (Heumann, 1975, p. 166). Indeed, the US Supreme Court has affirmed the constitutional legitimacy of this practice (*Brady v. US*, 1970; *Bordenkircher v. Hayes*, 1978).

Technically, the witness immunity procedure in itself does not involve any element of bargaining. It is an *ex parte* measure to eliminate the witness's privilege against self-incrimination, thereby enabling the government to compel his or her testimony. In practice, however, a grant of immunity is usually preceded by a negotiation between the prosecution and the witness for the purpose of smooth and fruitful execution of the witness examination. This negotiation gives the whole process the appearance of bargain justice, which would trigger resistance among Japanese.

As a matter of fact, such negotiation is not totally foreign to the practice of Japanese criminal procedure (Johnson, 1996, pp. 410–12;

Tamiya, 1982, p. 193; Ugawa, 1998, p. 37).[19] Indeed, a defense counsel might ask the prosecutor in charge of his client's case to suspend the prosecution or to apply to the court for a summary order imposing a light penalty or fine on the defendant.[20]

Prosecution and law enforcement people, however, believe that these practices are nothing more than discretionary extenuation, quite different from negotiation between two parties on equal footing (Sato, 1974, pp. 168ff). Although there seems to be room for questioning which would be fairer – to leave the decision entirely to the discretion of the prosecutor or to legitimate a procedurally safeguarded negotiation between the defense and the prosecutor – it is doubtful that the latter could ever occur, given the Japanese people's sense of justice and fairness.

As a matter of fact, the Tokyo public prosecutors recently dared to recommend, after serious discussion among the highest-ranking officials of all of the prosecution authorities, life imprisonment for one of the Aum cult defendants charged with a series of despicable offenses, including the sarin nerve gas attack on Tokyo's subway system which killed 12 passengers and subway employees, and injured nearly 3800 people. Their decision was based on the grounds that the defendant had "turned himself in" by spontaneously making confessions, after his arrest on another charge, which contributed significantly to confirming the suspected, but as yet unsubstantiated, offenses of the Aum cult group. This recommendation was accepted by the Tokyo District Court, which also highly evaluated the defendant's contribution to the clarification of the Aum cult offenses in sentencing him to life imprisonment.

Neither the prosecutors' recommendation nor the trial court's sentencing, however, could have been supported by the people, and therefore neither the prosecutors nor the court itself could have decided to make it, if the defendant were not deemed to have been disclosing the whole truth out of sincere remorse for his involvement in the offenses, rather than just incriminating other defendants in exchange for, or in expectation of, the authorities' lenient treatment of himself. Indeed, the same Tokyo public prosecutors later recommended the death sentence for another Aum cult defendant who also had cooperated in the investigation of the offenses, but was thought to have done so without volunteering facts disadvantageous to himself, mainly for the selfish purpose of protecting his own safety from revenge attacks by the cult group.

This makes a distinctive contrast with the contemporaneous Oklahoma City bombing trials in the US, in which one of the three alleged accomplices played an important role in testifying against the other two defendants in direct exchange for the granting of immunity.

Part VI Conclusion

In response to the Supreme Court's decision in the Lockheed case, the Japanese Ministry of Justice was reportedly planning to propose new organized crime legislation, including a witness immunity procedure. Some media representatives called this measure *"Shiho-Torihiki"* (bargaining of justice). Possibly in anticipation of a big controversy, the Ministry omitted the immunity clauses from the official proposals submitted to the Council on Legislation.[21]

As a responsible Justice Ministry official acknowledged in a Diet committee meeting,[22] the Ministry is still looking for an opportunity to introduce such a legislative proposal, which seems to be gradually gaining support among concerned scholars and lawyers (Taguchi, 1998, pp. 190–4; Sakamaki, 1999, p. 245).[23] This might suggest a possible change in the Japanese concept of the adversary system.

Considering the public sentiment concerning the Japanese sense of justice and fairness described above, however, there is no way of knowing whether the legislation will succeed. Its fate could be a touchstone of the Japanese adversary system.

Notes

1. Before the trial, the public prosecutor may ask a judge to examine as a witness a person who apparently possesses information relevant to the investigation, but who refuses to appear or to disclose such information voluntarily at the interview by the police or the prosecutor (CCP art. 226).
2. Article 248 of CCP provides, "If, after considering the character, age and situation of the offender, the gravity of the offense, the circumstances under which the offense was committed, and the conditions subsequent to the commission of the offense, prosecution is deemed unnecessary, prosecution need not be instituted."
3. The Supreme Court shall handle administrative matters involved in the management of the judiciary by way of its judicial conference that is composed of all the Justices and presided by the Chief Justice (The Courts Organization Act of 1947, §12).
4. Article 38(1) of the Japanese Constitution provides, "No person shall be compelled to testify against himself." This constitutional protection is often called in Japan "the right to remain silent."
5. Article 31 of the Japanese Constitution provides, "No person shall be deprived of life or liberty, nor shall any other criminal penalty be imposed, except according to procedure established by law." Although it does not include any specific words with such effects, the provision is generally interpreted to guarantee a due process protection similar to that of the 14th Amendment to the US Constitution.

6. For the full text of the opinions, see "Marubeni no Koso-Kikyaku wo Motomeru Iken" (1978, p. 197); "Shokutaku-Jinmon-Chosho ni kansuru Marubeni Bengodan Ikensho" (1978, p. 219).
7. Defendants Enomoto, Hiyama, and Tanaka were convicted and sentenced as follows: Tanaka received four years in prison and had to forfeit 500 million yen; Enomoto received a one-year suspended sentence; Hiyama received two and half years in prison. *Japan v. Tanaka,* 15 Kei-Sai Geppo 521 (Tokyo Dist. Ct. 1st Crim. Div. Judgment of October 12, 1983).
8. For the trial court opinions, see *Japan v. Osano,* 10 Kei-Sai Geppo 1256 (Tokyo Dist. Ct. 25th Crim. Div. Decision of September 21, 1978) ("Osano- and Kodama-routes"); *Japan v. Hashimoto,* 11 Kei-Sai Geppo 1269 (Tokyo Dist. Ct. 12th Crim. Div. Decision of October 30, 1979) ("Zennikku-route"). For the appellate court opinions, see *Osano v. Japan,* 37 Ko-Keishu 153 (Tokyo High Ct. 1st Crim. Div. Judgment of April 27, 1984), upholding *Japan v. Osano,* 13 Kei-Sai Geppo 577 (Tokyo Dist. Ct. 25th Crim. Div. Judgment of November 5, 1981) ("Osano-route." The indictment against Kodama was later dismissed because of the defendant's death); *Japan v. Hashimoto,* 39 Ko-Keishu 37 (Tokyo High Ct. 5th Crim. Div. Judgment of May 14, 1986), upholding *Japan v. Hashimoto,* 14 Kei-Sai Geppo 383 (Tokyo Dist. Ct. 12th Crim. Div. Judgment of January 26, 1982) ("Zennikku-route").
9. Former Prime Minister Tanaka had also filed an appeal with the Supreme Court, but the case against him was dismissed because of his death on December 16, 1993. The appeal by one of the former Marubeni officials had the same result, as did the appeals by Osano and Hashimoto in the other two routes. The appeal by Wakasa in the "Zennikku-route" had been rejected by the Supreme Court, 1436 Hanrei Jiho 3 (Sup. Ct. 3rd Petty Bench Judgment of September 18, 1992).
10. As a rare exception, the Commodity Exchange Act, before its elimination in 1954, had a provision that a person shall not be prosecuted or punished on the basis of the statement he is obliged to produce.
11. For a sampling of American cases concerning this facet of immunity, see *United States v. Quatermain,* Drax, 613 F.2d 38, 41 (3d Cir. 1980); *United States v. Winter,* 663 F.2d 1120, 1133 (1st Cir. 1981); *United States v. Anderson,* 778 F.2d 602, 606 (10th Cir. 1985); *United States v. Friedrick,* 842 F.2d 382, 393 n.14 (D.C.Cir. 1987); *United States v. Harvey,* 869 F.2d 1439, 1444 (11th Cir. 1989); *Surina v. Buckalew,* 629 P.2d 969, 979 (Alaska 1981); *Wright v. McAdory,* 536 So.2d 897, 902 (Miss. 1988). See also the US Department of Justice Manual 9-27.610 (1992).
12. Gesetz zur Änderung des Strafgesetzbuches, usw. und zur Einführung einer Kronzeugenregierung bei terroristischen Straftaten v. 9. 6. 1989 (BGBl. I. 1059), Art. 4 §1; Verbrechensbekämpfungsgesetz v. 28. 10. 1994 (BGBl. I. 3186), Art.5.
13. For instance, see *Doyle v. Hofstander,* 177 N.E. 489, 495 (N.Y. 1931); *Apodaka v. Viramontes,* 212 P.2d 425, 430 (NM 1949); *State v. Ashby,* 195 A.2d 635, 642 (N.J. 1963); *Bowie v. State,* 287 A.2d 782, 787 (Md.App. 1972); *Grand Jurors for Middlesex County for Year 1974 v. Wallace,* 343 N.E.2d 844, 845–6 (Mass. 1976); *Gipson v. State,* 375 So.2d 514, 515 (Ala. 1979); *Commonwealth v. Brown,* 619 S.W.2d 699, 701–2 (Ky. 1981); *State ex rel. Munn v. McKelvey,* 733 S.W.2d 765, 769 (Mo. 1987).

14. For the judges' statements, see *Osano v. Japan*, 1984, pp. 187–8; *Japan v. Hashimoto*, 1986, p. 52; *Tanaka v. Japan*, 1987, p. 122; *Japan v. Tanaka*, 1978, pp. 1524–5; *Japan v. Hashimoto*, 1979, pp. 1293–4.
15. For a sampling of American courts which have ruled on this issue of obligation, see *People v. Bogolowski*, 157 N.E.2d 181 (Ill. 1927); *State v. Hingle*, 139 So.2d 205, 210 (La. 1962); *State v. Ashby*, 1963, pp. 641–2; *People v. Brunner*, 108 Cal.Rptr. 501, 504–5 (1973). See also Note, 1974, pp. 338–40.
16. Article 35 of the Japanese Constitution provides,

    The right of all persons to be secure in their homes, papers and effects against entries, searches and seizures shall not be impaired except upon (separate) warrant issued (by a competent judicial officer) for adequate cause and particularly describing the place to be searched and things to be seized, or except (when an lawful arrest is made).

17. The October 1947 draft of the CCP, which was submitted to the Legal Section of the General Headquarters of the Allied Forces for review, specified a type of guilty plea procedure for noncapital cases. According to this provision, the trial court may find sufficient proof of guilt after determining that the defendant has pled guilty freely, with a full understanding of the charge, and that the plea is in conformity with the true facts in consideration of the other relevant materials.

    Supreme Court judgments holding that a defendant's open court confessions are not subject to the Constitution art. 38(3) *corpus delicti* requirement appeared to provide support for this provision. However, strong criticism of these Supreme Court judgments cast suspicion on the constitutionality of an arraignment system. See Dando (1948a, pp. 40–4), criticizing these Supreme Court judgments; Hirano (1958, pp. 232, 235 n. 2). In consideration of these arguments, the drafters finally decided to reject the system. They explicitly provided, in art. 319, that the accused shall not be convicted if his own confession, "whether made in open court or not," is the only proof against him (para. 2). The term "confession" includes "any admission of the accused which acknowledges himself to be guilty of the offense charged" (para. 3).
18. The Justice Ministry officials in charge of the CCP drafting gave similar reasons for rejecting the arraignment system (Nogi et al., 1948, pp. 156–7).
19. See also Atsumi (1994, p. 146), referring to an informal practice of the prosecutors to suspend the prosecution against those who have cooperated in breaking the case.
20. When the defendant has no objection, the public prosecutor may apply to a summary court judge for a summary order in a matter that comes within the jurisdiction of that court. The summary order states that the judge, after reviewing the documents and other evidence produced by the prosecutor, finds the defendant guilty, and shall impose a fine not exceeding 500,000 yen or a minor fine. The defendant does not appear in person before the judge. If the judge finds it improper to handle the case by a summary order, or if the defendant or the public prosecutor is not satisfied with the contents of the issued summary order and applies for formal trial, trial shall be conducted in the regular way (CCP, arts. 461–70).
21. *Homu-daijin Shimon* [The Matters Requested by Minister of Justice to the Council on Legislation for its Opinion] No. 42 of October 8, 1996, in

Kihonshiryoshu (1997, p. 145); *Soshikiteki na Hanzai ni Taishosuru tameno Keiji-ho Seibi Yoko Kosshi ni Kansuru Jimukyoku Sanko Shian* [Justice Ministry's Reference Draft for the Gist of the General Plan for the Organized Crime Legislation], in *Kihonshiryoshu* (1997, p. 148).

22. This statement was reported in *Asahi Shimbun,* November 26, 1997, p. 2.
23. See also Ugawa (1998, pp. 39–42), proposing to legitimate a more active use of prosecutorial discretion in exchange for the defendant's cooperation with criminal investigation and prosecution.

References

Alschuler, A.W. (1968) "The Prosecutor's Role in Plea Bargaining," *University of Chicago Law Review*, Vol. 36, p. 50.

—— (1979) "Plea Bargaining and Its History," *Law and Society Review*, Vol. 13, p. 211.

Atsumi, T. (1994) *Keijisosho ni okeru Jiyu to Seigi* [Liberty and Justice in Criminal Procedure] (Tokyo: Yuhikaku).

Bordenkircher v. Hayes, 434 US, 1978, 357.

Bradley, C.M. and J.L. Hoffmann (1996) "Public Perception, Justice, and the 'Search for Truth' in Criminal Cases," *Southern California Law Review*, Vol. 69, p. 1267.

Brady v. United States, 397 US, 1970, 742.

Brown v. Walker, 161 US, 1896, 591.

Casper, J.D. (1972) *American Criminal Justice* (Englewood Cliffs: Prentice-Hall).

Commonwealth v. Brady, 323 A.2d, 1974, 866.

The Courts Organization Act of 1947, §12.

Dando, S. (1948a) "Jihaku to Hokyo-shoko" [Confession and its Corroboration], *Horitsu Jiho*, Vol. 20, No. 4, p. 40.

—— (1948b) "Shin Keijisoshoho to Tojishashugi" [The New Code of Criminal Procedure and the Adversary System Principle], *Horitsu Jiho*, Vol. 20, No. 9, p. 1011.

—— (1965) *Japanese Criminal Procedure* (translated by B.J. George, Jr) (South Hackensack, NJ: Fred B. Rothman).

Doyle v. Hofstander, 177 NE, 1931, 489.

Enomoto v. Japan, 49 Keishu 1 (Sup. Ct. Grand Bench Judgment of February 22, 1995).

Finkelstein, M.O. (1975) "A Statistical Analysis of Guilty Plea Practices in the Federal Courts," *Harvard Law Review*, Vol. 89, p. 293.

Fujinaga, K. (1991) "Keiji-Menseki wo ataeteno Kyojutsu" [Statements Obtained in Exchange for Granting of Immunity], in S. Kawakami (ed.), *Keijisaiban Jitsumu Taikei*, Vol. XI (Tokyo: Seirin Shoin).

Heinz, A.M. and W.A. Kerstetter (1979) "Pretrial Settlement Conference," *Law and Society Review*, Vol. 13, p. 349.

Heumann, B.M. (1975) *Plea Bargaining* (Chicago: University of Chicago Press).

Hirano, R. (1958) *Keijisoshoho* [The Law of Criminal Procedure] (Tokyo: Yuhikaku).

Hogaku, Kyokai (ed.) (1953) *Chukai Nihonkoku Kenpo* [Commentaries on the Constitution of Japan], Vol. I (Tokyo: Yuhikaku).

Hotta, T. (1995) "Keiji-Menseki Seido wo fukumu Sosa no Kento wo" [Adoption of a Witness Immunity Procedure Should Be Considered in Criminal Investigation], *Asahi Shimbun*, March 4, p. 4.

Japan v. Fukumoto, 35 Keishu 426 (Sup. Ct. 2nd Petty Bench Judgment of June 26, 1981).

Japan v. Hashimoto, 32 Keishu 1672 (Sup. Ct. 1st. Petty Bench Judgment of September 7, 1978).

Japan v. Hashimoto, 11 Kei-Sai Geppo 1269 (Tokyo Dist. Ct. 12th Crim. Div. Decision of October 30, 1979) ("Zennikku-route").

Japan v. Hashimoto, 39 Ko-Keishu 37 (Tokyo High Ct. 5th Crim. Div. Judgment of May 14, 1986).

Japan v. Osano, 10 Kei-Sai Geppo 1256 (Tokyo Dist. Ct. 25th Crim. Div. Decision of September 21, 1978)("Osano- & Kodama-routes").

Japan v. Tanaka, 10 Kei-Sai Geppo 1514 (Tokyo Dist. Ct. 1st Crim. Div. Decision of December 20, 1978).

Japan v. Tanaka, 15 Kei-Sai Geppo 521 (Tokyo Dist. Ct. 1st Crim. Div. Judgment of October 12, 1983).

Johnson, D.T. (1996) "The Japanese Way of Justice: Prosecuting Crime in Japan", PhD dissertation submitted to the Graduate Division, University of California at Berkeley.

Kastiger v. United States, 406 US, 1972, 443.

Kihonshiryoshu: Soshikiteki Hanzai to Keijiho [Basic Materials on Organized Crime and the Criminal Law], (1997) Japanese Ministry of Justice, Criminal Legislation Section ed. (Tokyo: Yuhikaku).

Kleinknecht, T. and L. Meyer-Goßner (1995) *Strafprozeßordnung* (Kurzkommentar), 42nd edition. (Munich: C.H. Bech).

Kuh, R.H. (1975) "Plea Bargaining: Guidelines for the Manhattan District Attorney's Office," *Criminal Law Bulletin*, Vol. 11, p. 48.

LaFave, W.R. (1996) *Search and Seizure*, 3rd edn, Vol. I (St Paul: West).

LaFave, W.R. and J.H. Israel. (1984) *Criminal Procedure* (St Paul: West).

—— (1992) *Criminal Procedure*, 2nd edn. (St Paul: West).

"Marubeni no Koso-Kikyaku wo Motomeru Iken" [The Opinion of the Marubeni Defense for Dismissal of Indictment January 27, 1976], (1978) *Jurist*, No. 676, p. 197.

Matsumoto, I. (1984) "Sotsui Menjo" [Immunity from Prosecution], in Takada and Tamiya (eds), *Enshu Keijisoshoho* (Tokyo: Seirin Shoin).

Matsuo, K. (1972) "'Tojishashugi' ni tsuite" [On the Concept of 'Adversary System'], in *Keijisaiban no Kadai* (Tokyo: Yuhikaku).

Mitsui, M. (1980) "Shokutakujinmon to Lockheed Saiban" [The Entrusted Examination of the Witnesses and the Lockheed Decisions], Part II, *Jurist*, No. 721, p. 107.

Miyazawa, T. (1955) *Horitsugakutaikei Konmentaru: Nihonkoku Kenpo* [Systematic Commentaries on the Constitution of Japan] (Tokyo: Nihon Hyoronsha).

Nogi, S. et al. (1948) *Shin Keijisoshoho Gaisetsu* [Outline of the New Code of Criminal Procedure] (Tokyo: Tachibana Shobo).

Note (1974), "Judicial Supervision of Non-Statutory Immunity," *Journal of Criminal Law and Criminology*, Vol. 65, p. 334.

Osano v. Japan, 37 Ko-Keishu 153 (Tokyo High Ct. 1st Crim. Div. Judgment of April 27, 1984).

Powell v. Zuckert, 366 F.2d, 1966, 634.
Rhodes, W.M. (1979) "Plea Bargaining: Its Effect on Sentencing and Convictions in the District of Columbia," *Journal of Criminal Law and Criminology*, Vol. 70, p. 360.
Rubinstein, M.L. and T.J. White (1979) "Alaska's Ban on Plea Bargaining," *Law and Society Review*, Vol. 13, p. 367.
Sakamaki, T. (1999) "Keiji Menseki (Sotsui Menjo) Seido ni tsuite: Kyojutsu Kyosei Seido no Ripporonteki Kosatsu" [Comments on Legislative Adoption of Witness Immunity Procedure], *Jurist*, No. 1148, p. 245.
Sato, K. (1974) *Torihiki no Shakai* [Society of Bargaining] (Chuko Shinsho 379, Tokyo: Chuohkoron Sha).
"Shokutaku-Jinmon-Chosho ni kansuru Marubeni Bengodan Ikensho" [The Opinion of the Marubeni Defense on the Admissibility of the Depositions, February 22, 1978] (1978) *Jurist*, No. 676, p. 219.
State ex rel. Munn v. McKelvey, 733 S.W.2d, 1987, 765.
State v. Ashby, 195 A.2d, 1963, 635.
Stowe v. Devoy, 588 F.2d, 1978, 336.
Taguchi, M. (1998) "Rippo no Arikata to Keiji-Menseki, Shonin Hogo To" [Immunity and Witness Protection, and Basic Attitudes toward Organized Crime Legislation], *Keiho Zasshi*, Vol. 37, p. 188.
Tamiya, H. (1978) "Keiji Menseki ni tsuite" [On the Witness Immunity], *Jurist*, No. 676, p. 167.
—— (1982) *Keijisoshoho Nyumon* [Introduction to the Law of Criminal Procedure] (Tokyo: Yushindo).
—— (1991) "Keijisoho ni okeru Tojishashugi Ko" [An Analysis of the Concept of Adversary System], in *Keijiho no Shiso to Riron* (Tokyo: Daiichi Hok Shuppan).
Tanaka v. Japan, 40 Ko-Keishu 77 (Tokyo High Ct. 9th Crim. Div. Judgment of July 29, 1987).
Ugawa, H. (1998) "Shiho Torihiki wo Kangaeru" [Thinking about Bargaining of Justice], Part XVII, *Hanrei Jiho*, No. 1627, p. 36.
United States v. Salim, 855 F.2d, 1988, 944.
Wigmore, J.H. (1961) *Evidence in Trials at Common Law*, Vol. VIII (J.T. McNaughton rev.) (Boston: Little Brown).
Yamada, M. (1992) "Menseki ni yoru Shogen Kyosei" [Compulsory Testimony in Exchange for the Granting of Immunity], in K. Matsuo and M. Inouye (eds), *Keijisoshoho Hanrei Hyakusen*, 6th edn (Tokyo: Yuhikaku).
Yamakawa, Y. (1981) "Menseki ni yoru Shogen Kyosei" [Compelling Testimony by the Granting of Immunity], in R. Hirano et al. (eds), *Keijisoshoho Hanrei Taikei*, 4th edn (Tokyo: Yuhikaku).
Yokoyama, K. (1980) "Keiji Menseki" [Witness Immunity], *Keijisoshoho no Riron to Jitsumu, Bessatsu Hanrei Times* No. 7 (Tokyo: Hanrei Times Sha).

11
Critical Issues in the Lawmaking Policy of Japanese Criminal Procedure: the Wiretap Act and the Adversary System at the Pretrial Stage

Toshikuni Murai

In March of 1998, the Japanese government introduced three bills seeking to reform the criminal law and procedure with respect to the handling of organized crime. The first bill revised the Criminal Code to include offenses against money laundering. The second bill related to wiretaps as a means of investigation, and the third bill concerned witness protection.

On August 12, 1999, these three bills passed the Legislature. This chapter will focus on the second bill – wiretapping – in order to analyze Japanese policy-making in criminal procedure, with special focus on its relation to the adversary system.

Part I Debates on the constitutionality of wiretapping

Article 35 of the Japanese Constitution provides very strict limits on searches and seizures. In the light of this Article, a search and seizure will not be permitted without a separate "warrant issued for adequate cause and particularly describing the place to be searched and things to be seized." The warrant requirement under this Article is stricter than that of the Fourth Amendment to the United States Constitution. Under traditional American criminal procedure, "a search warrant will not issue upon an affidavit reciting only the anticipation of future offense. Rather, the allegations of a search warrant apply to conditions existing 'at the time of the issuance of the warrant'" (*US v. Roberts*, 1971, p. 787). However, recent cases have permitted anticipatory search warrants. In *US v. Ricciardelli* (1993, p. 10), the appellate court asserted that "probable cause doctrine does not require that the contraband to be seized must presently be located at the premises to be searched, only that there is probable cause to believe that a crime has been (or is being) committed and that evidence of it can likely be found at the described locus at the time of the search."

In Japan, similar arguments have been raised. Proponents of the Wiretapping Bill take the opinion that probable cause does not need to exist at the issuance of the warrant, but only at the time of the search. Opponents of the Wiretapping Bill contend that probable cause must exist when the warrant issued.

Professor Inouye, one of the main advocates of the bill, argues that Article 35 of the Japanese Constitution is based on the United States' Fourth Amendment (1997, p. 38). While I agree with this argument, it does not follow that we should interpret Article 35 in the same way as American courts have interpreted the Fourth Amendment. We can and should use the interpretation of the Fourth Amendment as an important reference tool for understanding Article 35.

First, to understand the original intent of the authors of Article 35, we must refer to the interpretation that was prevailing in the 1940s, when the Japanese Constitution was written. As I stated above, anticipatory search warrants were prohibited – even in the United States – until only recently. Hence the drafters of Article 35 would not have approved of anticipatory warrants in Japan.

Secondly, there is an important difference in structure between the Fourth Amendment and Article 35. The Fourth Amendment consists of two parts, "the first containing a general guarantee of freedom from 'unreasonable' searches, and the second specifying the conditions under which a warrant authorizing a search might be issued" (Landynski, 1966, pp. 42–3). The legislative history of this amendment indicates that this bifurcation was accidental; the founders did not attach any significant meaning to the division between the two clauses (Amar, 1991, pp. 1179–80). They viewed the two parts as making the same assertion: search and seizure without a warrant is unreasonable. Early courts had the same understanding as the founders, and they read the Fourth Amendment as a unitary pronouncement. But today, "it is clearly established that the first clause does provide some additional power" (LaFave, 1996, p. 4).

Japan's Article 35 differs in structure from the United States' Fourth Amendment in two key respects. Article 35 has just one clause requiring a warrant for any search and seizure, except for searches occurring incident to arrest. If taken literally, this statute does not permit any other kind of "reasonable" but warrantless search or seizure. Therefore, Japan's warrant requirement appears stricter than that of the United States.

Moreover, Article 35 requires "adequate cause" (*Seito na riyu*), rather than "probable cause," which the Fourth Amendment mandates. How different are these two terms? There are no evidentiary materials to explain why the legislators chose "adequate cause" instead of its American counterpart. But in Japan, we use the word *seito na* to express something right or fair; thus, it seems that the "cause" necessary for a Japanese search warrant must be not only quantitatively but qualitatively sufficient.

These structural differences require us to interpret more restrictively the warrant requirements of Article 35 than those of the Fourth Amendment. Given this, how should this strict standard affect our opinion concerning the constitutionality of wiretapping? The stricter the warrant requirement, the stronger the obstacle to permit anticipatory warrants, including wiretap warrants.

In issuing a wiretap warrant, the judge usually has to anticipate two events, future crime and future conversation – neither of which exists when he considers the warrant application. He must also foresee the connection between these two future events. This need to prophesize places too heavy a burden on the average judge; he does not have the skills or the foresight to predict the future from the past. Rather than being hindered by his inability, he will almost always grant an investigator's request for issuance of a warrant. In Japan, it is very rare for a judge to reject a request made by the police for a warrant, even under the present circumstances. For example, in 1996, only 0.8 percent of requests for search warrants were rejected! The rejection rate for wiretap warrants is certain to be even lower if evidence from the United States can be trusted. A recent report from the ACLU disclosed that only one wiretap request in the last eight years has been denied (1998).

Part II Assessment of the lawmaking policy in criminal procedure

The motivation to enact a law arises when people (1) recognize that some conflict exists between the current law (or its interpretation) and reality, and (2) believe that it is necessary to resolve this conflict.

Thus, in order to assess lawmaking policy, we must ask three distinct questions:

(a) whether the claimed conflicts between the current law (or its interpretation) and reality actually exist,
(b) if some conflicts do exist, whether it is appropiate to resolve them at all, and
(c) if it is appropriate to resolve these conflicts, is making a new law the best method for doing so?

Applying this framework to wiretap policy, I can only conclude that the Wiretapping Bill is bad law.

First, is there any evidence that some conflict exists between the current law and reality as they relate to the wiretaps? There is no provision in the current statutes to permit any kind of wiretap. On the contrary, Article 21 of the Japanese Constitution guarantees freedom of expression and unconditionally prohibits any violation of secrecy through any means of communication. Under a literal interpretation of these provisions, the Constitution prohibits any kind of wiretap. If the government wishes to implement a wiretap policy, the most orthodox method by which to do so involves revising the Constitution. However, constitutional amendments have proven unnecessary, as the Japanese Supreme Court has stated that the freedom of expression may be subject to restrictions based on the public welfare.[1]

Because the Code of Criminal Procedure (CCP) does not specifically authorize wiretapping as a form of inspection, certain scholars have argued that wiretapping violates Article 197 of the CCP, which prohibits the use of any measures except those contained in the CCP (see e.g. Hirano, 1958, p. 113). If the government agreed with the position taken by those scholars, Japan would need a new law to regulate wiretapping. However, in certain drug cases the courts have permitted wiretaps under existing law (see e.g. *Kofu* case, 1992; *Asahikawa* case, 1997). Given the courts' interpretation of the relevant law, there seems to be no conflict between the current laws (or cases) and reality.

However, if we look below the surface, we can find some serious conflicts between the current laws and the wiretapping practices of the police. In the *Kanagawa* case, the police illegally wiretapped the home telephone of a politician. They had no warrant and did not suspect him of any particular crimes. They implemented the wiretap just to collect some information on the political party to which he belonged. Although the prosecutor later admitted that the wiretaps were illegal, the government did not prosecute the police officers who had participated in the wiretapping. Even after the Kensatsu Shinsakai (the Committee for the Inquest of Prosecution) declared the prosecutor's decision inappropriate, the prosecutor did not bring charges against the police officers. This type of "benevolent paternalism" characterizes Japanese criminal justice (see Foote, Chapter 3, this volume).

Moreover, we can find many kinds of instruments for eavesdropping sold in stores, and the media often report news of illegal wiretapping. We do not have any effective measures – legal or otherwise – to combat such practices.

By considering real-world practices of the police, we find a significant conflict between law and reality. The *Kanagawa* case demonstrates wiretap practices prevailing in the real world. This kind of conflict has caused a serious violation of fundamental rights. To resolve this conflict, we need to have an effective tool for stopping illegal wiretapping.

The Wiretapping Bill which was passed by the Diet is not, however, a tool for *restricting* wiretaps. Instead it aims to *extend* wiretap practice far beyond that which is currently authorized by the courts. The bill gives the police power to intercept not only telephone communications but also e-mail and fax communications. It also allows police officers to request warrants for future crimes and to intercept communications relating to crimes other than those specified in the warrant.

Government officials claim that organized crime is causing serious problems in Japan and that the law enforcement officers should have new powers, including electronic surveillance, to fight this type of crime. Let us suppose that international public opinion regarding organized crime justifies the government's belief in its need for the Wiretap Bill. But why should we increase the power of the police at the price of a free society? I am afraid that the criminal justice system in Japan will lose its balance. The standpoint of the defense is very unstable in Japan. The bill will weaken it further.

The current criminal justice system in Japan provides wide discretion to the investigative authorities; as a result, there is considerable potential for intrusion on personal autonomy, as Prof. Daniel H. Foote emphasizes (Chapter 3, this volume).[2] The Wiretap Bill allows the police to collect private information from a suspect's home or office without giving him or her any previous warning. I do not think that a system which intrudes upon personal autonomy in this way can be adversarial.

Part III Conclusion

Traditionally, Japanese scholars have understood that the prevention of future crimes belongs to the "Gyosei Keisatsu" (administrative police), while the investigation of actual crimes belongs to the "Shiho Keisatsu" (judiciary police). If the judiciary police can get wiretaps based on predictions about future crimes, this boundary will blur and may cease to exist altogether.

Should we eliminate the distinction between the administrative and the judiciary functions of the police? I do not think so. In the United States, wiretap practice has allowed the police to move from the investigation of "an unknown criminal for a known crime" to the investigation of "an unknown crime from a known criminal." Given that such an expansion of police power is not traditional, even in American society, why should the Japanese people follow this lead?

In conclusion, I believe it is urgent that we Japanese design a law to prevent wiretaps in Japanese society. Such a law would help to restore the balance of power between suspects and police in our society.

Notes

1. Judgment of March 13, 1975, Saikosai [Supreme Court], 117.
2. The Japanese criminal justice system does not have a *Miranda*-type rule. At trial, an indigent defendant has the right to request assistance of appointed counsel. But the accused has no right to have defense counsel assigned before prosecution begins. In the 1990s, the Japan Federation of Bar Associations implemented a "duty attorney" scheme which provides free assistance of counsel for the first interview. But this program exists without any financial support from the state.

   Additionally, in Japan the accused cannot seek bail before prosecution. He or she can be detained without bail for a maximum of 23 days before prosecution. During this period, he or she is likely to be put into a police cell (Daiyo-Kangoku or substitute prison) and subject to exhaustive interrogation. Although some suspects request the presence of counsel for their interrogations, such requests are routinely denied.

References

ACLU Special Report (1998) "Big Brother in the Wires: Wiretapping in the Digital Age," Freedom Network, http://www.aclu.org/issues/cyber/wiretap_brother.html,1998 March 3, 1998.

Amar, A.R. (1991) "The Bill of Rights as a Constitution," *Yale Law Journal*, Vol. 100, p. 1131.

Asahikawa case, Judgment of May 15, 1997, Sapporo Kosai [High Court], 962 Hanrei Times 275.

Hirano, Ryuichi (1958) *Keijisoshoho* [Criminal Procedure] (Tokyo: Chikuma-Shobo).
Inouye, Masahito (1997) *Sosa-Shudan toshiteno Tsushin/Kaiwa no Boju* [Interception of Communication for the Investigation] (Tokyo: Yuhikau).
Kofu case, Judgment of October 15, 1992, Tokyo Kosai [High Court], 1443 Hanreijiho 154.
LaFave, W.R. (1996) *Search and Seizure: a Treatise on the Fourth Amendment*, 3rd edn (St Paul, Minn.: West Publishing).
Landynski, J. (1966) *Search and Seizure and the Supreme Court*, quoted in W.R. LaFave, *Search and Seizure: a Treatise on the Fourth Amendment*, 3rd edn (St Paul, Minn.: West Publishing, 1996).
US v. Ricciardelli (1993), 998 F.2d 8.
US v. Roberts (1971), 333 F.Supp. 786.

12

Miranda, Confessions, and Justice: Lessons for Japan?

Richard A. Leo

Part I Introduction

The interrogation of criminal suspects is universally regarded as one of the primary methods of solving crimes in all modern, democratic societies. This reliance on interrogation stems from a variety of sources: (1) the reflexive faith we (criminal justice officials, triers of fact, the public) place in confession statements; (2) the actual probative value of confession evidence (most confessions are capable of self-verification); and, in some societies, (3) the moral significance attached to the act of confessing itself. To almost everyone, it seems that confessions are inherently more reliable and more valuable than virtually any other type of evidence against a criminal offender – save, perhaps, a videotape capturing the suspect in the act. Some premodern societies (in which videotape technology did not exist) elevated confessions so far above other, competing forms of evidence that they came to be known as the "queen of proof;" when necessary, confessions were officially elicited by torture (Langbein, 1977). Although the routine use of torture to extract incriminating statements is no longer routine in most democratic societies (but see Cohen and Golan, 1991, 1992), the high status accorded to confession evidence remains.

While there may exist near universal agreement about the evidentiary importance of confessions, there are vast differences of opinion, both within and between societies, about how confessions should be legally regulated. In this chapter, I will evaluate how confessions have been legally regulated in one society (America) to draw lessons about how they may be regulated in another (Japan). In particular, I will address the following questions: To what extent would American *Miranda*-like warnings be feasible in Japan as a way of enforcing the constitutional privilege against self-incrimination? If implemented in Japan, would *Miranda*-like warnings be likely to succeed or fail? If *Miranda*-like warnings are neither likely to be implemented, nor likely to succeed if implemented, are there other policy reforms that might improve the quality of interrogation and confession in Japan and thus address the concerns raised by some Japanese defense attorneys and human rights activists? (see Takano, Chapter 8, this volume; Igarishi, 1984).

To answer these questions, I will first review the impact of the four-fold *Miranda* warnings on the ideology and practices of American police interrogators in the last third of the twentieth century. In light of what is known about *Miranda* in America, as well as the cultural and legal landscape of police interrogation and confessions in Japan, I will then analyze the feasibility of implementing *Miranda*-like warnings in Japan. And, finally, I will analyze the potential role of mandatory videotaping in improving both the quality of police interrogations and the reliability of confessions in Japan.

Part II Miranda in America: the first 33 years

Introduction

The United States Supreme Court sent shock waves through the legal community when it decided *Miranda v. Arizona* in 1966. The stated purpose of *Miranda* was to dispel the compulsion that the Supreme Court believed to be inherent in the police-dominated atmosphere of custodial questioning, and thus to empower the suspect to exercise his Fifth Amendment privilege against self-incrimination inside the interrogation room. To this end, the Supreme Court in *Miranda* required (1) that police warn every suspect of his or her constitutional rights to silence and counsel, as well as of the possible consequences of failing to exercise these rights, before commencing any custodial interrogation; and (2) that the state bear the burden of demonstrating that the suspect "voluntarily, knowingly and intelligently" waived these rights. If police failed to meet this burden, the suspect's statements would be excluded from evidence at trial (*Miranda v. Arizona*, 1966).

American police responded to the *Miranda* decision by creating a standard, printed admonition form from which they typically read the following *Miranda* warnings to a custodial suspect:

(a) You have the right to remain silent;
(b) Anything you say can and will be used against you in a court of law;

(c) You have the right to an attorney; and
(d) If you cannot afford an attorney, one will be appointed for you at no charge.

In some police departments, interrogators then ask the suspect one or both of the following two questions:

- Do you understand each of these rights that I have read to you?
- Having these rights in mind, do you wish to speak to me at this time?

The *Miranda* decision generated immediate political controversy. On the one side, police, prosecutors, newspaper editorials, and politicians loudly complained that the new *Miranda* requirements would "handcuff the police," and thus, for all practical purposes, put an end to valuable confessions from criminal suspects. This rhetoric suggested that *Miranda* would prevent police from solving a large percentage of their crimes, which would in turn prevent prosecutors from convicting, and prisons from incarcerating, a large percentage of violent criminals. *Miranda* thus would raise crime rates while demoralizing law enforcement and placing innocent lives in jeopardy. So intense was the moral panic precipitated by *Miranda* that, in 1968, Republican presidential candidates Richard Nixon and George Wallace used *Miranda* against Democratic presidential candidate Hubert Humphrey, who failed to defend either *Miranda* or the liberal Warren Court. Meanwhile, Congress attempted to invalidate legislatively *Miranda*'s presumption of coercion and rule of automatic suppression in the absence of a valid set of warnings or waiver (Baker, 1983; Graham, 1970; Leo and Thomas, 1998).

On the other side, some liberals, civil libertarians, and academic commentators also complained loudly that *Miranda*, by failing to mandate the presence of counsel prior to any custodial questioning, did not go far enough. Specifically, they charged that *Miranda* failed to empower custodial suspects to exercise their privilege against self-incrimination or to protect such suspects from coercive interrogation practices. In truth, *Miranda* represented something of an awkward compromise, a Supreme Court decision that read more like a legislative statute than a typical appellate court opinion and that, despite its high-minded intentions, seemed to leave virtually no one happy. Yet *Miranda* also represented the Supreme Court's attempt to balance the imperatives of crime control and due process in the interrogation room at a time in American history when the "third degree" practices of an earlier era remained a vivid memory, crime was steadily rising, and a counterculture challenging institutional authority and protesting societal inequalities had emerged (Caplan, 1984, 1985).

The early post-*Miranda* impact studies (1966–73)

Perhaps in response to the political controversy it generated, *Miranda* spawned a flurry of academic studies designed to measure the required warning and waiver regimen's impact on actual police interrogation practices, the confession rate, and the conviction rate. Undertaken within three years, and published within eight years of the *Miranda* decision itself, the dozen or so empirical impact studies appeared to put to rest the fear that *Miranda* was handcuffing the police, prosecutors, or the courts in their apprehension, conviction, or incarceration of violent criminals. Although each of the studies was limited to one geographical location, and most were methodologically flawed, this first generation of *Miranda* impact researchers arrived at a rough consensus, which would later be referred to as the "conventional wisdom" on *Miranda*'s real-world effects.

In short, these studies revealed that:

1. After an initial adjustment period, American police appeared to comply with the letter, but not necessarily the spirit, of the new *Miranda* requirements;
2. Despite these standard warnings, most criminal suspects routinely waived their constitutional rights and chose to speak to detectives;
3. The *Miranda* rules only marginally affected the ability of police to successfully elicit incriminating statements, admissions, and confessions from criminal suspects;
4. Once a waiver of rights had been obtained, the interrogation tactics and techniques did not appear to change as a result of *Miranda*;
5. Suspects continued to provide detectives with confessions and incriminating statements, though in some instances at a lower rate than prior to *Miranda*;
6. The clearance and conviction rate did not appear to be significantly affected by the *Miranda* requirements, though in some instances it too dropped; and
7. *Miranda* did not appear to undermine the effectiveness of criminal investigation in the way that the law enforcement community had initially feared.

The impact of *Miranda* today

For more than two decades after the first generation of *Miranda* impact studies, the conventional wisdom – that police, for the most part, complied with the letter of the *Miranda* ruling and that confession and conviction rates remained largely unaffected by the decision's code-like warning and waiver requirements – remained unchallenged, indeed unstudied. In the 1990s researchers began, once again, to empirically evaluate *Miranda*'s effects in the real world. No general consensus has yet emerged from this second generation of empirical studies about various aspects of *Miranda*'s influence on police practices and suspects' behavior, and researchers agree that more research is necessary to better understand *Miranda*'s ongoing impact (Thomas, 1996a). A few findings, however, are worth mentioning here. My own empirical study of nearly 200 interrogations in northern California revealed that police regularly complied with the *Miranda* warning and waiver regimen, that a majority of criminal suspects waived their *Miranda* rights, that most suspects were questioned for a relatively short period of time (92 percent of interrogations lasted less than two hours), and that a majority of those suspects (64 percent of the total sample, 76 percent of those who waived their rights) provided their interrogators with incriminating statements, admissions, or full confessions (Leo, 1996a, b). Cassell and Hayman (1996) also found that the vast majority of interrogated suspects waived their *Miranda* rights, that most interrogations did not last long, and that a sizeable percentage of suspects provided incriminating statements, admissions, or full confessions (see also Thomas, 1996b).

Cassell and his coauthors have argued, however, that *Miranda* has significantly harmed law enforcement by annually causing tens of thousands of guilty suspects (who presumably would otherwise have confessed to police and been convicted) to invoke *Miranda*, terminate interrogation, and go free. Cassell and his coauthors base this argument on a reassessement of the first generation of *Miranda* impact studies (Cassell, 1996), a study of screening sessions at the Salt Lake County, Utah District Attorney's Office during six weeks in 1994 (Cassell and Hayman, 1996), and an analysis of clearance rates from 1950 to 1995 (Cassell and Fowles, 1998). Cassell has breathed new life into the old (and largely discredited) argument that *Miranda* has handcuffed police and prosecutors' ability to apprehend, prosecute, convict, and incarcerate numerous guilty criminals. But he has also argued that *Miranda* endangers innumerable *innocent* suspects by preventing the police from obtaining confessions from truly guilty suspects who would exonerate innocents who have been wrongfully convicted (Cassell, 1998).

Cassell and his coauthors' views have not been accepted by the community of social scientists and legal scholars who have studied *Miranda*'s effects in the real world. Instead, Cassell and his coauthors have been repeatedly criticized for characterizing and interpreting data in a partisan manner, drawing unwarranted inferences, treating elaborate speculation as established fact, and overstating the evidence of *Miranda*'s harm (Schulhofer, 1996a, b, 1997; Thomas, 1996b, c; Leo and Ofshe, 1998; Donahue, 1998; Weisselberg, 1998; Leo and White, 1999). As Professor Stephen Schulhofer has written,

> at critical points in [Cassell's] analysis, data are cited selectively, sources are quoted out of context, weak studies showing negative impacts are uncritically accepted, and small methodological problems are invoked to discredit a no-harm conclusion when the same difficulties are present – even to a greater extent – in the negative-impact studies that Cassell chooses to feature. (Schulhofer, 1996a, p. 502)

Schulhofer goes on to describe Cassell's quantitative estimates of *Miranda*'s costs as "simply rhetoric" and "not a serious foundation for assessing social policy" (Schulhofer, 1996a, p. 546). While his arguments about *Miranda*'s harms to police and prosecutors lack adequate empirical support, Cassell has raised important and provocative questions that, all scholars agree, can only be resolved by more and better empirical research.

While there is not yet any conclusive research demonstrating that *Miranda* has had an adverse impact on the ability of law enforcement to apprehend, prosecute, and convict criminals, recent research has demonstrated how contemporary interrogators negotiate *Miranda* – that is, how they continue to interrogate effectively despite the possibility that suspects may invoke either the right to counsel or the right to silence. In the last one-third of a century, American interrogators have creatively adapted to *Miranda* by using a number of strategies to, in essence, outsmart suspects and creatively evade the spirit, if not the letter, of the law. Sometimes detectives recast the interrogation as merely "an interview" – by telling the suspect that he is not under arrest and free to leave at any time – thereby avoiding the necessity of issuing *Miranda* warnings at all (Leo, 1992). Sometimes interrogators attempt to downplay and to trivialize the *Miranda* warnings, treating them as a bureaucratic formality to which the natural response is a waiver (Leo, 1996b; Leo and White, forthcoming). Sometimes interrogators seek actively to persuade the suspect that he will obtain a material benefit and/or avoid a material harm *only* if he first waives his *Miranda* rights and speaks to police (Simon, 1991; Leo, 1996b; Leo and White, 1999). And sometimes

American detectives question "outside *Miranda*" – that is, they continue to interrogate a suspect who has invoked his *Miranda* right to silence and/or counsel by telling the suspect, falsely, that nothing he says after an invocation can be used against him in court. Although any resulting statements cannot be used against the defendant in the prosecution's case-in-chief, they can be used to impeach the suspect's testimony at trial if he takes the stand. Such statements, although taken in violation of *Miranda*, may also be used by police and prosecutors to uncover other witnesses and other evidence against the suspect (Weisselberg, 1998; Leo and White, 1999).

Part III *Miranda* in Japan?

Would a *Miranda*-like warning and waiver regime be feasible or desirable in Japan? To answer this question, I will briefly review the law, culture, and the practice of interrogation in Japan. I will argue that even if *Miranda*-like requirements were implemented in Japan, they would not be likely to change the behavior of suspects under interrogation, police methods of questioning, or, more generally, the cultural significance of confession in Japan. If the American experience teaches us anything, it is that police interrogators will creatively adapt to *Miranda*, that most suspects will waive their *Miranda* rights in any event, and that police and prosecutors will continue to successfully obtain confessions and convictions (most likely at similar rates) in spite of a *Miranda*-like system. Instead of advocating for the symbolically meaningful, but practically meaningless, *Miranda* warnings, Japanese defense attorneys and human rights activists should push for the mandatory videotaping of all custodial interrogations – a nonadversarial policy reform that would benefit everyone (including Japanese police and prosecutors) committed to the pursuit of truth and fairness in the Japanese criminal justice system.

The law of interrogation and confession in Japan

The textual provisions of the Japanese Constitution and Criminal Code regulating interrogation appear to be similar to many of those found in the American criminal justice system. Like the American system, the Japanese system provides for both a formal privilege against self-incrimination and a right to counsel. Like the American system, a suspect under custodial interrogation in the Japanese system must be informed of his right to remain silent and his right to designate an attorney. And like the American system, the Japanese criminal justice system prohibits the use of torture during interrogation. The penalty for violating the law in Japan, as in America, is the exclusion of the confession at trial (Foote, 1992).

However, here the formal similarity between the two system ends. Unlike the American system, the Japanese suspect under interrogation has no right to terminate police questioning (even if he asserts his right to silence) and no right to leave the interrogation room. He thus remains, in effect, under a duty to endure questioning. Moreover, indigent suspects do not have the right to choose free counsel until prosecution is instituted, and even if the suspect is not indigent (and thus can designate private counsel prior to indictment), defense attorneys are not permitted to attend interrogation sessions. The suspect's right to counsel does not attach until after indictment. In addition, the Criminal Code allows prosecutors to impose conditions (time, duration, and place) on meetings between the suspect and counsel during preindictment detention. Typically, Japanese prosecutors only permit the suspect to confer with counsel very briefly during preindictment detention, if at all. In short, the Japanese suspect may not refuse interrogation, may not leave the interrogation room, and may not have counsel present during interrogation (Foote, 1991, 1992; Suess, 1996; DeSombre, 1995).

Perhaps even more significantly, when police have probable cause and choose to arrest a suspect, they may interrogate the suspect, incommunicado and continuously, for up to 23 days in "substitute prisons" (i.e. the holding cells of police stations). This is possible because the law permits police to hold a suspect for up to 48 hours before releasing him or turning him over to the public prosecutor's office, which may hold the suspect for an additional 24 hours before taking any action. At the end of this 24-hour period, the prosecutor may request that a judge authorize detention for ten days. At the end of this ten-day period of detention, prosecutors may request that the judge authorize detention for another ten days, after which the prosecutors must either file an indictment or release the suspect. In the vast majority of cases, prosecutors apply for detention – and the judges routinely grant such requests – in order to obtain detailed confessions and derivative physical evidence against the suspect. Remarkably, the law permits police and prosecutors to detain suspects in substitute prisons and interrogate them incommunicado for 23 days *per count*! Thus, if Japanese interrogators should desire even more time for extensive, incommunicado interrogation, they merely need to arrest the suspect on other minor crimes, after which they can seek to renew the period of detention for another 23 days at a time (Foote, 1992).

In practice, then, the privilege against self-incrimination, the right to silence, and the right to counsel are meaningless for the suspect who must endure interrogation in Japan. As Daniel Foote (1991, p. 436) indicates,

> [F]ew people, innocent or not, have the fortitude to resist 23 days of interrogation. . . . Even if the suspect asserts the right to silence, it will not terminate the questioning; no matter how many times a suspect asserts that right nor how long he or she maintains absolute silence, the investigators may continue to talk to the suspect and address questions to him or her throughout the period of detention until the suspect gives in and begins to talk.

In addition, suspects who are broken and confess – and the overwhelming majority do – are not allowed to write their own confessions, but instead must sign summarized (and sometimes disputed) confession statements prepared by detectives. These summarized accounts – which are not verbatim accounts of the confession itself but the detectives' reconstructions – may be prepared long after the interrogation sessions have concluded (Foote, 1992).

The exclusionary rule – the rule whose purpose is to deter police misconduct by excluding improperly obtained evidence from use at trial proceedings against the accused – also operates as a weak control on police behavior during interrogation. In Japan, judges rarely suppress a confession, especially if it would appear to result in a guilty suspect going free, no matter how serious the allegations of abuse during interrogation. As Suess (1996, p. 318) further notes: "[W]hen the contents of the confession comport with other evidence and are accurate, interrogation questioning is not called into question. And even when a confession itself is thrown out, other evidence obtained as a result of that confession will remain admissible and support a conviction."

The law in action

With such weak controls on police investigative behavior, it should not be surprising that, in practice, Japanese interrogation appears to be routinely psychologically coercive. As we have seen, lengthy, incommunicado interrogation is permissible and common. In addition, Japanese police appear routinely to apply significant psychological pressure on suspects to confess, including promises of leniency and threats of greater punishment. As one detective told Miyazawa (1992, p. 161): "There aren't any confessions that are really voluntary. They're told that if they don't talk, they won't eat, won't smoke, won't meet with their families." These psychologically coercive techniques are, nevertheless, typically regarded as permissible by the Japanese courts.

The routine and extensive use of psychological coercion during interrogation is also due to the enormous significance attributed to confession in the Japanese criminal justice system. Japanese police believe a confession is necessary to successfully establish a case against the suspect (the suspect's motive as well as the facts of the crime), to receive an indictment and, ultimately, to obtain a conviction. Because Japanese police believe they will not be able to solve crimes without confessions, they regard confessions as superior to all other forms of evidence. As a result, Japanese police consider obtaining a full confession as one of their main functions, and, in the Japanese police culture of detecting, the inability to gain a confession is seen as a mark of failure. Perhaps not surprisingly, then, a full "90 percent of Japanese cases involve full confessions, and in most of the remainder the defendant confesses to all but certain elements of the crime" (Foote, 1992, p. 337). Largely as a result of the high confession rate, the Japanese criminal justice system, a prosecutor's paradise, boasts of a 99.8 percent conviction rate (Foote, 1992, p. 318; see also Johnson, 1996).

As with police, so too with Japanese prosecutors. Japanese prosecutors virtually demand confessions from custodial suspects. Also regarded by prosecutors as superior to all other forms of evidence, confessions are typically the heart of the state's case against the accused at trial. The value of confessions in Japan, however, is not merely evidentiary, but also rehabilitative – confession is seen as necessary to the acceptance of responsibility, moral catharsis, and reformation, a crucially important value in Japanese society (Haley, 1998). Because of this heavy reliance on confessions, both Japanese police and prosecutors are under considerable pressure to extract confessions once they believe a suspect to be guilty. As mentioned above, Japanese courts – typically concerned more with the reliability than with the voluntariness of the confession – rarely suppress a confession (no matter how psychologically coercive it appears to have been) if they believe the suspect to be guilty, and, moreover, explicitly grant more lenient sentences – sometimes suspended sentences – only to those suspects who have confessed and expressed a desire to reform (Foote, 1991, 1992; Suess, 1996; DeSombre, 1995).

The importance that police, prosecutors, and courts attribute to confessions reflects the values of Japanese society more generally. In Japanese society, as in the Japanese criminal justice system, an accused suspect is widely presumed guilty, and it is expected that he will confess, explain his misdeeds, and repent. The presumption of guilt in Japanese society is thus wed to a moral imperative to confess. This moral imperative reflects not only the pragmatic evidentiary value of confession evidence and the cultural norm that confession is necessary for moral catharsis and reform, but also a sense of deference to established authority. The Japanese culture of benevolent paternalism – which vests great trust and discretion in its police and prosecutors – emphasizes the necessity for such deference, as well as the necessity of confession, for the moral rehabilitation of the offender (Foote, 1992).

Would *Miranda* be feasible in Japan?

Given the expectations, discretion, and current practices of Japanese police and prosecutors, it is hard to imagine how a *Miranda*-like warning and waiver regime could possibly succeed in Japan – if by "success" we mean, as in the American context, that such warnings would dispel the inherent coercion of police-dominated interrogation, level the playing field between the interrogator and suspect, and empower the informed suspect to terminate interrogation by asserting his constitutional right to silence and/or counsel. In Japan, such lofty ideals could be accomplished only if other rules of criminal procedure – such as the duty to submit to questioning or the laws permitting police to interrogate a suspect incommunicado for 23 days – were changed as well. This seems unlikely. *Miranda*-like warnings, by themselves, would hardly dispel the heavy psychological coercion inherent in contemporary Japanese interrogation practices.

To succeed in Japan, *Miranda*-like warnings would also have to transform the entire culture of Japanese detecting, so much so that Japanese interrogators would have to be induced or compelled to read suspects their rights, to permit suspects to invoke them, and, when invoked, to terminate the interrogation. This new approach would have to take place despite the high (evidentiary and rehabilitative) value Japanese police and prosecutors place on confession evidence and despite the fact that Japanese police detectives regard the failure to obtain a confession as an impermissible mark of failure (Miyazawa, 1992). As with a change in the law of interrogation, a change in the Japanese police culture also seems plainly unrealistic.

Instead, even if *Miranda*-like warnings were implemented in Japan, it is likely that police and prosecutors would creatively adapt to them without lessening their ability to successfully coerce confessions. Learning from the American experience, perhaps Japanese interrogators would recast interrogations as interviews and thus obviate the legal necessity of issuing any warnings. Or perhaps they would treat the warnings in a perfunctory manner, signaling to the suspect that the warnings are a mere bureaucratic triviality for whom automatic waiver should be a foregone conclusion. Or perhaps interrogators would read the warnings to suspects in good faith but simply ignore any invocation (should any suspects actually invoke their *Miranda* rights) and claim otherwise in courtroom "swearing contests" that they are sure to win. Or perhaps interrogators would question outside *Miranda* and simply use the fruits of otherwise inadmissible confessions to inculpate the defendant.

And even if Japanese interrogators defied these predictions and followed both the letter and the spirit of a *Miranda*-like warnings and waiver regime, it is hard to imagine that prosecutors and judges would suddenly change their orientation to interrogation and confession. Prosecutors and courts are unlikely to honor a suspect's claims when he has confessed but alleged that the *Miranda* warnings were improperly read, not read at all, or simply not waived. Instead, Japanese prosecutors, like their American counterparts, would likely use *Miranda* to their advantage – by claiming it as a symbol of police professionalism, by insisting that the police are always telling the truth in every "swearing contest," and by using the fact of a *Miranda* waiver as evidence of a confession's voluntariness, even though the two lines of legal inquiry are largely separate. So too would Japanese judges, like their generally conservative American counterparts, almost certainly presume the voluntariness of virtually every *Miranda* waiver and then treat the entirety of post-*Miranda* interrogation as voluntary because the suspect initialled the preprinted *Miranda* waiver form. If the confession appeared to be unreliable on its face, the judge would likely suppress it (if at all) on voluntariness, not *Miranda*-violation, grounds. As Wayne Westling and Vicky Waye (1998, p. 504) have written in another context,"the cautioning of suspects may strengthen the chimera of voluntary collaboration between interrogator and suspect."

But such speculation is nearly futile, for even if the rules of criminal procedure, the culture of Japanese policing, and the crime control orientation of Japanese prosecutors and judges could somehow be changed – itself a conjunction of events with a lower probability than elephants suddenly mutating wings and learning to fly – the rest of Japanese culture would have to change too. Given the degree to which the Japanese expect and value confession and redemption, it is hard to imagine that the Japanese media and public would go for American-invented constitutional rights that quite clearly allow the criminally accused to impede the pursuit of truth in the legal process. For in the benevolently paternalistic Japanese criminal justice system, unlike in America, confessions are regarded as serving the interest of not only the state, but also the accused. The blocking of confessions, via *Miranda*-like warnings, would be perceived not only to impede the pursuit of truth in Japanese criminal justice, but also to prevent some defendants from taking moral responsibility for their offenses, and thus from repenting and reintegrating into society (Foote, 1992).

The glaringly obvious fact missed by *Miranda* advocates in Japan is that a *Miranda*-like warning and waiver regime can only "succeed" in a truly adversarial criminal justice system and culture. Despite the Western influence on the Japanese Criminal Code and Constitution, the Japanese criminal justice system is not adversarial, and the adoption of *Miranda*-like warnings will not make it any more adversarial. If I am correct, Japanese defense attorneys and human rights activists who wish to improve the quality of criminal justice in Japan – by reducing the coerciveness of Japanese police interrogation as well as the number of false confessions and miscarriages of justice – might look to other, nonadversarial policy reforms to accomplish their goals.

Videotaping interrogations

The goals of Japanese defense attorneys and human rights activists – as well as those of Japanese police and prosecutors who are committed to eliciting truthful confessions through fair interrogation procedures – could be served by a requirement that all custodial interrogations be audio- or videotaped in their entirety. The mandatory requirement of tape recording is a nonadversarial policy reform that, unlike the creation or restriction of constitutional rights, does not structurally alter the balance of advantage between the prosecution and the defense. In other words, videotapes are not biased in favor of either the state or the accused. Instead, they are merely a medium for preserving the truth of the interrogation and any resulting confessions – the centerpiece of most criminal cases in Japan – so that *all* criminal justice officials can more readily ascertain what exactly occurred inside the interrogation room.

Videotaping creates an objective, comprehensive, and reviewable record of what transpired during questioning, from which all parties – suspects, police, prosecutors, judges, the public – can make accurate and informed decisions about the interrogation process and the resulting confessions (see Geller, 1992; Leo, 1996b; Westling and Waye, 1998). Tape recording would thus render the process of interrogation in Japan visible, without intruding on the prerogative of interrogators to question suspects, without lessening the willingness of suspects to speak to police, and without undermining any rights currently accorded to suspects. Rendering visible (the currently invisible) process of interrogation in Japan would factually resolve any "swearing contests" between the accused and the detectives, would protect police detectives and suspects from any false allegations made by the other, would facilitate more effective and more efficient case processing, and would lend greater professionalism and legitimacy to the Japanese criminal justice system. The tape recording of interrogations is thus in all parties' self-interest.

Tape recording benefits police detectives for a number of reasons. First and foremost, it protects them against false accusations of impropriety, misconduct, or abuse by creating a record that can demonstrate when such allegations are false. The videotaping of interrogations would thus likely reduce the number of false allegations made against police, and make such allegations more easy to resolve. Second, without intruding on detectives' ability to question suspects, videotaping would improve the quality of interrogation and criminal investigation. Videotaping would allow interrogators to compare a suspect's present account to earlier statements, thereby improving their ability to spot inconsistencies. It would allow detectives to play an accomplice's taped confession for an uncooperative suspect. It would allow detectives to use videotaped admissions against coconspirators more effectively than written statements. It would allow other detectives to monitor the questioning from outside the interrogation room and to feed in strategic suggestions via a closed circuit monitor. It would allow police departments to use videotapes as training materials to educate interrogators about which methods and strategies are most effective (Geller, 1992). And it would offer police management a tool with which to rein in detectives who may be exercising their discretion inappropriately. Third, tape recording would save police departments time and money by allowing interrogators to question suspects with fewer distractions, by obviating the need for a second interrogator to be present to take notes, and by reducing the amount of time interrogators spend testifying about the interrogation in court. Fourth, videotaping interrogations, by leading to greater openness and fewer allegations of misconduct, would promote greater respect for police procedures and police professionalism.

The mandatory videorecording of all interrogations would also benefit Japanese prosecutors and judges. Videotaping permits both prosecutors and the courts to evaluate the voluntariness and the veracity of a confession with far greater accuracy than when the court is left merely with the conflicting testimony of a suspect and his interrogators. By providing a more reliable and accurate fact-finding record, prosecutors would be in a more informed position to make charging decisions, and judges would be better able to make decisions about a confession's admissibility.

By promoting more accurate and reliable fact-finding, the mandatory tape recording of interrogations would also benefit suspects and their defense attorneys. First, tape recording should deter some police misconduct and abuse during interrogation by restraining overzealous detectives who might otherwise resort to impermissible or illegal techniques, especially in high-profile cases in which little or no evidence exists against the suspect. If, however, the interrogator coerced a confession, the tape would reveal the interrogator's activities to the prosecutor, defense, and judge. The videotaping of interrogation would thus encourage fairer treatment of all suspects during interrogation. Second, tape recording would offer suspects greater protection against the possibility of a wrongful conviction based on a false confession. By creating an objective record of the entire interrogation, videotaping would permit the courts to more adequately evaluate the custodial pressures and interrogation techniques that might have given rise to a false confession, as well as the likely reliability of the statement itself.

The mandatory taping of police interrogations would also benefit the Japanese public. It is in everyone's best interest for police to interrogate custodial suspects fairly and legally, to separate the innocent from the guilty, and to exude integrity, professionalism, and legitimacy. By promoting more accurate and reliable fact-finding, by leaving behind an objective record of interrogation for all parties to review, and by creating a safeguard against false accusations and false confessions, the mandatory videotaping of custodial interrogation promotes the public interest. The use of videotaping would therefore complement police officers', prosecutors', and the Japanese public's extant commitment to truth-finding in the criminal justice system. As Suess (1996, p. 307) has written, "Japanese police, prosecutors, judges and many defense lawyers accept that 'getting at the truth,' which includes a suspect's or defendant's confession, is in the interest of both society and the individual."

In sum, electronically recording custodial interrogations promotes the goals of accurate fact-finding, fair treatment, and accountability in the legal process. By creating an objective and reviewable record of police questioning, videotaping protects police from false accusations of impropriety at the same time that it protects suspects against legally impermissible police practices and provides the public with a greater safeguard against both false confessions and the potential for wrongfully convicting the innocent. Videotaping preserves the most probative evidence available of a suspect's guilt, and thus serves the larger interests of the Japanese criminal justice system, rather than the particular interests of any one of the parties. It is therefore not surprising that the taping of police interrogations has either become a mandatory or a common practice in other democratic countries, including England, Canada, Australia and parts of America.

Part IV Conclusion

In this chapter, I have analyzed whether a *Miranda*-like warning and waiver regime could be successfully implemented in Japan. I first reviewed the social science and legal scholarship on the impact of *Miranda* on interrogation practices and suspect behavior in America during the last one-third of the twentieth century. The consensus of the first generation of *Miranda* impact studies (1966–73) was that police, for the most part, complied with the letter of the *Miranda* ruling and that confession and conviction rates remained largely unaffected by the decision's code-like warning and waiver requirements. The subsequent empirical research on *Miranda*'s real-world effects has not weakened this conclusion, but has shown how modern police detectives have creatively adapted to *Miranda* – by recasting an interrogation as an interview so that *Miranda* warnings need not be given; by downplaying or trivializing the significance of *Miranda* waivers; by persuading suspects that they will receive only a material benefit, or avoid a material harm, if they waive their rights; and by questioning suspects "outside *Miranda*." Despite *Miranda*'s warning and waiver requirements, most suspects continue to waive their rights, and police and prosecutors continue to obtain a high number of confessions and convictions.

In this chapter, I also reviewed the contemporary law and practice of interrogation in Japan. Despite the American influence on the Japanese Constitution and Criminal Code, Japanese police and prosecutors have tremendous power and discretion to aggressively investigate crimes and interrogate criminal suspects. The custodial suspect in Japan has no right to terminate police questioning, no right to leave the interrogation room, and no right to have counsel present during questioning. Moreover, prosecutors may impose the conditions (time, duration, and place) on meetings between the suspect and counsel during preindictment detention. Perhaps most significantly, police may interrogate a suspect, continuously and incommunicado, for up to 23 days (per count!) in "substitute prisons" prior to indictment. Thus, in practice, the privilege against self-incrimination, the right to silence, and the right to counsel are meaningless for the suspect who must endure interrogation in Japan. It should therefore not be surprising that Japanese interrogation appears to be routinely psychologically coercive and that virtually all defendants eventually make either partial admissions or full confessions to the offenses of which they are accused.

The routine and extensive use of psychological coercion during interrogation is due not only to the enabling laws of Japanese criminal procedure, but also to the enormous evidentiary and cultural significance of confessions in the Japanese criminal justice system. Japanese police and prosecutors regard confessions as superior to all other forms of evidence and therefore as often necessary for charging and conviction. As a result, Japanese police are under enormous pressure to obtain confessions, and Japanese prosecutors typically make the confession the centerpiece of the state's case against the accused at trial. Japanese courts rarely suppress confession statements, even those obtained under highly questionable circumstances, and the exclusionary rule thus operates as a weak, if not ineffectual, control on investigators' behaviors.

A confession is extremely important to police and prosecutors not only because of its evidentiary value, but also because of its rehabilitative value in Japanese culture more generally. Japanese police and prosecutors believe confessions are necessary for the suspect to accept moral responsibility for his offense, to repent, and to begin the process of rehabilitation and reintegration. Because of the cultural significance of confession and rehabilitation, judges grant more lenient sentences to those suspects who have confessed and expressed a desire to reform. The importance that police, prosecutors, and courts attribute to confessions reflects the values of Japanese society more generally. In Japanese society, as in the Japanese criminal justice system, an accused suspect is widely presumed guilty, and it is expected that he will confess, explain his misdeeds, and repent.

Based on the enabling rules of criminal procedure and current practices of Japanese police and prosecutors, as well as the popular beliefs and cultural expectations of Japanese society more generally, it is hard to imagine how a *Miranda*-like warning and waiver regime could possibly succeed in Japan. To succeed, *Miranda* warnings would have to be linked to a massive reform of other rules of criminal procedure, such as the duty to submit to questioning or the laws permitting police to interrogate a suspect for 23 days continuously per offense, outside of the presence of counsel, prior to indictment. Such a sea change in Japanese criminal justice seems highly unlikely, if not just plain fanciful. In addition to transforming the other, highly enabling rules of Japanese criminal procedure, a successful *Miranda* revolution in Japanese criminal justice would also have to transform the culture of Japanese detecting, the crime control orientation of Japanese prosecutors and judges, and the value placed on confession and rehabilitation in Japanese culture more generally. In light of these established practices and cultural values, it is hard to imagine that the Japanese media and public would go for American-invented, self-serving constitutional rights that quite clearly allow the criminally accused to impede the fact-finding process.

Finally, I have argued in this chapter that Japanese defense attorneys and human rights activists should support the mandatory videotaping of all custodial interrogations in their entirety. Unlike the zero-sum *Miranda* warnings, mandatory videotaping would benefit all parties – police, prosecutors, judges, defense attorneys, criminal suspects, and the public – by promoting accurate and reliable fact-finding, by leaving behind an objective record of the interrogation for all parties to review, by offering an additional safeguard against false accusations of police misconduct as well as wrongful convictions based on false confessions, and by lending greater professionalism and openness to the criminal justice process. Without intruding on the prerogative of interrogators to question suspects or lessening the willingness of suspects to speak to police, tape recording would improve the quality of interrogation, save time and resources, and lead to more effective and efficient case processing. In a criminal justice system whose values and practices are benevolently paternalistic, rather than adversarial, it is hard to imagine a more universally favorable policy reform.

References

Baker, Liva (1983) *Miranda: Crime, Law and Politics* (New York: Athenum Press).

Caplan, Gerald (1984) "*Miranda* Revisited," *Yale Law Journal*, Vol. 93, pp. 1375–85.

—— (1985) "Questioning *Miranda*," *Vanderbilt Law Review*, Vol. 38, pp. 1417–76.

Cassell, Paul (1996) "*Miranda*'s Social Costs: an Empirical Reassessment," *Northwestern University Law Review*, Vol. 90, pp. 387–499.

—— (1998) "Protecting the Innocent from False Confessions and Lost Confessions – and from *Miranda*," *The Journal of Criminal Law and Criminology*, Vol. 88, pp. 497–556.

Cassell, Paul and Richard Fowles (1998) "Handcuffing the Cops? A Thirty-Year Perspective on *Miranda*'s Harmful Effects on Law Enforcement," *Stanford Law Review*, Vol. 50, pp. 1055–145.

Cassell, Paul and Bret Hayman (1996) "Police Interrogation in the 1990s: an Empirical Study of the Effects of *Miranda*," *U.C.L.A. Law Review*, Vol. 43, pp. 839–931.

Cohen, Stanley and Daphna Golan (1991) *The Interrogation of Palestinians during the Intifida: Ill-Treatment, "Moderate Physical Pressure" or Torture?* (B'tselem, Israel: The Israeli Information Center for Human Rights in the Occupied Territories).

Cohen, Stanley and Daphna Golan (1992) *The Interrogation of Palestinians during the Intifida: Follow-up to March 1991 B'tselem Report* (B'tselem, Israel: The Israeli Information Center for Human Rights in the Occupied Territories).

DeSombre, Jean Choi (1995) "Comparing the Notions of the Japanese and the U.S. Criminal Justice System: an Examination of Pretrial Rights of the Criminally Accused in Japan and the United States," *Pacific Basin Law Journal*, Vol. 14, pp. 103–45.

Donahue III, John (1998) "Did *Miranda* Diminish Police Effectiveness?" *Stanford Law Review*, Vol. 50, pp. 1147–80.

Foote, Daniel (1991) "Confessions and the Right to Silence in Japan," *Georgetown Journal of International and Comparative Law*, Vol. 21, pp. 415–88.

—— (1992) "The Benevolent Paternalism of Japanese Criminal Justice," *California Law Review*, Vol. 80, pp. 317–90.

Geller, William A. (1992) "Police Videotaping of Suspect Interrogations and Confessions". A Report to the National Institute of Justice. Unpublished manuscript.

Graham, Fred P. (1970) *The Self-Inflicted Wound* (New York: Macmillan Company).

Haley, John (1998) *The Spirit of Japanese Law* (Athens, Ga: University of Georgia Press).

Igarishi, Futaba (1984) "Crime, Confession, and Control in Contemporary Japan," *Law in Context*, Vol. 2, pp. 1–30.

Johnson, David T. (1996) "The Japanese Way of Justice: Prosecuting Crime in Japan". Unpublished doctoral dissertation.

Langbein, John (1977) *Torture and the Law of Proof* (Chicago: University of Chicago Press).

Leo, Richard A. (1992) "From Coercion to Deception: the Changing Nature of Police Interrogation in America," *Crime, Law, and Social Change: an International Journal*, Vol. 18, Nos 1–2 (September), pp. 35–59.

—— (1996a) "Inside the Interrogation Room," *The Journal of Criminal Law and Criminology*, Vol. 86, No. 2, pp. 266–303.

—— (1996b) "The Impact of *Miranda* Revisited," *The Journal of Criminal Law and Criminology*, Vol. 86, No. 3, pp. 621–92.

Leo, Richard A. and Richard J. Ofshe (1998) "Using the Innocent to Scapegoat *Miranda*: Another Reply to Paul Cassell," *The Journal of Criminal Law and Criminology*, Vol. 88, No. 2, pp. 557–77.

Leo, Richard A. and George C. Thomas III (1998) (eds) *The Miranda Debate: Law, Justice and Policing* (Boston: Northeastern University Press).

Leo, Richard A. and Welsh S. White (1999) "Adapting to *Miranda*: Modern Interrogators' Strategies for Dealing with the Obstacles Posed by *Miranda*," *The Minnesota Law Review*, Vol. 84, No. 2, pp. 387–472.

Miranda v. Arizona, 386 US 436 (1966).

Miyazawa, Setsuo (1992) *Policing on Japan: a Study On Making Crime* (Albany: State University of New York Press).

Schulhofer, Stephen J. (1996a) "*Miranda*'s Practical Effect: Substantial Benefits and Vanishingly Small Social Costs," *Northwestern University Law Review*, Vol. 90, pp. 500–63.

—— (1996b) "*Miranda* and Clearance Rates," *Northwestern University Law Review*, Vol. 91, pp. 278–94.

—— (1997) "Bashing *Miranda* Is Unjustified – and Harmful," *Harvard Journal of Law and Public Policy*, Vol. 20, pp. 347–73.

Simon, David (1991) *Homicide: a Year on the Killing Streets* (Boston: Houghton Mifflin Company).

Suess, David A. (1996) "Paternalism versus Pugnacity: the Right to Counsel in Japan and the United States," *Indiana Law Journal*, Vol. 72, pp. 291–333.

Thomas, George C. III. (1996a) "Is *Miranda* a Real-World Failure? A Plea for More (and Better) Empirical Evidence," *U.C.L.A. Law Review*, Vol. 43, pp. 821–37.

—— (1996b) "Plain Talk about the *Miranda* Empirical Debate: a 'Steady-State' Theory of Confessions," *U.C.L.A. Law Review*, Vol. 43, pp. 933–59.

—— (1996c) "Telling Half-Truths: While *Miranda* Is Not Immune from Questioning, Advocacy Cannot Replace Careful Scholarship," *Legal Times*, August 12, pp. 20, 24.

Weisselberg, Charles (1998) "Saving *Miranda*," *Cornell Law Review*, Vol. 84, pp. 109–92.

Westling, Wayne and Vicki Waye (1998) "Videotaping Police Interrogations: Lessons from Australia," *American Journal of Criminal Law*, Vol. 25, pp. 493–543.

13
The Administration of Juvenile Justice in Japan: Focus on Adversarial Justice

Nobuyoshi Araki

Part I A short history and summary of juvenile justice procedure in Japan

The first Juvenile Law in Japan was enacted in 1923 (the Old Law). The Old Law was completely revised by the second Juvenile Law in 1948 (the Present Law). Under the Old Law, the public prosecutor reviewed all cases of crimes committed by youths aged 14–17 and selected the cases which should be handled by the adult criminal court. The public prosecutor sent the remaining cases to the administrative juvenile section. Under the Present Law, all of the juvenile crime cases (for crimes committed by youths aged 14–19) are sent directly to the Family Court. The public prosecutor has no discretionary power to file juvenile cases in an adult court (Araki, 1998). If the crime was committed by a juvenile between the ages of 16 and 19, the Family Court has the power to send the case back to the public prosecutor, whereupon he or she is forced to file the case in the district court.[1]

Under the Present Law, the Family Court follows the doctrine of *parens patrie* with respect to its juvenile clients, much as has traditionally been done in the United States and England (Tappan, 1949). The Family Court probation officer, after receiving the formal order from the Family Court judge, must investigate the social background of the youth to gather information which will help the judge decide how to treat the juvenile. The investigation includes interviews with the offender, his or her parents, teachers, and peers. If the probation officer thinks that the juvenile may not be guilty of the crime with which he or she is charged, the probation officer must immediately suspend the investigation and ask the Family Court judge to hold a fact-finding hearing first.

In addition to this investigative role, the probation officer and others try to help the juvenile repair his or her relationships with family, school, workshop, and so on. When the probation officer is successful in this task, there is no need to send the juvenile to a training school.

Japan has few strict rules which govern juvenile court procedure. Article 22 of Juvenile Law provides only as follows: "The Hearing shall be conducted in a mild atmosphere with warm consideration. The Hearing shall not be open to the public." In other words, the proceedings should be informal rather than formal. The hearsay rule does not apply in juvenile court hearings; all of the written documents prepared by the police and the public prosecutor are sent to the court in advance and are introduced as evidence. Hearings are inquisitorial, rather than adversarial.

The juvenile has the right to counsel, but the counselor need not be an attorney. The Family Court judge may appoint a lay person, such as a parent, teacher, or volunteer, as the youth's counsel. The public prosecutor has no right to attend the juvenile court hearing and no right to appeal the decision of the court.[2]

The juvenile can appeal the court's decision to the High Court. However, despite the arguments the juvenile makes in his or her appeal, there is no stay of the Family Court sentencing order; he or she may be sent to training school pending appeal. Following appeal, there is no retrial within the juvenile justice system.

During the early part of 1998, various government officials in Japan considered the state of the juvenile justice system. All, it seems, suggested some form of revision. According to a member of the Supreme Court, the current procedure mandated by the Juvenile Law – which does not allow the public prosecutor to attend the hearing – is not appropriate for modern juvenile court cases.[3] When a juvenile pleads not guilty, according to this official, the public prosecutor should participate in the hearing. Moreover, if the Family Court finds the juvenile not guilty, the prosecutor should have the right to appeal. Minister of Justice Shimoinaba insisted that Japan change the age of court jurisdiction in two ways: (1) Japan should lower the age at which a juvenile can be tried as an adult and (2) Japan should lower the minimum age at which a juvenile can be held criminally responsible by the juvenile court. The Juvenile Law Committee of the Liberal Democratic Party agreed with the revisions suggested above.

Victims of juvenile crimes, particularly the families of murder victims, are lobbying to open up the juvenile court hearings to the public. They insist that they have a right to learn the details of the crime and of the offender's background.

Part II Should we introduce the adversary system into juvenile court procedure?

When the juvenile and his counselor plead not guilty, does the inquisitorial system sufficiently protect the juvenile? All of the evidence, including written statements and summaries prepared by police officers and the public prosecutor, is sent directly to the Family Court judge at the time the case is filed. The judge then reads these documents before the protective detention hearing, and then reads them again before the adjudication hearing. The judge's main task at the hearings is to confirm the facts (about which he or she has already read) and to ask some questions of the juvenile concerning the details which remained unclear in the police documents.

The juvenile and his or her counsel are able to present a defense, although the public prosecutor has no chance of attending the hearing or to get detailed information about the case. Hence, the youth and his or her counselor are not always at a disadvantage in the courtroom, compared with the prosecutor. In fact, they may stand a good chance of defeating the charges. But is this possibility a reality or a facade? If we discuss it formally or superficially, this possibility is real. But under the inquisitorial system, the judge cannot be a neutral fact-finder, and thus these apparent defense benefits vanish in the reality of the courtroom.

For most of the cases filed in the juvenile court, the juvenile does not present a defense. In order to make his findings of fact, the judge reads the documents submitted by the police and the prosecutor. If the offender does present a defense (which is rare) which shakes the judge's belief in the prosecution's evidence, the judge may ask the prosecutor or the police to begin a supplementary investigation. While this approach sounds fair, it invites fraud. To gather useful and important evidence a few months later is almost impossible. Consequently, the police see the judge's order as a license to develop more consistent and persuasive written testimony, or to force an important witness to change his or her testimony. Most of the juvenile court judges in Japan do not question the credibility of newly sent evidence. This trust stems from two sources. First, judges and prosecutors advance through the career system, thereby regarding each other as colleagues.[4] Additionally, because they typically hear cases in which no defense is presented, judges have grown accustomed to relying on documents submitted by the prosecutor.[5]

Should the adversary system be introduced into Japan's juvenile court proceedings? The aim of the Juvenile Law in Japan is the "wholesome rearing of juveniles" to be achieved by "carry[ing] out protective measures relating to the character correction and environmental adjustment."[6] However, many scholars and critics, including the Ministry of Justice, insist that the purpose of the juvenile justice system has changed from "wholesome rearing" to "punishment." Others believe that, while "wholesome rearing" remains the mission of the juvenile court, Japan needs to make some changes. But what type of changes would adversariness entail?

Should the Japanese juvenile court procedure be divided into two parts, the fact-finding adjudication hearing and the "protective measures" hearing? If the procedure is bifurcated to allow the prosecutor to participate in the adjudicatory phase, should the prosecutor also be permitted to attend the "protective measures" hearing? At this second hearing, the prosecutor is likely to seek punishment in accordance with adult criminal standards. Hence, to keep "wholesome rearing" as the principal aim and focus of the juvenile court, the prosecutor should be barred from the second phase.

Even a superficial adversarial system demands the presence of an attorney as defense counsel. In 1995, according to the judicial statistics, among 188,409 juvenile cases, private attorneys were present in only 2116 cases (1.1 percent), and other (nonattorney) counselors were present in an additional 141 cases (Shiho Tokei Nenpo – Syonenhen, 1995). If the adversary system is introduced into the juvenile court, can the JFBA afford to provide private attorneys for each juvenile? Given the current shortage of attorneys in Japan this is unlikely. Will resources force us to provide right to counsel only in certain types of cases? True adversariness would require us to establish a court-appointed, or public defender system to guarantee right to counsel for *all* juvenile offenders.[7]

Adversarial justice would be good for factual dispute resolution. When the juvenile and his or her counsel assert that the charges are false, the adversarial procedure should govern the fact-finding process. The judge should be forced to listen to evidence and arguments presented in court by both the defense and the prosecutor.

However, allowing the prosecutor to participate in disputed fact-finding hearings is likely to lead to prosecutors' participation in nondisputed cases as well. Judges who have expressed an opinion on this topic contend that the prosecutor's attendance at the hearing increases the public's confidence in the court's decision. Yet in cases involving no factual dispute, the prosecutor will not contribute much (if anything) to the actual hearing; his or her presence should thus not affect the public's perception of the proceedings. I suspect that the judges also want to allow the public prosecutor to attend the second stage to hear arguments in support of punishment, to validate the judges' own position concerning the purpose of sentencing. Placing the prosecutor in court will serve, then, both to increase the prosecutor's power and to reinforce punishment for juvenile crimes. In sum, if we graft a superficial form of the adversarial system onto our juvenile court procedure, the original objective of the juvenile law will disappear altogether.

Notes

1. See Code of Criminal Procedure, article 248, and Juvenile Law articles 20 and 45.
2. The juvenile law does not adequately address lesser included offenses or appropriate ways to handle pleas of not guilty.
3. Since 1948, the Ministry of Justice has sought to increase the authority of the public prosecutor, citing due process concerns. However, to enlarge the public prosecutor's power means to embrace "tough justice" or punishment, rather than youth welfare, as the justification of the juvenile justice system. Interestingly, the Japanese motivation conflicts with the writings of American jurists, such as Justice Fortas in *In Re Gault,* 387 US 1 (1967), who sought to protect the juvenile from unfair adjudication and incarceration.
4. Under the career system, the judge has no experience acting as a private attorney, because he or she is trained only as a judge. By working with the same prosecutors for many years, the judge comes to regard the public prosecutors as colleagues.
5. Because there is no jury trial system in Japan, even in adult courts, judges become more comfortable relying on written statements and other forms of hearsay.
6. See article 1 of the Juvenile Law.
7. A few years ago, Japanese associations established a "private attorneys on duty" system for adult offenders, otherwise known as the "duty lawyer" scheme. An accused can call a phone number and obtain free legal advice, but each person can call only once. Although this system is not yet supported by a national budget, it may be the first step toward expanding a nationwide court-appointed attorney system in Japan.

References

Araki, Nobuyoshi (1998) "How to Familiarize the Citizen with the Criminal Justice System," *Rikkyo Hogaku,* Vol. 49, pp. 18–36.

In Re Gault, 387 US 1 (1967).

Shiho Tokei Nenpo – Syonenhen, 1995 (Japanese Supreme Court statistics, 1996).

Tappan, Paul (1949) *Juvenile Delinquency* (New York: McGraw-Hill).

14

European Trends toward Adversary Styles in Criminal Procedure and Evidence

Gordon Van Kessel

Part I Introduction

This chapter describes recent European trends in criminal procedure and evidence, examining the many varieties of adjudicatory methods in Continental countries and suggesting some approaches for Japan in its effort to reform and to modernize its system of criminal justice. In brief, Continental countries are moving away from traditional inquisitory or nonadversary procedures toward more adversary-style systems, as well as toward greater uniformity among national systems of criminal justice.

At the outset, however, a few cautions are necessary. First, many people in common-law countries misunderstand the nature of foreign systems of justice. They have an instinctive aversion to anything labeled "inquisitory" and fail to distinguish between ancient inquisitions of Continental Europe, which relied on inhumane practices to extract confessions, and modern "less-inquisitory-somewhat adversary" (which I prefer to call "inquiry") systems now in place in virtually every Continental country. Contrary to perceptions prevalent in common-law countries, modern Continental systems do not rely on torture or presume defendants guilty until they establish their innocence.

The modern, Continental inquiry systems of criminal justice are official, judicial inquiries, rather than contests between opposing parties; the primary responsibility for presentation of the evidence rests with the judge rather than with opposing counsel. The inquiry trial is characterized by an activist judge who is familiar with the facts of the case, calls and first questions the witnesses, and takes responsibility for arriving at an accurate and just result.

Collateral characteristics of inquiry systems include the following:

1. A unitary court of professional judges (or in serious cases, a mixed bench of professional and lay judges) that decides both legal and factual issues, as opposed to the common-law jury trial in which the judge declares the law and the jury finds the facts;
2. A unitary trial in which the tribunal determines questions of guilt and punishment in one proceeding;
3. A continuous, flexible procedure from pretrial through appeal in which the pretrial stage is emphasized and the trial is just one phase of fact-finding, rather than its centerpiece;
4. An informal trial procedure and an absence of complex rules of evidence regarding direct and cross-examination, hearsay, and character evidence;
5. Strong reliance on defendant as source of testimonial evidence; and
6. The absence or limited use of plea bargaining, particularly in serious cases.

A second caution concerns the assumption that adversary and inquiry systems exist as entirely separate forms of adjudication. In fact, there is no clear line between adversary and inquiry systems. No modern civilized country has a pure adversary or nonadversary system. All are "mixed" to some degree, with Continental systems even more diversely mixed than common-law systems (Van Den Wyngaert, 1993).

Finally, some contradictions appear in contemporary trends in European criminal justice. With greater European economic integration and the shift toward more adversary-style procedures on the Continent, there is more "common thinking" among member states of the European Union, which is accompanied by a pronounced movement toward uniformity among national systems of justice (Fennell et al., 1995; Markesinis, 1994). This trend toward common procedures is evident even between European common-law countries (such as England and Scotland) and traditional Continental civil law systems (such as France and Italy) (Amodio and Selvaggi, 1989). On the other hand, considerable diversity remains, not only between common-law and civil law countries, but among Continental countries themselves, whose justice systems are even less uniform than those of their common-law neighbors. Variations from country to country in the degree of movement toward adversary procedures account for much of the diversity among Continental systems. While most countries are changing gradually, a few are experiencing earthquake-like shifts in their procedural structures through wholesale adoption of adversary-style modes of adjudication (Van Cleave, 1997; Pizzi and Marafioti, 1992).

With these cautions in mind, we can safely say that Continental systems are moving away from traditional inquiry-style procedures and toward more adversary-style methods of adjudication (Bradley, 1993, 1996; Markesinis, 1994; Trouille, 1994). They also are moving toward greater uniformity, particularly in terms of commonly accepted standards of fairness. These trends are apparent in the increasing prominence of the parties and their lawyers, the diminishing authority of professional judges, the greater importance and complexity of the rules of procedure and evidence, the shift in emphasis from the pretrial to the trial phase of adjudication, the lessening of the inquiry system's traditional reliance on the accused as a source of testimonial evidence, and the increasing reliance on alternatives to the traditional trial (Van Kessel, 1986, 1992, 1999).

I will describe these trends and speculate on their underlying causes, including European economic integration, the international perspectives on criminal justice, and cultural shifts affecting attitudes toward the individual's relationship to government and society. Finally, I will point out the advantages of converging, yet diverse, procedural systems and discuss some implications for the Japanese system of criminal procedure.

Part II Major Continental trends

Increasing prominence of the parties and their lawyers

Party authority is on the increase throughout Continental Europe, with both prosecutors and defense lawyers becoming more active and more partisan (Bradley, 1996; Johnsen, 1996; Andenaes, 1993, p. 464). At the trial, this trend is evident in the movement toward allowing lawyers to question witnesses directly, rather than through the presiding judge. Prosecutorial power during the pretrial phase has grown with the decline of the investigating magistrate. Rapidly increasing caseloads have led to greater use of plea bargaining analogues, which tend to be controlled by prosecutors rather than by judges. Increases in the severity of sentences have also enhanced prosecutorial powers. On the other hand, greater emphasis on the rights of the accused has given more authority to both defendants and defense lawyers. For example,

Continental expansion of the right to examine witnesses has given defendants greater authority to demand that prosecutors present evidence in a form that is subject to challenge at trial.

With increasing party authority, Continental lawyers are tending to view themselves as more partisan. For the most part, Continental prosecutors, particularly in France and the Netherlands, are still perceived in their traditional role as "the standing part of the judiciary," but increasingly they tend to be regarded as separate from the judiciary – in essence, a separate party in a contest with the defense. Defense lawyers are also becoming more contentious. Throughout Continental Europe, and particularly in Germany, defense attorneys seem to be more aggressive in contesting and challenging the government's evidence.

Diminishing judicial authority

Decreased use of the investigating magistrate – the *juge d'instruction* – in many countries and its elimination in others has reduced judicial authority during the pretrial process. Even in France, the *juge d'instruction* is controversial. Official commissions have proposed its abolition, and its use has been diminishing (Freccero, 1994; Delmas-Marty, 1994).

Although judges still dominate trials in most Continental countries, judicial authority is eroding, quite dramatically in some countries. The most radical changes have taken place in Italy, where, in serious cases, adoption of a quasi-adversary system has greatly enhanced the authority of the parties at the expense of judicial power. But even in countries that have maintained traditional inquiry systems, judicial authority is on the decline (Dubber, 1997, p. 580). For example, the trend toward allowing direct questioning of witnesses by the parties at the trial (as in Germany) places lawyers between the judge and the evidence in a way that is contrary to the traditional judge-dominated inquiry trial. Even in France, the status of the all-powerful trial judge is under fire (Trouille, 1994, p. 743). Some regard the presiding judge's interventions and questioning of witnesses as excessive influence on the fact-finders and propose looking to English-style judges who supervise proceedings and sum up but do not question the witnesses. Finally, in some countries such as the Netherlands, one finds less rigorous enforcement of the judges' traditional duty to provide detailed written reasons supporting the decisions (Nijboer, 1993, p. 8).

Increasing importance and complexity of the rules of procedure and evidence

(1) Adoption or expansion of both extrinsic and intrinsic exclusionary rules of evidence

Extrinsic exclusionary rules of evidence, including search and seizure rules and exclusion of confessions for failure to caution suspects regarding the right to silence, are on the increase throughout Europe (Bradley, 1993, pp. 173, 219). Intrinsic exclusionary rules also are expanding, leading to more emphasis on the right to confront witnesses and less use of derivative evidence such as hearsay. While on the Continent, recognition of the weaknesses of hearsay and limits on its use have ancient origins, traditional Continental systems of criminal justice have been, and to a great extent still are, extremely lenient in the use of hearsay evidence (Damaska, 1992, p. 436). However, Continental courts today increasingly recognize the weaknesses of secondary evidence and restrict its use in some manner. Many modern judge-dominated systems (Germany and Scandinavian countries in particular) have principles analogous to American hearsay rules which are designed to assure that the best, most reliable evidence available is presented and to give the accused the opportunity to challenge prosecution witnesses. In many countries restrictions on secondary evidence are rapidly increasing. Greater importance is being placed on oral evidence and confrontation between witnesses and the accused at the trial, while less reliance is placed on written forms of proof (Freccero, 1994; Amodio and Selvaggi, 1989). In Spanish jury trials, for example, prior inconsistent statements of witnesses, including the accused, are not admissible for their truth, except for testimony taken in an adversary context which cannot be repeated at trial (Thaman, 1998).

(2) Adoption of common-law-style procedures to shield the fact-finder from improper evidence

Procedures designed to protect fact-finders from improper or potentially prejudicial evidence have been implemented in many Continental countries. One such method is to remove illegally obtained evidence from the dossier. The French *nullité* procedure allows the defendant to apply to the Chambre d'Accusation of the Cour d'Appel to declare an investigative act or procedure null and void, resulting in exclusion of the evidence. Upon such declaration, any evidence so obtained is removed from the dossier and no reference may be made to it in any subsequent proceedings (Field and West, 1995, p. 490). Another approach is to create a "dual-file" system. Under the new Italian procedure, the judge does not receive the entire dossier, but only the charging documents, physical evidence, and evidence gathered during the *incidente probatorio* (Amodio and Selvaggi, 1989). The rest must be presented at the trial by the parties. Thus, the judge must rely on opening statements and presentation of evidence by the lawyers. The new Spanish jury trial procedure incorporates a dual-file procedure similar to Italy's and is aimed at both eliminating the investigatory dossier from the trial and increasing orality and immediacy. Trial use of evidence gathered during the pretrial investigation is limited. The former testimony in the trial file is limited to depositions of witnesses who will not be available at trial and who were previously confronted and examined by the opposing parties. This elimination of the traditionally all-powerful dossier is designed to bolster orality and immediacy principles at the trial and to enhance the objectivity of the judge (Thaman, 1998, p. 282).

Shift in emphasis from the pretrial to the trial phase

Traditional inquiry procedure strongly emphasizes the pretrial stage of criminal cases. In serious cases the investigating magistrate supervises a formal preliminary process which is governed by detailed, precise rules. During this stage, the case is fully investigated, points of dispute are identified and clarified, and a reliable record is compiled. But decreasing use of written and increasing use of oral evidence, as well as the elimination or reduced role of the investigating magistrate in some countries, has resulted in more witnesses being examined at the trial. Consequently, the trial stage has been rehabilitated and has become a more significant part of the fact-finding process.

In some countries, this shift in emphasis has been deliberately designed to give greater importance to the trial. For example, Italy's procedural changes were designed to emphasize the trial and to make the pretrial phase less crucial (Freccero, 1994). Spain's new jury procedure has increased the importance of the trial as the primary truth-determining arena. As a result, pretrial procedure has been shortened and the length of trials has increased. The new Spanish jury trials take longer than judge trials, but much less time than jury trials in the United States. Most homicide jury trials last no more than three days, although a few have lasted more than a week (Thaman, 1998).

Reducing reliance on the accused as a source of testimonial evidence

Following the decline of the ordeal and other ancient modes of proof which had been based on divine intervention, Continental inquisitory systems routinely employed a system of judicially authorized torture to force confessions from defendants (Langbein, 1977a). Trials were conducted in secret and were based on written summaries of statements of witnesses and on compulsory interrogations of the accused (Damaska, 1973; Esmein, 1913, pp. 288–350; Volkmann-Schluck, 1981, pp. 2–3). Following the Enlightenment which swept across Europe in the eighteenth century, the leading states of Europe abolished judicial torture and discarded other pernicious aspects of old inquisitory trials (Schlesinger et al., 1977).

Despite these humanizing reforms, modern inquiry systems still place great reliance on the accused as a source of testimonial evidence. The abolition of torture did not end pressures on defendants to speak and to confess guilt. As Professor Damaska (1978) has noted, following the abolition of torture, milder coercive devices appeared and the chase for confessions continued, "only in ways less brutal though sometimes more perfidious."

Contemporary Continental systems utilize a variety of procedural devices to convince the accused to speak. During the pretrial stage, lenient rules with respect to assertion of the right to silence permit continued questioning of one who wishes to remain silent or requests counsel, and many countries restrict or deny the right to counsel to suspects during initial police questioning (Van Kessel, 1998). At trial, pressures to speak arise from the unitary nature of the trial, which induces a defendant to answer questions on the issue of guilt if he wishes to speak on sentencing. Also, the presiding judge as one of the fact-finders of the mixed court has studied the dossier and is aware of any refusal of the defendant to provide his side of the case. Finally, the informal, judicially controlled inquiry procedure marginalizes defense counsel and allows the judge to turn to the defendant for an explanation of the facts, thereby focusing the proceedings strongly on the accused.

However, with recent widespread recognition of a right to silence and a privilege against self-incrimination as elements of fundamental fairness, pressures on the accused to speak have been diminishing to some extent, and there has been a gradual reduction in reliance on the accused as a source of testimonial evidence. The United Nations International Covenant on Civil and Political Rights (ICCPR) (1992) explicitly recognizes a privilege against self-incrimination. Section 14(3) states that "in the determination of any crim. charge, everyone shall be entitled to the following minimum guarantees . . . (g) Not to be compelled to testify against himself or to confess guilt." In the early 1990s, decisions of the European Court on Human Rights (which sets human rights standards for the 41 countries that are members of the Council of Europe) announced in *Funke v. France* (1993) that, although the European Convention on Human Rights contains no explicit guarantee of a right to silence, "there could be no doubt that the right to remain silent under police questioning and the privilege against self-incrimination are generally recognized international standards which lay at the heart of the notion of a fair procedure under Article 6 [which guarantees the right to a fair and public hearing]." The court found the privilege closely linked to the presumption of innocence contained in Article 6, section 2 of the Convention, and the court's emphasis on free will as a basis of these rights suggests that the court will apply them liberally.

Moreover, there is at present near-universal agreement among Continental countries on the existence of a right to silence and on certain fundamental aspects of that right. All recognize some form of the right to silence and the privilege against self-incrimination in both the pretrial and trial stages of a criminal case. Finally, the silence right is being brought to life on the Continent as countries move toward more adversary procedures, which recognize a broader and more aggressive role for lawyers (Hatchard et al., 1996, p. 233). Nevertheless, at present, the right to silence in Continental countries is rather anemic, certainly much weaker than in America. Despite the technical prohibitions on drawing adverse inferences from the accused's silence in most countries, numerous procedural devices operate to pressure defendants to speak and to confess.

England, however, is bucking the European trend toward expansion of the right to silence. While access to counsel during police questioning had been severely restricted before the mid-1980s, the Police and Criminal Evidence Act 1984 (PACE) established a statutory right of access to a solicitor, as well as a right not to be held incommunicado (Burke and Brown, 1997). Sections 6.6 and 6.8 of the Codes of Practice which supplement the statute state that, with certain exceptions, "a person who asks for legal advice may not be interviewed or continue to be interviewed until he has received it" and provide that the person must be allowed to have a solicitor present whenever he is interviewed if a solicitor is available. While access to a solicitor may be denied on specified grounds, it is not proper to deny access based on the fear that the solicitor will advise the suspect to remain silent. Exclusion of a solicitor by the police is possible only if the officer is unable properly to put questions to the suspect or in other cases where clearly justified.

However, the presence of counsel does not shut down police questioning. First, English rules do not prohibit further police questioning when a suspect has requested a solicitor as long as the solicitor has advised the suspect and is allowed to be present during the interview (Zuckerman, 1989). Second, the role of counsel during police questioning is quite different from that of lawyers in the United States. The Law Society's guidelines on advising suspects during police station interviews make clear that the solicitor is not present to prevent the interview but to see that the interrogation is conducted fairly (Cape, 1994; Roberts, 1993).

Despite the limited effect of the presence of solicitors during stationhouse interviews, with the adoption of PACE in 1984 and its implementation in 1986, studies found that British confession rates began to decline towards American levels (Baldwin, 1993). Some speculated that this decrease was associated with the increased use of solicitors who discouraged suspects from confessing where the evidence against them was weak. The fear arose that guilty defendants were using the right to silence, in conjunction with the new access to solicitors, to escape convictions. As a result, Parliament enacted the Criminal Justice and Public Order Act of 1994, which permitted the trier of fact to draw adverse inferences from both silence during police interrogation and silence at trial (Archbold, 1998, pp. 15–227). The caution was altered from a simple statement of the right to silence and warning that what is said may be used as evidence, to include an admonition that the defendant's case may be harmed by failure to mention something on which defendant later relies in court. In addition, special warning provisions were enacted which apply to failure to answer questions concerning incriminating circumstances (such as presence at the scene of the crime), and which do not allow a defense to be raised at trial which had not been raised earlier. Cases soon made clear that that adverse inferences would not be limited to exceptional situations and that trial judges would have broad discretion in authorizing juries to draw adverse inferences from silence.

With the 1994 Act, the proportion of English suspects refusing to answer questions appears to be shrinking. A recent study of police interviews found that while a greater proportion of police station detainees requested legal advice during the early post-PACE years, both the rate of statements and the rate of confessions increased from before the 1994 Act (Burke and Brown, 1997; HMSO, 1997). The English experience shows that it is possible to give defense lawyers a wider role during the pretrial investigation without impairing access to the defendant as a testimonial resource.

Growing reliance on trial alternatives

As Continental countries move toward more adversary forms of trial procedure, increasingly they are seeking alternatives to trial (Van Cleave, 1997). Such alternative procedures involve enhanced party control and represent a shift to more adversary forms of pretrial procedures. For example, in Germany, as in traditional inquiry countries, there is no technical plea procedure, yet Germany is no longer the "land without plea bargaining" as once characterized by Professor John Langbein. Today, plea bargaining in the form of a negotiated settlement is common practice in 20–30 percent of German criminal cases (Dubber, 1997, p. 550).

Some countries have gone further and have formally recognized the plea process. Italy adopted the common-law plea procedure and codified a plea bargaining practice involving automatic one-third discounts for guilty pleas in minor and moderately serious cases (Freccero, 1994; Pizzi and Marafioti, 1992; Van Cleave, 1997). In nonjury cases in Spain, defendants may stipulate conformity with the prosecution's most serious charges and be sentenced at a reduced level (Thaman, 1998, p. 311). In Spanish jury cases, the parties may reach *conformidad* after taking of the evidence, in which case the judge discharges the jury and pronounces a reduced sentence if the defendant accepts the facts as stated in the pleadings.

Part III Instruments and underlying causes of current trends

The influence of international and domestic law

A new global dimension to comparative and international law is emerging throughout the Western world (Frase, 1998). This trend is particularly pronounced in Europe, where the European Court of Human Rights (ECHR) in recent years has informed many European countries of ways in which domestic systems are unfair. Taking a rather activist approach and interpreting the Convention in light of contemporary circumstances, the court has established a common floor of procedural rights with an adversary-style tilt which places greater importance on the trial (as opposed to pretrial) stage and on the oral (as opposed to the written) form of proof. In light of the increasing primacy of international law, the ECHR's effect has been felt widely throughout Europe, and its influence is likely to increase (Spencer, 1994; Field and West, 1995; Schermers, 1994a, b).

Europeans generally accept the "monist theory" of international law – upon ratification, a treaty is integrated into the domestic legal system, becomes directly enforceable, and takes precedence over ordinary domestic rules. The principle is strongest in the Netherlands, where the Constitution provides that international treaties take priority over all domestic legislation, including the Constitution itself. Indeed, Dutch courts have repeatedly refused to apply domestic legislation on the ground that it conflicted with the Convention or other treaty obligations. In several other countries, treaties rank immediately after the Constitution, but take priority over domestic legislation. In others (Germany and Italy), treaties are incorporated into domestic law and are at the same level as legislation. Even Britain is now following the current trend toward the primacy of international over domestic law. While until recently, the Convention had not been directly enforceable in British courts, in 1998 the English government adopted the Human Rights Act which incorporated the Convention into the law of the United Kingdom.

Furthermore, in areas of criminal justice relating to economic matters covered by European Union laws, decisions of the Court of Justice in Luxembourg impose on all members uniform standards of proportionality and fundamental rights, which take precedence over national laws and are strongly felt in contexts relating to criminal justice. Although the Convention is not itself a provision of the EU treaty, the Court of Justice, in the exercise of its inherent power to identify a basis for the protection of human rights in EU law, draws inspiration from international treaties for the protection of human rights which Member States have adopted (Baker, 1998). Thus, the European Court of Justice has largely incorporated the human rights norms contained in the Convention into EU law; in those areas subject to EU law, the Convention is now indirectly a part of the national laws of member nations (Schermers, 1994b, pp. 170–4; Brown-Wilkinson, 1994, p. 202).

In view of the importance of international law, one is tempted to conclude that its mandates are the primary cause of the current European movement to adversary procedures. However, international tribunals are only one factor. In large part, adversary trends are the result of fundamental changes in domestic law which in turn stem from shifts in European social attitudes and values. For example, radical shifts to adversary procedures, such as those which have occurred in Italy and in Spain, were the result of legislative action rather than of international law. Furthermore, decisions of domestic courts, particularly decisions of national Constitutional courts, are of increasing significance, which is in part a consequence of growing acceptance of Constitutional review and a trend toward a more activist domestic judiciary.

Diminishing complacency with respect to the merits of domestic systems of justice

Continentals generally admire their modern criminal justice systems, noting the strong contrasts with pre-Enlightenment inquisitory practices and proudly pointing to a competent, objective judiciary and a prosecutorial system that seeks both to protect the innocent and to convict the guilty. Recently, however, defenders of Continental systems have been more willing to recognize their weaknesses.

Focusing on the investigating magistrate, for example, Continentals often warn that judicial pretrial investigation leads to excessive delay, lengthy pretrial detention of suspects, and the compromising of judicial neutrality. A number of countries have either abolished the investigating magistrate or severely reduced its powers. The 1988 Italian Code replaced the instruction judge with a more neutral judge and gave greater authority to the parties in order to open up the system consistent with a modern democratic society (Pizzi and Marafioti, 1992, p. 5; Nijboer, 1993, p. 79). The new Spanish jury procedure retains the investigating magistrate, but with reduced powers, in order to leave presentation of evidence to the trial phase (Thaman, 1998, p. 273).

During the trial phase, the dominance of the judge creates an appearance of partiality, often placing the judge in the difficult position of maintaining objectivity while playing an active part in the proceedings (Rossett, 1972; Kotz, 1981). Finally, the dominant role of the Continental trial judge occasionally leads to lazy, unprepared lawyers who defer too much to judicial authority.

Scholars and judges are also increasingly critical of the inquiry systems' strong reliance on the written case file, which tends to compromise the quality of fact-finding by overreliance on the pretrial investigation of the magistrate and the police. Strong reliance on evidence compiled during the pretrial stage endangers judicial objectivity and makes dispassionate evaluation of the evidence at trial more difficult. A judge who, prior to trial, studies the case file developed by the police and prosecutor may tend to reach a conclusion at an early stage and to be impervious to contradictory evidence later developed at trial. The trial then tends to be a review and affirmation of what took place during the pretrial investigation. Trial judges become, in effect, prisoners of the fact-gatherer. These concerns tend to reinforce the trend toward procedures that give lawyers more authority and that place greater importance on examination of witnesses at the trial stage.

Increasing openness to global perspectives

Around the world, but particularly in Europe, there is an increasing interest in comparative and foreign law on the part of European academics, judges, and politicians (Van Kessel, 1999, pp. 487–501). For example, the Spanish Parliament's adoption of a jury of nine citizens was inspired by the number of jurors in the French *cour d'assises*, and the English recently have shown great interest in aspects of foreign justice systems, particularly the *juge d'instruction* (Thaman, 1998, p. 263). This more open attitude toward foreign systems is due to a number of factors. Membership in the EU contributes to the capacity of lawyers to make comparisons that underlie the successful use of foreign law in the process of law reform (Edward, 1994). Also, increasing openness to foreign and international law is facilitated by the growth of information-sharing technologies such as the Internet and is enhanced by the recognition of shared similarities between adversary and inquiry systems (Frase, 1998, p. 22).

Cultural, economic, and political changes

Across Europe, and perhaps around the world, confidence in government is diminishing and the social compact is in decline. This trend has affected popular views toward systems of criminal justice, which historically had relied on a paternalistic, family-oriented judicial system in which citizens regard the state as a benevolent protector that generally can be trusted. The trend toward less confidence in decisions of government institutions and civil servants signals a greater public acceptance of dispersal of authority away from the judiciary and to the parties and their lawyers – the principal characteristics of adversary procedure (Nye, 1997; Thaman, 1995). The causes of this declining confidence are subject to speculation, but they probably include greater racial, ethnic, and religious diversity, the decline of shared norms, the realignment of political authority, and an increasingly powerful and critical media. These trends bolster individual autonomy, which emphasizes competition and accepts the notion of winning and losing (Bradley, 1996). Individualism also supports giving defendants and their lawyers wider choices during the pretrial phase in contexts such as plea bargaining, as well as greater authority at trial.

America's enhanced prestige and influence in the post-cold war world has also increased the attractiveness of its individualistic, competitive procedures. During the cold war, there were two competing military, economic, and political systems. With the collapse of the Soviet Union, American institutions have enjoyed enhanced respect, particularly in the economic context, where one finds an increased acceptance of American-style capitalism, privatization, and competition. Finally, the American criminal trial of the 1990s is a most entertaining civic theater. Combative lawyering and confrontational questioning of live witnesses are much more exciting than an inquiry by a neutral judge based on a written case file. Taken together, these factors no doubt have accelerated the movement away from the family model of criminal procedure and toward more open, competitive, and adversary forms of adjudication (Amodio and Selvaggi, 1989; Bradley and Hoffman, 1996; Freccero, 1994).

Part IV Implications of European procedural shifts

Caution signs regarding the pace and duration of current European trends toward adversary procedures

Despite current trends, the movement toward adversary procedures should not be overstated. There remain vast differences in cultural values between Europeans and Americans, and there is no reason to believe that Europeans will adopt adversary procedures wholesale. While confidence in government has declined somewhat, Europeans still expect the government to play a powerful role, both socially and economically. Furthermore, although Spain and Russia are experimenting with the common-law-style jury trial, there is little sentiment on the Continent to adopt the common-law jury trial or to increase the degree of lay participation in mixed courts (Bradley, 1996). In fact, the trend in criminal cases is away from even the limited lay participation in modern Continental mixed courts (Dubber, 1997).

Finally, one finds some dissatisfaction on the Continent with shifts to adversary procedures (Nijboer, 1993; Fennell et al., 1995; Damaska, 1997). In France, the Delmas-Marty Committee recommended reforms which would limit the powers of the investigating magistrate and expand defense rights in order to fully implement the *principe du contradictoire* (Field and West, 1995; Detmas-Marty, 1994). The reforms were enacted by a socialist government in January 1993, but were rescinded by a conservative government later that same year. In Italy, adversary-inspired reforms of 1989 have had only limited success.

Common-law countries moving in the opposite direction

Common-law countries are tending to move away from the excesses of adversary forms of adjudication, as well as from lay participation in fact-finding. England has shown a growing interest in Continental forms of procedure. Following the revelation of injustices arising from convictions based on coerced confessions, English reformers looked to the Continental investigating judge. While importation of the investigating judge was rejected, England has embraced a number of traditional inquiry-type procedures, such as open pretrial discovery and restrictions on the right to silence. In America also, much criticism has been leveled against the excesses of the American form of adversary criminal procedure, particularly after the O.J. Simpson case. Critics of the American system have tended to look to Continental models for guides to reform, such as authorizing freer admission of hearsay evidence and requiring greater judicial control in the trial of criminal cases (Bradley and Hoffman, 1996; Ar nella, 1996; Selinger, 1997).

Moreover, common-law countries are moving away from lay participation in fact-finding by reducing reliance on the jury (Damaska, 1997a, p. 127; Doran and Jackson, 1997, p. 155). In common-law jurisdictions around the globe, there has been a marked increase in criminal bench trials. In England, a criminal defendant's right to jury trial was seriously weakened in the 1970s, and this trend has continued (Jackson and Doran, 1997, pp. 161–4). No country is more wedded to the jury trial than the United States, but even there, with plea bargaining and bench trials on the increase, full-dress jury trials represent a minuscule fraction of the total number of criminal cases.

What are the implications of the common-law trend away from use of the lay jury? If, as some contend, the jury is intimately connected to adversary procedure, such that its adoption accelerates the movement toward adversary-style systems, one might speculate that the contrary is true – that diminishing use of the jury will tend to bring about less adversary forms of criminal procedure in the United States.

The negative aspects of adversary procedure and skepticism regarding legal transplants

The negative aspects of adversary procedures are evident to most Continentals, and there is considerable skepticism on the Continent regarding radical movements toward adversary procedures, particularly Italian and Spanish styles. Increasing party power may lead to an imbalance in which the prosecutor has excessive authority. With increased prosecutorial power and decreased judicial authority, there is a greater need for vigorous, probing, and aggressive defense attorneys. A strong defense bar is necessary for a proper balance – it is an essential aspect of a fair adversary system. Currently in Europe, powers of the prosecutor are increasing, and with the decline of the investigating magistrate and rapidly increasing caseloads, prosecutors are tempted to place excessive reliance on dossiers developed by police. In this environment, probing and inquiring defense attorneys are essential.

Also, adversary procedures, when taken to extremes, tend to place too little importance on truth and equality. The movement toward common-law adversary styles of proof-taking leads to a subtle value shift in which the importance of truth discovery is diminished and compliance with procedural rules takes on greater significance. Adversary procedures also entail a greater willingness to accept the inequality that results from lawyers with diverse abilities and resources. This reduction in equality tends to diminish the legitimacy of the system in the eyes of the public and may lead to lack of confidence in government institutions.

Moreover, there seems to be a connection between punishment and procedure. Extremes in adversary procedures tend to promote harsher punishments in order to encourage waiver of trial rights and acceptance of alternative means of resolving cases (Pizzi, 1996, pp. 66–7). Complicated procedural systems tend to inflict harsh punishments since they must pressure defendants into accepting plea bargains. Harsh punishments in turn encourage even more emphasis on procedure. In the United States, for example, some contend that adversary extremes have contributed to a pronounced shift from rehabilitation to punishment, resulting in increased criminal penalties and incarceration rates. The American conflict model, with its winners and losers, has supported the acceptance of harsher punishments (Mauer, 1994), which in turn has led to greater acceptance of the notion that it is proper for the defendant to fight the system and to refuse to cooperate by speaking or otherwise providing relevant evidence. This contentiousness, of course, lengthens the adjudication process and contributes to the need for stronger punishments in order to pressure defendants into accepting alternatives to full trials.

An emphasis on punishment as opposed to rehabilitation conflicts with the family model of criminal procedure, which values acceptance of responsibility, rehabilitation, and integration back into society and which enjoys strong support in most Continental countries. A family-based procedural system generally limits the severity of punishments while encouraging suspects to accept responsibility for their conduct.

Finally, there is considerable skepticism concerning the feasibility of legal transplants and the desirability of "convergence" of legal systems. While some extol the advantages of legal transplants, others are less optimistic concerning the workability of transplanting procedural aspects from one distinct system to another, whether involving Continental importation of Anglo-American forms of procedure or American importation of Continental procedures (Boari, 1997). Comparativists have cautioned that useful borrowing from other systems depends on a proper understanding of what is being borrowed in its native context. The success of procedural innovations appears to depend as much on the institutional context in which justice is administered in a particular country as on the quality of the transplants themselves. As Professor Damaska (1997b, p. 851) put it, "The music of the law changes, so to speak, when the musical instruments and the players are no longer the same."

Part V Conclusion

The advantages of converging, yet diverse, procedural systems

Despite the negative aspects of adversary procedure and the dangers of procedural borrowing, the convergence of fundamental values and procedures in Europe has led to a greater willingness to consider foreign transplants, including the prospect of adopting the best attributes of diverse systems (Delmas-Marty, 1994; Frase, 1998). Moreover, global diversity provides a laboratory of procedural systems with different approaches to achieving justice. For example, the adversary system and the jury trial, although usually found together, are not essential to each other. In fact, mixed systems are the norm throughout Europe. Adversary systems are often found without a common-law jury, and inquiry systems may be found together with a common-law jury. Moreover, countries that currently are experimenting with jury trials often utilize unique forms of quasi-adversary procedures (Thaman, 1992, 1995; Merino-Blanco, 1996). With great Continental diversity, numerous options are available. There now exists a wide variety of procedural possibilities, which, together with shared perspectives on fundamental rights in criminal cases, provides a solid foundation for procedural experimentation. Furthermore, decisions of the European Court of Human Rights provide helpful guideposts since they describe procedural guarantees that are designed to apply to both the common law and civil law systems of modern European countries.

Implications for Japan

With the many diverse options in the global marketplace of procedural systems, Japanese reformers might ask whether Japan should look to America's superadversary system or to England's more moderate adversary procedures or to Continental Europe's even less adversary, inquiry-style systems. I suggest that Japan look less to the superadversary system in the US as its model but focus more on the moderate, less adversary systems of England and Continental Europe. A criminal justice system must be consistent with a country's cultural and institutional environment. European styles seem to fit best with Japanese culture, whereas a wider cultural gap appears between the United States and Japan. Thus, the best solution for Japan may be a common-law adversary system which has been "filtered through a European lens" and which is similar to the quasi-adversary systems that are developing on the Continent today. For example, adoption of police interrogation rules similar to those operating in England, which provide for tape recording and for the presence of lawyers, but which encourage suspects to speak, would guarantee greater protection for criminal suspects while not undercutting reliability of trials through the loss of important evidence (Van Kessel, 1998). Such procedures would also better fit with Japan's culture of cooperation and responsibility than would American rules, which discourage suspects from providing their side of the case and deter them from speaking with the police and from testifying at trial.

However, a note of caution is in order. The extremely powerful position of Japanese prosecutors presents an obstacle to greater movement toward adversary procedures, since a fair and effective adversary system requires a balance between prosecutorial and defense powers. Increasing the rights of defendants and the powers of defense attorneys would provide a better balance. But if it is not possible to check the excessive power of Japanese prosecutors by enhancing the role of defense lawyers, Japan might consider correcting the imbalance by increasing the independence and authority of judges and moving back toward a modern Continental-style inquiry system. Of course, Japan might best consider enhancing the powers of both defense lawyers and judges, and possibly bringing back the jury trial, in order to check the excessive power of prosecutors. However, this approach presents two hurdles: First, a fair inquiry-style system requires a truly independent judiciary, a difficult goal given the authority of the Ministry of Justice to demote judges or to assign them to disagreeable regions. Second, there is at present no equivalent in Japan of the European Court of Human Rights to guard against judicial bias and to promote a balance between prosecutorial and defense forces.

In any event, social and economic changes may propel criminal justice reform in Japan. The Japanese are moving slowly toward a more individualistic society and a more open, competitive, and capitalistic economy. Both shifts emphasize the very factors which form the foundations of the adversary system – individuality as opposed to group harmony, competitiveness as opposed to cooperation, and combative procedures involving winners and losers, as opposed to a family model of adjudication. These social and economic trends are also consistent with the adversary system's emphasis on the trial as a decisive conflict-resolving procedure.

Thus, Japan's social and economic shifts may lead to its joining the global move toward more adversary procedures based on international human rights standards. It might even be possible that Japanese lawyers, judges, and academics will someday be part of procedural shifts which eventually will lead to a stronger, fairer, and more adversary system of criminal justice.

References

Amodio, Ennio and Eugenio Selvaggi (1989) "An Accusatorial System in a Civil Law Country: the 1988 Italian Code of Criminal Procedure," *Temple Law Review,* Vol. 62, p. 1211.

Andenaes, Johannes (1993) "Criminal Law, Criminology and Criminal Procedure," *Journal of International Law and Practice,* Vol. 2, p. 431.

Archbold, John Frederick (1998) *Criminal Pleading, Evidence and Practice* (London: Sweet & Maxwell).

Arenella, Peter (1996) "Forward: O.J. Lessons," *Southern California Law Review,* Vol. 69, p. 1233.

Baker, Estella (1998) "Taking European Criminal Law Seriously," *Criminal Law Review,* p. 361.

Baldwin, John (1993) "Legal Advice at the Police Station," *Criminal Law Review,* p. 371.

Boari, Nicoli (1997) "On the Efficiency of Penal Systems: Several Lessons from the Italian Experience," *International Review of Law and Economics,* Vol. 17, p. 115.

Bradly, Craig M. (1993) "The Emerging International Consensus as to Criminal Procedure Rules," *Michigan Journal of International Law,* Vol. 14, p. 171.

—— (1996) "The Convergence of the Continental and Common Law Model of Criminal Procedure," *Criminal Law Forum,* Vol. 7, p. 471.

Bradley, Craig M. and Joseph L. Hoffman (1996) "Public Perception, Justice, and the 'Search for Truth' in Criminal Cases," *Southern California Law Review,* Vol. 69, p. 1267.

Brown-Wilkinson, Lord (1994) "Some Comparative Reflections," in Basil Markesinis (ed.), *The Gradual Convergence* (New York: Oxford University Press).

Burke, Tom and David Brown (1997) "In Police Custody: Police Powers and Suspects' Rights under the Revised PACE Codes of Practice," *Home Office Research Study* (London: Home Office Research and Statistics Directorate).

Cape, Ed (1994) "Police Interrogation and Interruption," *New Law Journal*, Vol. 144, p. 120.

Damaska, Mirjan R. (1973) "Evidentiary Barriers to Conviction and Two Models of Criminal Procedure: a Comparative Study," *University of Pennsylvania Law Review*, Vol. 121, p. 506.

—— (1975) "Presentation of Evidence and Factfinding Precision," *University of Pennsylvania Law Review*, Vol. 123, p. 1083.

—— (1978) "Book Review: the Death of Legal Torture," *Yale Law Journal*, Vol. 87, p. 860.

—— (1986) *Faces of Justice and State Authority* (New Haven: Yale University Press).

—— (1992) "Of Hearsay and Its Analogues," *Minnesota Law Review* Vol. 76, p. 425 (book review).

—— (1997a) *Evidence Law Adrift* (New Haven: Yale University Press).

—— (1997b) "The Uncertain Fate of Evidentiary Transplants: Anglo-American and Continental Experiments," *American Journal of Comparative Law*, Vol. 45, pp. 839–52.

Delmas-Marty, Mireille (1994) "The Juge d'instruction: Do the English Really Need Him?" in Basil Markesinis (ed.), *The Gradual Convergence* (New York: Oxford University Press).

Doran, Sean and John Jackson (1997) "The Case for Jury Waiver," *Criminal Law Review*, p. 155.

Doran, Sean, John D. Jackson and Michael L. Seigel (1995) "Rethinking Adversariness in Nonjury Criminal Trials," *American Journal of Criminal Law*, Vol. 23, p. 1.

Dubber, Marcus Durk (1997) "American Plea Bargains, German Law Judges, and the Crisis of Criminal Procedure," *Stanford Law Review* Vol. 49, p. 547.

Edward, David (1994) "The Scottish Reactions – an Epilogue," in Basil Markesinis (ed.), *The Gradual Convergence* (New York: Oxford University Press).

Esmein, Adhemar (1913) *A History of Continental Criminal Procedure* (Boston: Little, Brown & Co.).

Fennell, Phil et al. (1995) *Criminal Justice in Europe: a Comparative Study* (New York: Oxford University Press).

Field, Stuart and Andrew West (1995) "A Tale of Two Reforms: French Defense Rights and Police Powers in Transition," *Criminal Law Forum*, Vol. 6, p. 473.

Frase, Richard S. (1998) "Main-streaming Comparative Criminal Justice: How to Incorporate Comparative and International Concepts and Materials into Basic Criminal Law and Procedure Courses," *West Virginia Law Review*, Vol. 100, p. 773.

Freccero, Stephen P. (1994) "An Introduction to the New Italian Criminal Procedure," *American Journal of Criminal Law*, Vol. 21, p. 345.

Hatchard, John, Barbara Huber and Richard Vogler (1996) *Comparative Criminal Procedure* (London: BIICL).

"HMSO 1992 Research Study No. 3", Summarized at *Criminal Law Review*, 1993, 161.

Jackson, J.D. (1991) "Curtailing the Right of Silence: Lessons from Northern Ireland," *Criminal Law Review*, 404.
Jackson, John and Sean Doran (1997) "Juries and Judges: a View from across the Atlantic," *A.B.A. Criminal Justice Journal*, p. 16.
Johnsen, Jon T. (1996) "The Jury Trial from a Norwegian Perspective," [Unpublished paper presented at the University of California, Center for the Study of Law and Society, March 4, 1996, on file with the author.]
Kotz, Hein (1981) "The Reform of the Adversary Process," *University of Chicago Law Review*, Vol. 48, p. 478.
Langbein, John (1977a) *Comparative Criminal Procedure: Germany* (St Paul: West Publishing Co.).
—— (1997b) *Torture and the Law of Proof: Europe and England in the Ancient Regime* (Chicago: University of Chicago Press).
—— (1994) "The Historical Origins of the Privilege against Self-Incrimination at Common Law," *Michigan Law Review*, Vol. 92, p. 1047.
Markesinis, Basil (1994) "Learning from Europe and Learning in Europe," in Basil Markesinis (ed.), *The Gradual Convergence* (New York: Oxford University Press).
Mauer, Marc (1994) "Americans behind Bars: the International Use of Incarceration, 1992–1993," in *The Sentencing Project* (Washington, DC: The Sentencing Project).
Merino-Blanco, Elena (1996) *The Spanish Legal System* (London: Sweet & Maxwell).
Nijboer, Johannes (1993) "The American Adversarial System in Criminal Cases: Between Ideology and Reality," *Cardozo Journal of International and Comparative Law*, Vol. 5, p. 79.
Nye, Jr, Joseph S. (1997) "In Government We Don't Trust; Declining Confidence of People in Their Governments," *Foreign Policy*, Vol. 108, p. 99.
Pizzi, William (1996) "Punishment and Procedure: a Different View of the American Criminal Justice System," *Constitutional Commentary*, Vol. 13, p. 55.
Pizzi, William and Luca Marafioti (1992) "The New Italian Code of Criminal Procedure: the Difficulties of Building an Adversarial Trial System on a Civil Law Foundation," *Yale Journal of International Law*, Vol. 17, pp. 1–18.
Rene, David (1980) *English Law and French Law* (London: Stevens).
Roberts, David (1993) "Questioning the Suspect; the Solicitor's Role," *Criminal Law Review*, 368.
Rossett, Arthur (1972) "Trial and Discretion in Dutch Criminal Procedure," *U.C.L.A. Law Review*, p. 353.
Schermers, Henry G. (1994a) "The Eleventh Protocol to the European Convention on Human Rights," *European Law Review*, Vol. 19, p. 367.
—— (1994b) "The European Community and the European Convention on Human Rights: Their Effect on National Law," in Basil Markesinis (ed.), *The Gradual Convergence* (New York: Oxford University Press).
Schlesinger, Rudolf B. (1977) "Comparative Criminal Procedure: a Plea for Utilizing Foreign Experience," *Buffalo Law Review*, Vol. 26, p. 361.
Schlesinger, Rudolf B., Hans Wolfgang Baade, Mirjan R. Damaska, and Peter E. Herzog (1998) *Comparative Law*, 5th edn. (New York: Foundation Press).
Selinger, Carl M. (1997) "Dramatizing on Film the Uneasy Role of the American Criminal Defense Lawyer: True Believer," *Oklahoma City University Law Review*, Vol. 22, p. 223.

Smith, A.T.H. (1999) "The Human Rights Act 1998 and the Criminal Lawyer: the Constitutional Context," *Criminal Law Review,* 251.

Spencer, J.R. (1994a) "Orality and the Evidence of Absent Witnesses," *Criminal Law Review*, p. 628.

—— (1994b) "French and English Criminal Procedure," in Basil Markesinis (ed.), *The Gradual Convergence* (New York: Oxford University Press).

Thaman, Stephen C. (1995) "The Resurrection of Trial by Jury in Russia," *Stanford Journal of International Law,* Vol. 31, p. 61.

—— (1998) "Spain Returns to Trial by Jury," *Hastings International and Comparative Law Review*, Vol. 21, pp. 241, 304–73, 388.

Trouille, Helen (1994) "A Look at French Criminal Procedure," *Criminal Law Review,* p. 735.

United Nations International Covenant on Civil and Political Rights (ICCPR) (1992).

Van Cleave, Rachel A. (1997) "An Offer You Can't Refuse? Punishment without Trial in Italy and the United States: the Search for Truth and an Efficient Criminal Justice System," *Emory International Law Review,* Vol. 11, p. 419.

Van Den Wyngaert, Christine (1993) *Criminal Procedure Systems in the European Community* (London: Butterworths).

Van Kessel, Gordon (1986) "The Suspect as a Source of Testimonial Evidence, a Comparison of the English and American Approaches," *Hastings Law Journal,* Vol. 38, p. 1.

—— (1992) "Adversary Excesses in the American Criminal Trial," *Notre Dame Law Review*, Vol.67, p. 403.

—— (1999) "European Perspectives on the Accused as a Source of Testimonial Evidence," *West Virginia Law Review*, Vol. 100, p. 799.

Volkmann-Schluck, Thomas (1981) "Continental European Criminal Procedures: True or Illusive Model?" *American Journal of Criminal Law*, Vol. 9, p. 1.

Wadham, John and Helen Mountfield (1999) *Blackstone's Guide to the Human Rights Act 1998* (London: Blackstone).

Zuckerman, A.A.S. (1989) *The Principles of Criminal Evidence* (New York: Oxford University Press).

Case

Funk v. France (Feb. 1993) Series A, Vol. 256-A.

Appendix
Summary of and Comments on Recommendations of the Judicial Reform Council (2001)

Setsuo Miyazawa

Note. The essays in this volume were written shortly after the Judicial Reform Council was established. The Council presented its final recommendations to Prime Minister Jun'ichiro Koizumi on June 12, 2001 (for an official translation, see "Recommendations of the Justice System Reform Council – For a Justice System to Support Japan in the 21st Century," at http://www.kantei.go.jp/foreign/judiciary/2001/0612report.html). Its recommendations in the field of criminal justice should be reviewed here (Eds).

The mandate of the Judicial Reform Council was very broad and ambitious. Article 2 of the Law Concerning Establishment of the Judicial Reform Council promulgated on June 9, 1999 stipulates that

> The Judicial Reform Council shall consider fundamental measures necessary for judicial reform and judicial infrastructure arrangement by defining the role of the Japanese administration of justice in the 21st century. The agenda of the Council may include the realization of a more accessible and user-friendly judicial system, public participation in the judicial system, redefinition of the legal profession and reinforcement of its function. The Council shall state its opinion to the Cabinet based on the results from investigations and deliberations conducted according to the preceding provision.

Thirteen members were appointed, including three male law professors, three male lawyers, two professors in economics and accounting (one of whom is a woman), two male businessmen, one male labor union leader, one leader of a women's organization, and a female novelist. Koji Sato, a constitutional law professor at Kyoto University, was the Chairman of the Council. Masahito Inouye, a contributor to this book and the youngest of the three law professors, quickly took the lead on several issues, including legal education, public participation in the administration of justice, and criminal justice. The third law professor was in the field of civil justice. The three lawyers included a former president of the JFBA, a former chief judge of the Hiroshima High Court, and a former head of the Nagoya High Prosecutor's Office. The former JFBA president often represented the most reformist positions in the deliberation, while the former prosecutor usually took the most conservative position, particularly on criminal justice. The Council was supported by a Secretariat formed under it, with a prosecutor serving as the Secretary General.

The Council held public hearings in four places and visited the United States, Germany, France, and the United Kingdom. Deliberation was made public through closed circuit TV, and summaries and complete transcripts were published on the Council's website.

At the beginning of Chapter I (Fundamental Philosophy and Directions for Reform of the Justice System) of its final report, the Council presents its understanding of the Japanese society and its own mission:

> Approximately one hundred years have passed since the compilation of the Civil Code and over fifty years since the establishment of the Constitution of Japan . . . this Council has determined that the fundamental task for reform of the justice system is to define clearly "what we must do to transform both the spirit of the law and the rule of law into the flesh and blood of this country, so that they become 'the shape of our country'" and "what is necessary to realize, in the true sense, respect for individuals (Article 13 of the Constitution) and popular sovereignty (Article 1), on which the Constitution of Japan is based."

In short, the Council believes that the rule of law has not taken root in Japan's 130-year history of modernization; government agencies have ruled the country without being subject to meaningful legal regulations, and the people have relied on these government agencies to promote and protect their interests. In the remainder of Chapter I, the Council criticizes the reliance on unregulated government and recommends downsizing of government agencies under the rubric of administrative reform and deregulation. The Council further encourages the Japanese people to become actively involved in shaping their country, both through participation in the political process and the use of law in challenging government agencies and in forming relationships among themselves. Hence, "[t]he judicial branch, which is based on the concept of the rule of law and places all parties concerned in an equal position . . . must, along with the political branches, be a pillar to support the 'space of the public good'."

The Council's final recommendations cover a wide range of issues. The two principal ideas are (1) to expand the judiciary and the legal profession and to make them more accessible to the public, and (2) to strengthen the democratic basis of the administration of justice. Therefore, among innumerable recommendations, the Council recommended tripling of the number of new lawyers per year (from 1000 to 3000) by about 2010 and introducing lay judges (*saiban-in*) who will decide certain serious criminal cases in conjunction with professional judges. Furthermore, the Council recommended establishing graduate professional law schools (*hoka daigakuin*) in 2004 as the core of the new system designed to produce a larger number of better-educated lawyers.

Strengthening the democratic basis of the administration of justice seems to require a firm commitment to the rule of law. In the area of criminal justice, one would expect this commitment to be reflected in treatment of law enforcement, criminal defendants, and the courts: police and prosecutors would be under more stringent legal regulations in their activities, the position of the accused vis-à-vis the state would be buttressed, and the criminal courts would carefully scrutinize the legality of police investigations and the prosecution's burden to prove guilt beyond a reasonable doubt. The Council, however, manifested a different understanding of the commitment to rule of law:

> The purposes of criminal justice are to maintain the social order and to secure the safety of the people by accurately identifying crimes and arresting criminals, by finding out the truth of cases through fair procedures, and by fairly and speedily realizing the authority of punishment, bearing in mind the maintenance of public welfare and the guarantee of individual fundamental human rights. . . . In other words, the discovery of the substantive truth – finding out the truth of the case, pursuant to the guarantee of due process, is demanded. . . .

This pronouncement reflects an essentially inquisitorial philosophy on criminal justice. Although the Council always mentions the need to maintain due process and to respect human rights, the main purpose of the criminal justice system is clearly the speedy punishment of the criminal. The primacy of truth-finding as a main function of the criminal justice system is mentioned in various places. For instance, in the section concerning the questioning of suspects, the Council says that "[t]he questioning of a suspect, so long as it is conducted properly, contributes to the discovery of the truth, and, in the event the suspect who actually committed the crime truly regrets the crime and confessions, it also contributes to his or her rehabilitation." This has been the position taken by police and prosecutors who want to maintain the present system.

In accordance with this view, the Council seemed to place great importance on the expediency of criminal trials; it made the following recommendations:

- A new preparatory procedure presided over by the court should be introduced in order to sort out the contested issues and to establish a clear plan for the proceedings in advance of the first trial date. To achieve the thorough ordering and clarification of the contested issues, it is necessary to expand the disclosure of evidence. For that purpose, rules regarding the timing and the scope of the disclosure of evidence should be clearly set forth by law . . .
- Trials should be in principle held over consecutive days . . .
- A system should be established that enables defense counsel to concentrate on individual criminal cases, including the establishment of the public criminal defense system; . . .

Under these guidelines, the judge would have more power to manage the litigation. But note that the Council itself did not set rules on disclosure of evidence; it simply left the matter to the subsequent legislative process that will likely be controlled by the Justice Ministry. Those who want to establish a system that compels disclosure of prosecution evidence thoroughly and quickly will surely find an uphill battle in the legislature. Even the public criminal defense system is proposed mainly as a measure to speed up criminal trials, rather than as a measure to strengthen the criminal defense bar.

Regarding the new public defense system, the Council recommends the following:

- A public defense system for suspects should be introduced, and a continuous defense structure covering both the suspect stage and the defendant stage should be established.
- The organization that manages the public defense should be fair and independent . . .
- The above-mentioned organization should take responsibility for the administration of the system . . . it is critical to establish a structure that can support the effective implementation of the new popular participation system in the trial proceedings.
- . . . the autonomy and the independence of the defense activity in the individual case must not be damaged even under the public defense system . . .
- The bar associations . . . bear a serious responsibility to ensure the quality of the defense activity and should autonomously develop suitable arrangements for it.

The expansion of free criminal defense counsel from the trial stage to the investigation stage is clearly a progressive step toward strengthening the position of the accused in Japan. Increasing the public expenditure on criminal defense lawyering is a move in the same direction. However, the scope of these reforms will depend largely on the institutions which create and supervise the nationwide public defense system. While it is not clear that the JFBA will be the organization that implements the system, it seems clear that the Justice Ministry will obtain the supervisory power. Much is left to the legislative process, and it is not at all clear whether the new public criminal defense system will promote more aggressive and adversarial defense activities.

The Council also recommended expansion of criminal defense work in juvenile justice. As of November 2000, the family court may ask the prosecutor to participate in the fact-finding process in cases of intentional homicide or when the crime is punishable by imprisonment for two years or longer. In cases in which the prosecutor is called in, the court must appoint a defense counsel as an attendant to the juvenile. The Council recommended further study concerning the expansion of this public attendant system to other cases.

The Council's recommendations concerning the position of the accused and defense counsel during a criminal investigation were disappointing to reform advocates:

- Consideration should continue to be given to the reform, and improvement of both the systemic and operational aspects . . . in order to prevent and rectify the improper custody of suspects and of defendants.
- A system should be introduced that imposes the duty of making a written record, for every occasion of questioning, in order to ensure the propriety of questioning of suspects.

It is apparent that these recommendations are merely for show (or are toothless reforms). In explanatory notes, the Council acknowledged that many aspects of the present system have been criticized, particularly in light of international human rights, and defends its nondecision by stating the following:

> Various concerns have been pointed out regarding the custody of suspects and of defendants, such as how *daiyo kangoku* (use of custody facilities in police stations in lieu of detention facilities) should be, possible introduction of pre-indictment bail system, how defense counsel's right to meet with suspects in detention should be, issuance of warrants, and how determinations with respect to requests for post-indictment release on bail should be (Recommendation of the United Nations Human Rights Committee, etc.). It is difficult to reach a concrete immediate conclusion on these matters, because there are various ways of thinking arising from differences in assessments of the current state of affairs. . . .

Since the Council accepted the position that confessions are indispensable in finding truth and rehabilitating criminals, it is natural that the Council rejected any reforms that would make it difficult to obtain confessions. It is also clear that nothing can be changed if police and prosecutors are determined to oppose reforms.

The Council repeated a similar argument regarding possible measures to increase the transparency of the questioning of suspects (and the consequent reliability of their statements).

- . . . while there are some opinions that audio and video recording of the questioning itself and the attendance of the defense counsel at the questioning are necessary, it is difficult to decide with certainty whether to introduce such measures at this stage because careful attention should be paid to such measures with regard to the function and significance of the questioning of suspects in the whole structure of the criminal procedure.

Similarly, changing the present system to allow the suspect in custody to refuse to answer questions was not recommended.

In short, while a radical increase in the total number of defense attorneys and the establishment of a public criminal defense system would make defense counsel more available to suspects, those defense attorneys cannot do much during the investigation stage. Moreover, they must face a very rapid trial without having a guarantee that prosecutors will disclose all of their evidence well in advance of the trial. Depending on how it is designed, the proposed organization that would implement the public criminal defense system might further limit criminal defense activities. The JFBA and others who wanted measures that were not adopted by the Council will face an uphill battle in introducing reforms that would exceed the Council's recommendations.

On the other hand, prosecutors did not get what they wanted – the immunity system. The Council says that "there are issues concerning whether the immunity system meets the legal sentiment and sense of fairness of the Japanese people, so it is difficult to reach an immediate conclusion . . ."

Finally, the Council recommends a new system that combines elements of the Anglo-American jury system and the German lay assessor system: a group of local citizens randomly selected on a case-by-case basis would decide both facts and law in conjunction with professional judges. Such lay citizens, called *saiban-in* (meaning members of adjudication), will participate as follows:

- Applicable cases should be cases of serious crime to which heavy penalties attach.
- No distinction should be made based on whether the defendant admits or denies the charge.
- Defendants should not be allowed to refuse trial by a judicial panel of judges and *saiban-in*.

The actual range of applicable cases is left to the legislative process, but an arraignment system was not introduced, and the trial by a hybrid panel is mandatory:

- Judges and *saiban-in* should deliberate and make decisions both on guilt and on the sentence together. In the deliberations, *saiban-in* should possess generally equivalent authority to that of judges; and in the hearing process, *saiban-in* should possess appropriate authority including the authority to question witnesses.
- The number of judges and *saiban-in* on one judicial panel and the method of deciding the verdict should be determined appropriately, giving consideration to the need to ensure the autonomous and meaningful participation of *saiban-in* and the need to ensure the effectiveness of deliberations . . .
- However, a minimum requirement should be that a decision adverse to a defendant cannot be made on the basis of a majority of either the judges or the *saiban-in* alone.

The composition of the panel has become a focus of the debate after the publication of Council's recommendations. Those who wish to prevent a situation where professional judges overwhelm lay judges propose to include a far larger number of lay citizens; those who argue that lay citizens should participate in proceedings mainly to assist professional judges propose that the number of lay citizens should be equal to or less than that of professional judges. Again a vital element is left to the subsequent legislative process.

Will the presence of lay judges strengthen the position of either the accused or the prosecution? As far as we can tell from the media reports about public sentiments concerning a series of serious cases in recent years, it seems possible that the participation of lay judges will lead to a general increase in the penalties given to convicted offenders.

In short, the Council's recommendations will not significantly strengthen the position of the accused or restore the balance between the two sides. Particularly disappointing is the Council's failure to change any legal provisions regarding criminal investigation and the rights of suspects and defense attorneys during the investigation stage. It remains to be seen whether and how the defense bar will renew its efforts to establish a truly independent organization for the new public criminal defense system, so that an organized bar of full-time criminal defense specialists will emerge.

Index